ROAD TO INAMURA

THE ROAD TO
INAMURA

by
LEWIS BUSH

ILLUSTRATED

CHARLES E. TUTTLE COMPANY
Rutland, Vermont & Tokyo, Japan

For
Claire *and* Edmund Blunden
With Affection and Esteem

Representatives
Continental Europe : Boxerbooks, Inc., *Zurich*
British Isles : Prentice-Hall International, Inc., *London*
Australasia : Paul Flesch & Co., Pty. Ltd., *Melbourne*
Canada : M. G. Hurtig Ltd., *Edmonton*

Published by the Charles E. Tuttle Company, Inc.
of Rutland, Vermont & Tokyo, Japan
with editorial offices at
Suido 1-chome, 2-6, Bunkyo-ku, Tokyo, Japan

© *1972 by Charles E. Tuttle Co., Inc.*

Library of Congress Catalog Card No. 78-171996

International Standard Book No. 0-8048-1014-1

First edition published 1961 by Robert Hale Limited, London
First Tuttle edition published 1972

0223-000290-4615
PRINTED IN JAPAN

ILLUSTRATIONS

ACKNOWLEDGEMENTS

The copyright of illustration no. 1 is held by Mr. Saburo Yasuda;
no. 10, by the Imperial War Museum, London; no. 14, by BOAC;
no. 15, by the Japan Broadcasting Corporation (NHK); and no. 16,
by the Tokyo Broadcasting System.

Chapter One

I

WE SAT in the dining car of the train which was speeding towards her native place; past paddy-fields where men, women and even children sloshed about in the mud assisted by oxen in preparing for rice planting, and here and there spring flowers embroidered the precise divisions between the fields and the banks of the railway and irrigation ditches.

Bluish-grey hills and mountains crept heavenwards from the plain to the right, and to the left the rugged peaks, capped with snow and in bold relief above the mirror-like streak above the pine-trees that was Lake Biwa.

The railway skirted the old trunk road flanked with ancient pines, gnarled, twisted and bent into the most fantastic shapes, past villages and hamlets of thatched and grey tiled roofs, dominated by imposing temples, past bamboo groves and stone gateways of Shinto shrines, and the red lacquered wooden ones which lead to the abode of Inari Sama, the deity of the Harvest. We clattered over rivers and streams now swollen by the melting mountain snows, and the only fault to find was in the seemingly inevitable and unsightly advertisements for pocket tonics, beer, sake; radios, cosmetics and other commodities, with which the Japanese clutter up their countryside.

But so attractive did everything seem to me that spring morning that I had soon forgotten the ordeal which lay before us. For it was not usual for a native daughter of a small Japanese town to marry in opposition to the wishes of her parents, and unthinkable that she should bring home a six-foot-two husband with grey eyes, blonde hair, and by native standards an extremely long nose. It was quite obviously going to cause as great a sensation as might be provided in the daughter of a Southern gentleman turning up in Mississippi with the Wild Man from Borneo on her arm.

Fellow passengers appeared to find us both of more than unusual interest. Across the aisle an aged man, a woman's fur stole around his neck, sucked his teeth and beamed at me most kindly whenever I chanced to look his way; a couple of children, their faces smeared with chocolate, seemed to find me funny-making to an extreme, and a military officer, displaying an imposing array of medals who had given up trying to engage me in conversation in Russian, on being satisfied that I was not a dangerous Communist agitator viewed me with what appeared to be a certain tolerance. I had listened to one convivial gentleman

7

who had stripped down to his heavy long-handled under-wear and vest give a rendition of "Tipperary" for my benefit and with whom I had exchanged numerous cups of sake and vows of friendship between my country and Japan, listened to his opinions concerning the virtues of the Prince of Wales, King George V, Abraham Lincoln, as well as his condemnation of our lack of understanding of what Japan was doing to bring peace and prosperity to China and Manchuria and had sighed with relief when his spouse had dragged him away just in time to get out at their stop.

But it was herself who bore the brunt of all the friendliness and inquisitiveness, and as she was dressed for those days outside of Tokyo like a being out of another world, our fellow travellers seemed to find it quite incredible that she spoke their language and incomprehensible that she should be of their race!

She looked smart and lovely in a very chic blue dress trimmed with little bits of fur, and her hair peeked out from beneath a smart little hat from which hung a wisp of veil, and it was a toss-up whether this ensemble or my stature, eyes and nose, were the greater attractions for our kimono and otherwise clad companions.

As I stood up, after having paid the bill, every eye in that dining car was focused upon us and all beamed their satisfaction, even the somewhat stern-visaged military man, with our having provided interest. But while herself was returning the bow of the aged man opposite I chanced to look down and, to my horror, there draped around her ankles was a filmy, flimsy garment! My hair seemed to bristle, my face was on fire as I gasped: "For God's sake! Your pants have fallen down!" But she just went on exchanging courtesies with the old man who appeared to know her family, to increase my discomfort gave me a wistful smile and caused me to break out in a sweat, and then she just dropped her handkerchief, bent down, and handkerchief and that preposterous article which until then I must confess I had found by no means unattractive, were swept into her handbag before any had the chance to discover the cause of my obvious and sudden embarrass-ment.

I slumped back into the seat, wiped my brow and called for another bottle of beer, and her inquiry as to whether I possessed a safety-pin seemed just about the last straw. The waitress kindly obliged, and after she disappeared for a few minutes to the toilet we made a successful move to our seats.

"God almighty! Can't you even do your pants up properly?" I snorted.

"But I cannot help it if a button breaks."

"Buttons shouldn't break. This is a fine start to the day. What an embarrassing thing to happen, in front of all those people, too!"

"But nobody did see, did they?"

"Well, I don't know. They were probably too polite to show

that they did. Anyhow you'd be better off with no pants at all than going around with that bit of rubbish draped round you!"

"Please don't be so foolish," she said with a half smile. "I am sorry. But you'd better get our things together because we'll have to change in five minutes."

I realized that my ridiculous boorishness had surprised and hurt her, mumbled an apology, smiled, she smiled back at me, and we both burst out laughing and did not stop until we were pulling into the junction where we had to change trains.

II

We stepped out on to the platform to be confronted with quite a crowd which included porters, and other railway officials, and in the centre of which was a chap dressed in a morning suit who immediately came forward and started a bowing contest with Kaneko. Indeed they both bowed so much, a bow appearing to be a sort of punctuation mark to break up each sentence they uttered and were so close together for this sort of thing that at any moment I expected there would be a crack of skulls, and I prayed that with all this bowing the safety-pin would hold, for the station-master had appeared and was introduced, and a chap with a notebook who had newshawk written all over him.

And whilst herself was reciprocating the courtesies all were sizing me up and down. There was a sort of hush as she motioned me forward and introduced morning-suit as her cousin.

I stood my distance and gave him bow for bow and I felt that things were not going to be too bad with this chap dressing up in formal attire for the occasion. The newspaperman then took the stage to inquire as to my age, height, weight, preferences in food and drink, reasons why I had married, opinions on Manchuria, the League of Nations, the attitude of Lancashire towards the Japanese cotton industry, and when he'd finished a policeman took his place to ask almost the same questions all over again.

Outside the station an ancient taxi waited and such a crowd had gathered that it was with difficulty that the driver was able to gain the open road.

We were soon bowling and rattling along a very bumpy highway by the side of the lake. Herself jabbered away with cousin who would occasionally smile at me as if he approved and although the detraining welcome had been somewhat wearing yet everyone had been so friendly that much of my previous misgiving had now evaporated.

"Ibuki San!" said cousin, pointing to a sizeable snow-capped mountain where herself explained a Japanese St. George had in the remote ages run a Japanese dragon or other monster to earth.

"Some years ago the Prince of Wales cruised on Lake Biwa in a special vessel built for the purpose," confided cousin. I expressed suitable gratification on hearing this but felt that the Duke of

Windsor had certainly arrived in the area under somewhat more favourable circumstances than myself.

He seemed most anxious that I noted all the items of interest and pointed to a giant statue of a Buddhist divinity whose face I found resembled that of my great aunt.

"Very nice of your cousin to put on formal attire to meet us," I observed.

She laughed. "Oh, he had to attend a funeral much earlier this morning." It occurred to me that she might have allowed me to retain my impression of having merited the ceremonial attire.

We entered a sleepy-looking town where it seemed that the entire population was out to witness our arrival and after negotiating what seemed a labyrinth of extremely narrow lanes drew up before a house which stood on the other side of a swift running stream spanned by a narrow bridge.

Herself stumbled out of the car to start the bowing business all over again with a crowd which included men and women, old and young, some with perambulators, with babies on their backs, a policeman, a man with a bicycle, on the carrier of which was a miniature theatre and balloons and paper windmills streaming from the handlebars, and there was an old crone who appeared to be about ninety who had black-lacquered teeth. Whether my in-laws were present I had no means of knowing and after making my obeisances was led across the tiny bridge to the house.

I slipped off my shoes and stepped up on to the raised flooring to deal my head a sounding crack against a beam. This brought forth expressions of alarm from the elder folk, great mirth from the youngsters, a painful lump on my cranium, and a sense of dire foreboding.

A skinny, grey-haired old lady sat awaiting us in a large inner room whose only furniture was a black-lacquered table which stood out in sharp contrast against the spotless, cream coloured *tatami* and who was introduced as Kaneko's father's widowed sister whose husband had been engaged in the development of the railways in Formosa. A few uncles, two brothers, several cousins and other male and female relatives now made their appearance and to whom, despite my aching knees and thighs I continued my exercises from the waist. But there was still no sign of my parents-in-law and although herself assured me that they were at home making preparations for our reception yet I could not help feeling that I was probably about as welcome as the German measles.

A young man staggered in with a huge wicker chair which he placed on the veranda and beckoned me to relax. But this I simply could not do; for if these Japanese squatted down with their legs tucked under their posteriors, then I would do likewise, even though I should emulate Daruma, said to have been the founder of Zen Buddhism, and believed to have sat in meditation for nine years until his backside rotted away.

But while I was declining the offer of comfort and on the point of giving way a policeman took the chair and, after clearing his throat with several hawks, surveyed me with intense interest and then announced that he would have to see my passport. He thumbed through the pages, nodding his approval at the various notations, but when he was about to hand it back to me Kaneko suggested that he would perhaps gain a clearer understanding if he read it the right way up. This was unkind of her because by now the populace was showing great interest from outside the veranda and having been duly impressed by the officer's ability to fathom such a document now simply rolled with laughter. However, he took it all in good part, slapped himself on his close-shaven head, and then howled with merriment. But it was Kaneko's passport which created the greatest impression, especially when in response to the policeman's request for a translation of the preamble it was realized that she was no longer a Japanese and that a certain high panjundrum by the name of Mr. Anthony Eden, his Majesty's Principal Secretary of State for Foreign Affairs etc., etc., had even instructed, nay commanded, all of his Majesty's hirelings throughout the world to give her all the assistance of which she might stand in need.

It was passed around, admired; complications started to arise over *"Honi Soit Qui Mal y Pense"*, but were fortunately interrupted by aunt who had been whisking up some sort of brew in a stone bowl with what looked like a shaving brush and who now pressed upon me some extremely sweet cake and then handed me the bowl of frothy green liquid which I found tasted like some very disagreeable medicine. And although I politely expressed satisfaction with my first taste of powdered green tea, she then bustled away to return with a tray on which was a pot of coffee, milk and sugar, and a cup decorated with roses like a Victorian chamber pot.

"We always drank coffee in Formosa," she confided, "My husband always had his whisky, and we used to go to the hotel at Taihoku where they had ballroom dancing."

She appeared to be a genial old soul and I felt that we were going to get along fine and so I produced a bottle of Johnnie Walker from my bag. But, just as the policeman and various others, including aunt, were about to join me in a nip there was a blood-curdling scream and into the room rushed an extra-ordinary looking female, her eyes shining, her hair in disarray, and yelling as if she were pursued by all the devils out of hell.

"Good heavens! Who is she, and what is the matter?" I gasped.

"Oh, it is only cousin Kimi. She says we've brought the Fox God with us and it is in her stomach again."

The rosy-cheeked and somewhat buxom young woman now rolled upon the *tatami* and seemed in shocking pain. The women-folk sought to soothe her, the men behaved as if nothing extraordinary was happening, and the children chuckled with glee.

But relief now appeared in a summons to the parental home

and after some difficulty in making my numbed legs operate we were soon together with what seemed a vast concourse including the young man bearing the wicker chair, on our way.

It was little more than five minutes' walk, but as herself was compelled to indulge in bowing spells with old friends who appeared from almost every house we passed we made slow and embarrassing progress.

Every house seemed alike as two peas; there were no pavements and the wooden barred fronts were flush with the roadway, which gave them a somewhat gloomy appearance. In feudal days a rigid code laid down what type of house a man might erect, according to his rank, and only samurai and above were entitled to gateways. And the merchant class, then at the bottom of the social scale, took every care not to be presumptuous in any way and hid whatever wealth it might possess behind gloomy and unostentatious exteriors. But if their frontages were narrow, yet I was to find that many such houses not only possessed great depth but concealed fine storehouses built in the classic style as well as landscape gardens with their rocks, stone lanterns and bridges, lakes, streams, rivers of sand and pebbles, in the designing of which the Japanese have no peers.

Mother-in-law, truly a tiny person, even for a Japanese, could not conceal her joy at seeing her daughter, and the warmth of her smile for me seemed to imply that odd though I might be, yet if I were Kaneko's choice then it was quite all right with her. But while I was now introduced to several other male relatives there was still no sign of father-in-law and sensing my inquiring manner herself informed me that he was away on business but expected at any moment.

It seemed that all the multitude of relatives peculiar to most Japanese families stretching to the children of cousins thrice removed had come from all over the county for the occasion and, although partitions had been removed to provide one large room which now extended back to the small garden, people seemed to be in every nook and corner of the house as well as squatting on the edge of the raised flooring, and even in the garden and the front porch.

The wicker chair had now been brought in but I remained adamant in my desire to conform with custom, despite the extreme discomfort of squatting Japanese style, and the article remained untenanted.

Then, just after another session of the sweet cakes and bitter powdered tea, there was an ominous sort of hush and a very large man made his appearance. He was dressed impeccably in kimono, over the lower part of which he wore the pleated, skirt-like *hakama*. Close-cropped white hair was in contrast with his bushy black eyebrows and his tanned skin, and he sat down without at first paying any attention to anyone and I thought he resembled a very disgruntled, handsome old bull. To his daughter's obeisances he merely nodded and grunted, then he looked up, I made my bow, extended my hand, which he ignored, and stared at me.

He then arose and went over to a large cupboard which he opened to reveal a magnificent altar in which squatted an image of the Buddha and two of his disciples, gilded vases, several faded photographs and tablets bearing Japanese ideographs. He lit several candles, prostrated himself, and then started a rumbling sort of prayer which he punctuated by now and then clapping his hands. I was awestruck and decidedly uncomfortable for I imagined that he was invoking the aid of Buddha in an effort to rid himself of this unwanted son-in-law. But his prayer ceased as abruptly as it had started and herself went forward and paid her respects to her departed ancestors, and on being motioned forward I tried my best to emulate her actions with as much dignity as my aching limbs would permit.

Father-in-law then sat down before me once again, put his hand to his waistband and drew forth a dagger in a case. And just as I expected to be subjected to some terrible heathenish form of bloodletting ceremony he withdrew a long pipe from the case, the thimble-like bowl of which he proceeded to fill with a fine hairy looking tobacco, lit it from the fire-bowl, took a couple of draws, tapped it out, stood up and dragged the wicker chair before me and his look was a veritable command that I sit down and stop playing at trying to be a Japanese.

It seemed that ceremony was now at an end, judging by the general merriment of all except father-in-law, and after I was relaxed in the welcome comfort of that ugly chair I handed the old man my little gift in the form of two bottles of Johnnie Walker—Black Label at that. He mumbled his thanks and put them side by side in the *tokonoma*—the place of honour, and then with bows to all excused himself on the grounds of having most important business which called him elsewhere.

III

What seemed to be a most sumptuous banquet was now prepared with many tables laid end to end to form one long one and on which attractive dishes were set out containing raw fish, red and white, decorated with sprigs of various herbs, and other rather exotic-looking foods. But if I felt any doubt about the taste of what was set before me, yet I had never seen food so artistically embellished and such variety of exquisite porcelain. And if father-in-law had not exactly exuded warmth in his welcome, mother-in-law, relatives and friends of the family certainly made up for it. Countless vows of eternal friendship were exchanged over the sake cups, a one-armed man arrived with a bottle of whisky—bottled, according to the label, in of all places Buckingham Palace, but which by its fiery taste must have come from a rocket fuel centre. And just as I was beginning to enjoy "*sukiyaki*" a boy arrived on a bicycle with a box from which for my benefit only was disgorged a plate of rice covered with flaming yellow curry, two fried lobsters, and a plate of steak and vegetables, all stone cold, which I was informed father-in-law had ordered in the belief that local fare could hardly be to my liking!

A very subdued Kimi—with the Fox in her stomach—joined the party somewhat belatedly, and by the amount of food she ate that Fox had been indulging in a prolonged fast.

The skinny old aunt from Formosa was in her element. "All foreigners smell of butter and cheese," she announced, "and I suppose we Japanese smell of pickled turnip.

"When we went to Formosa the head-hunters could smell us out. Oh, yes! And once when my husband was surveying they swooped down on our little settlement. He, Kimi and I, hid in the toilet—yes, right in it, and when we emerged there were the bodies of our friends—minus their heads!"

And then, much to our embarrassment, the old girl desired to know whether we indulged in what she considered was the disgusting Western habit of kissing?

The arrival of a teacher of English from the local middle school who exacted my promise to talk to his pupils robbed the company of any anticipated amusement from this subject, and by the time he had excused himself the old woman was voicing her opinion on the iniquity of eating meat, although she confessed that she liked it.

There was no stopping her, she took charge of the proceedings in the absence of father-in-law for she was the senior member of the family present, and mother-in-law just did not count.

By the time the guests started to leave I had been promised fishing excursions, mountain climbing, visits to silk filatures, initiation into the mysteries of brewing sake, invitations to shrines and temples, rowing and sailing on the lake, and had promised to visit families in the countryside spread it seemed over the entire prefecture. My cup of happiness was almost full. But I still entertained doubts about Kaneko's stern-visaged father. However, she seemed happy and smiled her pleasure, and expressed the opinion that as I had made a great hit with the aunt from Formosa she considered this meant that our battle with father was all over, bar the shouting.

For what seemed a very long time the womenfolk disappeared, leaving the one-armed man to press more of his Buckingham Palace whisky upon me. There was no denying him but I managed to just swill it round my mouth and then rid myself of the fiery fluid in pretending to sip at a cup of tea. For I had long heard that whisky, even the best, did not go well with sake.

> "Sake and whisky,
> Mighty risky.
> Sake and beer,
> All is clear."

And experience has proved to me that whoever composed that little jingle knew what he was talking about.

When the women folk reappeared one-armed Cho-San was sent on his way and I was led upstairs to find a bed prepared fit for a king. There were not only thick blankets piled about two feet thick, but as these were designed for a normal Japanese and not for a six-footer an arrangement of cushions had been contrived so that my feet would not stick out.

A light cotton kimono was then produced, plus a thick padded one, and I was ordered to divest myself of my clothing and prepare for a bath. These garments were up around my knees and this started a discussion on how best to make me suitable Japanese clothes, it finally being decided that three lengths would serve to make me two kimono.

The bathroom was small, scrupulously clean and the bath itself made of iron, heated from below, and which had a wooden grating to prevent one burning the feet. The old aunt hung about instructing me in the use of the contraption and if Kaneko had not got her out of the way I feel sure she would have washed my back. I soaped and washed myself outside the bath, rinsed off, and then got inside. But the wooden grating came loose, and I hopped out and scalded myself on the side of the beastly thing to find the grating floating on the top of that very hot water. And try as I might I could not wedge it into place. A *Goyemonburo*—Goyemon bath—has ever since possessed a special sort of terror for me, and I always shudder to think of the wretched robber, Ishikawa Goyemon, who gave his name to the contraption through having been boiled alive in one a few hundred years ago on the dried up part of the river bed at Kyoto.

It was obvious that herself had much to talk of with her family and so I was easily persuaded to retire, and I lay there with all the events of my life flashing through my mind with the speed of film passing through a projector and each memory a single frame.

Outside there was a sharp clap-clapping sound, repeated at intervals and drawing nearer and nearer, followed by the noise of a piece of iron being dragged over the ground. Unable to control my curiosity I got up and slid aside the wooden shutter in time to see father-in-law pass by clapping two pieces of wood together and followed by a man trailing an iron rod.

It seemed ages before Kaneko came to bed. She was not unduly pessimistic, said that her father had made little comment one way or other. But I was not really interested. All I wanted to know was why he was traipsing around knocking a couple of wooden blocks together to keep folk from their sleep.

"Oh that! Why, it is our house's turn for the fire watch, and father has to do that once every hour around the block throughout the night."

"Oh, really! I thought it was just another Japanese rite in which he was trying to exorcize the evil spirit of the barbarian from his hearth."

"He is a hard-headed man," she replied. "Be patient. I think he likes you, but he has for so long been telling people that he would never allow me to darken his doorstep again—that I had disgraced the family, so that he must put up a show until he finds his own way out."

Chapter Two

I

I WAS awakened by the sound of someone groaning and moaning as if in great pain or sorrow; sometimes it was a sort of low chatter, then a kind of shuddering note crept in, and occasionally a wail. I shook herself.

"I think something is wrong. Someone seems to be ill."

She rubbed her eyes, and sat up.

"Oh, go to sleep, it is only father greeting the sunrise and praying to his gods."

"What! And does he do it every day?"

"Yes, and it will go on for sometime, because after this he'll begin all over again before the Buddhist altar."

I did not see father-in-law for some days. He was up at crack of dawn to prepare the offerings for his Shinto God shelf and his Buddhist altar, and to say his noisy prayers, and he was out of the house before I was about and did not return until I was in bed.

He certainly appeared to be very religious, and mother-in-law, too, for Kaneko was very soon having to instruct me concerning my unwitting offences against some of her mother's pet gods. There was the God of the Kitchen whom I apparently offended by cleaning my shoes in his domain, the God of the Well was put out because I left my shaving brush on the side of his abode and, as I was informed that there were several million of these Shinto Gods, I realized that I had better tread warily.

Visitors began to arrive even before breakfast and, apart from the inevitable bean paste soup which I found quite palatable and which is said to be very good for smokers as it is supposed to clear away the harmful effects of nicotine, this Japanese meal of soup, rice, pickles, and sometimes fish, has always appeared to me to be most unsatisfactory.

Nagahama, a typical Japanese country town, possessed quite a thriving silk industry, was famous for the production of a special crêpe silk called *chirimen*, and the manufacture of mosquito nets, and velvet. The thump, thump, of looms could be heard almost everywhere and, as velvet in particular was very much a home industry, in many homes a single loom was operated by the women folk. Between the lake and the hills and mountains to the rear is a wide plain devoted chiefly to the growing of rice, amid which are numerous quaint old world hamlets and villages with their thatched houses and many splendid temples and shrines, and through which clear streams tumble down to Lake Biwa. The people of this part of Omi, or Shiga prefecture called Goshu, are very conservative, and for centuries have been renowned as thrifty and shrewd merchants. Some of Japan's greatest business houses were founded by men from Goshu, and it used to be said of them that: "where they had passed the grass would no longer grow". But the fine temples and shrines bear testimony to their devotion to religion, and although Goshu experiences severe winters, has suffered periods of great drought as well as the effects of earthquakes, yet its people have remained independent and proud to an extreme.

Enormous wooden structures in eight of its main streets house the splendid floats brought out once each year for Nagahama's famous festival, one of the finest in the land and of which its inhabitants are justly proud. This originated in the time of Hideyoshi, the great sixteenth century warrior who rose from obscurity to become generalissimo of the Empire, who was even bent on conquering China, and who gave Nagahama, where he built his first castle, a large sum of money to commemorate the birth of his first son. This the townsfolk decided to use in building the great and ornate floats for what was to become known as the Nagahama Matsuri which has since then, excepting for a break during World War II taken place each year in October to draw visitors from all over the country.

Lake Biwa, said to have been formed in the remote ages during an upheaval of the earth when Mount Fuji arose in the east, abounds in fish and particularly the sweet trout and roach, the latter prepared with rice to form what is known as *"Funa Sushi"* and esteemed for heart diseases, apoplexy, even as an aphrodisiac, but the smell of which is worse than that of a very ripe Limburger cheese.

In the park by the shore are some stone ramparts, all that remains of the once proud stronghold of Hideyoshi.

A few miles away at Hikone the well-preserved and attractive castle of the Ii Clan nestles amid the pines of a hilly promontory, and to the West is a pinnacle shaped island named Chikubushima, a place of shrines and temples where Benten, goddess of many virtues presides, whither flock pilgrims and sightseers in the excursion steamers that ply between the prefectural capital at Otsu and the tiny ports and landing places around the lake.

And, as if silent vanguards of the shape of things to come, the great chimneys of the factory adjoining the park belched forth smoke in production of cotton and other textiles to flood the markets of Asia with inexpensive goods as Lancashire and the newspapers of Manchester rumbled with anguish in complaints against "slave labour" and the "rice-fed workers of Japan", as if a Japanese switch to bread and butter, marmalade and kippers, and bacon and eggs, could solve the difficulties of an industry which appeared to regard a world monopoly as a sort of divine right; and the chauvinistic Japanese Press countered by telling its readers that the dastardly British cut off the hands of Indians to prevent them earning their curry and rice by competing with the millworkers of Lancashire.

For days I made the round of relatives and friends of the family in town and in the countryside accompanied by brothers-in-law, and One-armed Cho, who seemed to have developed a great attachment to me. The children believed that he'd lost his arm in some deed of derring-do in the Russo-Japanese War, but mother-in-law confided that it had been snipped off by a railway train when he decided to sleep on the tracks after a prolonged drinking session. A puck-like little man, he always wore kimono too short for him, a broad smile, and seemed to spend most of his time with children whom he'd entertain with stories and by manipulating a doll which he stuck on the stump of his arm. He'd wasted a small fortune left him by his father in collecting all kinds of birds, expensive imported dogs, and in entertaining his friends. And when his money was gone and debts had been paid by a thrifty brother his relatives had found him a room somewhere in town, guaranteed his meals and hoped he would behave. He was the veritable god of all children and was always with the young-sters, in their homes, in the school playgrounds, playing with them in the lakeside park, and invariably with an infant he'd been minding for someone or other strapped on his back. He was obviously light in the head, but I soon came to regard him as the most lovable and perhaps the most carefree and happy person I had ever met.

II

The boy continued to arrive on his bicycle with the box of cold fish, the inevitable curry and rice, and beefsteak, sent in to the order of my extraordinarily difficult but obviously not ungenerous father-in-law, and it was when exploring the town and I came upon a fat, jolly looking man standing outside a shop who wished me good evening! in English, and invited me into his establish-ment, that I found the source of my special fare.

It proved to be a small restaurant, with tables and chairs, and on a shelf behind a bar were bottles of "White Pig", "Corvan's Gin", the "Buckingham Palace" whisky, and other Japanese versions of the "Water of Life", gin, brandy, ver-mouth, etc.

Two pointers, a setter, and a couple of nondescript dogs, barked a welcome as I entered and, after begging me to take a seat, he disappeared to return with a bottle of Old Parr. He apologized for the quality of food he'd been sending me on father-in-law's orders and prepared an excellent meal. He said that for many years he'd served in the Empress liners of the Canadian Pacific Steamship Co. Mishima San was indeed a fine cook when he pleased and we became good friends; but as he was intolerant of bureaucracy and worldly he was at that time regarded by the local police as something of a dangerous reactionary who was probably in the pay of Moscow.

Wherever I went I attracted a crowd or a band of followers, for a foreigner in those parts was indeed a rarity. Down the line at Omi-Hachiman lived a worthy American missionary who'd established a school and an architectural college with the assistance of a benevolent countryman who'd given him the manufacturing rights of a healing balm known throughout the world from Buffalo, N.Y., where it had been conceived, to Puntas Arenas and Timbuctoo, and which was always to be found in Japanese barbershops where it was used for soothing the ravages caused by the razor.

I had come to love life upon the *tatami* which was always so clean and shining. The clip-clop of the *geta*, the pipe of the noodle-seller, the whistle of the man who cleaned out smoking pipes with steam, the clack-clack and jangling of the firewatchers, even the racket of the pieces of bamboo to which strips of cotton and silk were attached for dusting and which simply flicked the dirt from one place to another and poked holes in paper screens and windows and which came to be my pet aversion was music to my ears. The *tokonoma* was never without its vase, or trays of flowers or sprigs of leaves or berries, and neither was the lavatory, the plumbing of which was primitive to an extreme but which was always sweetened with a pungent but attractive incense.

And there was seldom a dull moment.

One morning little Jiro from next door was crying and displaying his diminutive penis on which there was a pimple. "He has been doing something wrong in the lavatory," said his mother, "probably spitting in it, and the god is punishing him." When one of my young relatives developed a toothache he was packed off to the railway station to return smiling with a bright red chop on his jaw and announced that the pain had gone. The station man had chopped his jaw with the ideographs for Tokyo and in this manner sent the pain on its way to the capital.

One evening the local millionaire called for me in a car and whisked me off to a restaurant where I was overwhelmed with country geisha and serving maids begging me to teach them to dance to the tunes provided by a portable gramophone, and returned home my chin stinking to high heaven of the pomade from their hair. I was visited by teachers of English from middle schools all over the countryside and by students who begged me to tutor them for their entrance examinations to higher schools and universities, the father of one even offering to open a special school for this purpose.

However, I had not been able to get close to father-in-law who persisted in avoiding me; cousin Kimi was liable to appear at any odd hour, day and night, to put on a screaming spell concerning the Fox and other evils we had brought with us, and had even harangued me in the street, and there was the tussle with the old aunt from Formosa.

All had been so kind, especially hard working mother-in-law and, as I wished to do some shopping I decided that we'd invite her and a young brother-in-law to Kyoto for the day. All arrangements had been made and we were to leave on the following morning when that night the aunt stormed into the house and demanded an explanation from mother-in-law as to why she was going on a journey without first consulting her and obtaining her permission. What Kaneko told her I could not understand, but it was enough to bring about a first-class row, in the middle of which Kimi had another fit and the old harridan then turned, and pointing to me announced that she would arrange that herself and I be divorced immediately.

"You'd better go for a walk," said Kaneko. And realizing that I could do no good staying there I strolled down to the lakeside, terribly unhappy that I had been the cause of sowing discord, but furious with the old aunt, and then set off for Mishima's restaurant where over many bottles of the excellent Japanese beer, I told him my troubles.

He laughed. "Don't take any notice of that old woman. She has been a pest to the family ever since she came back from Formosa. All believe that it was she who sent poor Kimi crazy in marrying her off to a drunken wastrel who divorced her as soon as he had borrowed all he could from her father."

"Oh, I am not worrying for myself, but for the family, especially my wife's mother," I replied. "And it is obvious that I am a terrible embarrassment to the old man."

"Don't worry about him. He is all right. His friends are always on to him about his hard-headedness. He'll come round in time, you wait and see!"

Just then a geisha appeared with whom I had danced at a party. She was willowy, with the long classic type of face, reminiscent of the beauties of another age depicted by Utamaro, Hiroshige and other wood-block print artists.

Hideya was her name and, after we had exchanged greetings she invited me to a nearby Japanese restaurant, I was in no condition to refuse but, on the contrary, felt quite inspired.

However, no sooner had Hideya started to assist me to forget my troubles than cousin of the morning suit appeared and insisted that it was time for me to go home.

All was quiet in the household and Kaneko and her mother sat awaiting me, the old lady showing signs of tears.

"I have apologized to aunt," said herself. "And tomorrow morning we shall go there together so that you can make your apologies."

"What on earth are you talking about, woman? Why should you, your mother or I, apologize to her?"

"Oh, please. Do let me handle this trouble. This is a Japanese affair. Aunt is father's elder sister. Mother has been persecuted by her since her marriage, aunt even tried to have mother divorced from father. But such is the Japanese family system. If we do not smooth things over mother will suffer, everyone will suffer, but if we apologize to aunt, which will not cost us anything, everything will be all right."

"Good heavens! Do you think I would allow you to be insulted in this way by my aunt?"

"Yes, I know. But you are in Japan and in a very conservative part of the country, so please do this for me. Do you think I like it? Of course I hate the whole business. But I know that it is the wisest course."

I pondered the matter. I could see that she was really boiling with anger but knew that I must do everything possible to make her happy and so agreed, on condition that we leave without delay.

"But, in a few days the cherry trees in the park will blossom and the whole family will have a party under the trees. Tomorrow I have promised that we'll go together to visit an old friend of the family who particularly wishes to meet you. We must stay until after the cherry-blossom party."

"Well, as you wish, but after that we must go—to Tokyo or to Kobe, or back to Hong Kong—and we'll not come back until they ask us on their bended knees."

"Oh, don't be silly. And now go and have a bath."

"Oh! So you even want me to suffer again in that terrible iron contraption like that poor bloody robber they boiled alive in the thing?"

What mother-in-law must have thought if she saw the aftermath of that remark I do not know, but she probably resigned herself to the fact that her daughter had succumbed to shocking foreign habits.

III

Faint hints of pink were beginning to fleck the trees in the lakeside park, in temple and shrine grounds, in hamlets and villages and on the hillsides, and the atmosphere was charged with a sort of impatient expectancy and all seemed like a father awaiting the news as to whether his spouse had delivered him a boy or girl.

Houses were thrown open to the four winds and bedding out to air in the warm, spring sun, as herself and I entered a very conventional type of house which turned out to be that of a wholesale stationer and paper merchant.

A sturdy, good natured looking, middle-aged man arose from beside a large porcelain firebowl, bade us welcome, and was introduced to me as a remote relative.

He clapped his hands and called a name and immediately a strikingly handsome woman whom he introduced as his wife appeared who ushered us along a corridor into the heart of the premises until we came to a large room which overlooked a most exquisite rock and pine-clad garden.

As is the custom I was made to sit with my back to the place of honour but I had sufficient time to glimpse a superb arrangement of flowers and a scroll painting executed in Indian ink.

The house seemed to be of great age and the woodwork shone with the sheen of polished rosewood.

Sweet cakes and bitter, green powdered tea, having been served, after appropriate remarks had been made by herself concerning the excellence of the tea-making utensils and the bowls in which it was served. Then individual tables were placed before us by the wife, on which were raw-fish garnished with tiny leaves and with a dab of horseradish resting upon a slice of carrot, together with a tiny dish of soy, as well as sake and beer.

And after the usual expressions of admiration concerning the manner in which I handled my chopsticks, surprise that I liked raw-fish, my height, and niceties concerning the health of my parents, both expressed the opinion that we must stay, no matter what inconveniences I might have to endure, that their home was always open to us, and that they would support us against any prejudices within the family or from without. But if this and the splendid repast were not enough this kindly man then commenced to display for my benefit a collection of porcelain, scrolls, wood-ware, lacquer, each piece of which was taken from a white store-house which stood at the side of the garden, and when the room resembled the emporium of an antique and fine art dealer invited me to select something which should serve to remind us of their friendship.

There were dishes and bowls and vases of the white and blue Hizen ware, Satsuma and Kutani porcelain, various articles of lacquer, old steel mirrors, a bronze figure of Kwannon—Goddess of Mercy, incense burners, cloisonné ware, an exquisite little ship —the treasure ship of the Seven Lucky Gods carved in ivory, and a figure carved in wood and beautifully painted of a benevolent looking and ruddy-cheeked old man with white hair and whiskers, dressed in a pale blue gown with a black cap upon his head and who carried a bamboo rake.

"Please select one of these poor things," our host insisted. I turned to herself for guidance. But she would have nothing to do with a choice and, there being no help for it, I took up the figure of the old man.

"I was hoping you'd choose that; it is most appropriate," he remarked, and left the room to return with another figure about half the size, of a sweet-faced old lady dressed in long, flowing robes and carrying a broom.

He placed the two figures before me and said, "I could not give you the old man Jo, without his beloved wife Uba, for they are the symbols of wedded bliss. I am sorry that I do not have the real mate of the old man, but she was destroyed in a fire many years ago. But Kaneko will explain their significance and their story, which is perhaps the oldest in our literature."

Herself then related very simply the story of the ancient pine-tree of Takasago in which dwelt the spirit of a maiden who was seen by Izanagi, one of the creative divinities, who fell in love with her and took her for his wife. Both lived to a very great age and died at the same time on the same day, since when their spirits have abided in the tree. They resume human shape only on moon-lit nights when they revisit the scenes of their worldly happiness and go about their work of gathering pine-needles. The two figures, called Jotomba, are placed in the bridal room of newly-weds, and their story, "The Song of Takasago" is often sung or recited at wedding ceremonies.

We were deeply moved by Sato San's great kindness, and Jo and Uba were very dear to us until they were taken from our flat at Kai Tak, Hong Kong, in December 1941 with all the rest of our possessions by Chinese looters or the Japanese military. Since then I have come across many figures of old man Jo and his beloved wife and sometimes they are accompanied by a crane or a stag; but I have not found any which could replace those which really brought us so much happiness in the difficult days when we badly needed moral support and which were given us by one whose sincerity and desire for our happiness is an unforgettable and cherished memory.

Chapter Three

I

PAPER lanterns had been strung amid the trees in the lakeside park now crowned with the delicate pink cherry blossoms, their branches entwining to provide a great circular bower through which the rays of the sun pierced down from an almost cloudless pale-blue sky to dapple the shaded grass with patches of amber brightness.

The lake was a sparkling mirror; the mountains on the far shore great mauve masses in the haze created by the warmth of the sun and now streaked with but faint rivulets of snow.

A shrike screamed down on unwary sparrows, the crows seemed to caw-caw their joy, and kites perched on the stone ramparts of the ancient castle like priests in profound meditation.

I had arisen very early, but not in time to catch a glimpse of father-in-law who had awakened me as usual with the precision of an alarm clock by his loud invocations towards his gods, and after breakfast set out with One-armed Cho, my young brother-in-law and sundry young children, armed with bundles of clean straw matting and boxes and bundles of crockery and cooking utensils in order to stake out a claim for the family cherry-viewing party which was to take place that evening and which I had now decided would be my Swan Song, as far as Nagahama was concerned. For despite all the great kindness shown me by everyone, yet father-in-law's attitude and the fact that I was a terrible embarrassment to him and had hurt his pride, had convinced me that to remain longer at this stage would only aggravate matters and even bring great unhappiness between Kaneko and myself.

We spread the matting beneath the trees on a tiny hillock but a few yards from the shore. Here and there men were driving red painted stakes into the ground on top of which they fixed lanterns made of bamboo with white, paper windows.

Food and drink stalls were being set up and everywhere children and womenfolk were like ourselves staking out the family matting.

A little toddler, a girl about five years of age, came running up to where I sat smoking with my back against a tree.

"*O'Hayo, Hana-kami San!*" she cried with glee, "*O'Hayo!*"—"Good morning, Mr. Nose-Paper!"

This was my nickname with the very young, and I immediately whipped out some tissue from my pocket and gave her the treatment.

There used to be a little jingle about Kobe..."Where the

women all wear *Obis*, and the kids have running noses," composed
by an American Marine officer who was studying the language.

In those days a running nose was the one feature which seemed
to mar all the charm of the very young, and I had started my own
campaign with the children of the family and relatives which
soon embraced any youngsters who attached themselves to me.

Certain doctors used to say that it had something to do with
diet and the fact remains that with the post-war improvements in
feeding and, especially the consumption of milk, butter and meat
proteins, it is no longer a characteristic of Japanese children.

Having been instructed to stay put and look after our claim,
after a picnic lunch with Cho and our brood, brother-in-law
returned pushing a perambulator loaded with a charcoal
brazier, fuel, cushions, various kinds of food, and large bottles
of sake, plus a case of Kirin beer. And, no sooner had we unloaded
all this than to my horror Hidesaburo, a whimsical farmer relative,
staggered up with aunt from Formosa's great wicker chair on his
back, accompanied by a gang of interested children. Then came
aunt herself, all smiles, having apparently buried and completely
forgotten the hatchet, and Kimi, decked out in her best and really
looking quite pretty, and by her rational manner, appearing to
have got rid of the Fox, other female relatives and more and
more children. There was not a man around except One-armed
Cho and soon aunt had a vast group around from all the other
camping sites to which she was obviously holding forth on me
and my idiosyncrasies. And from the nods and smiles and stares I
might have been the prize exhibit in a museum or zoo. So I fled to
the lakeside, pushed out a boat and rowed towards the far shore.

The boat was too small, the oars too short, so that I was continually smiting my knees, but I pulled away and was soon some
three hundred yards away where I rested and found myself bathed
in sweat and so removed my jacket and sweater. It was like a
summer day, perfect for a swim. The water was certainly cold to
the touch, but it occurred to me that a dip would anyway absolve
me from having to endure that iron bathing contraption that
night and so I stripped down to my underpants, secured the oars
and plunged in.

The shock of that icy, lake water simply staggered me; I gasped
and choked, struck out furiously to try to warm my aching bones,
and looking shorewards saw a couple of boats coming my way and
a multitude of folk gathered at the water's edge.

The only way to get back into the boat seemed over the stern
and I grabbed hold of the flimsy craft and heaved myself up-
wards, with the result that under went the stern, and I was
floundering about in a submerged craft with my clothing floating
up around my ears and my shoes floating out of reach.

By the time I had that wretched boat afloat, upside down it
is true, three boatloads of laughing schoolboys were on the scene.
They retrieved my shoes and socks and other garments and got
the boat in tow, but I refused to be rescued and swam behind

them to the shore with the firm conviction that herself would not be pleased, father-in-law less so, and that I had made a perfect fool of myself.

By the crowd which had gathered, including Kaneko, who looked far from pleased, her mother who appeared anxious, and a policeman whose many gold teeth flashed in a broad smile, I might have been emerging from a successful attempt on the English Channel.

But what made things all the more embarrassing, was the fact that my thin white underpants had been rendered all but transparent, and I had to wade the final ten yards or so in six inches of water!

"What an exhibition you have made of yourself!" muttered Kaneko as she wrapped One-armed Cho's kimono around me, and he stood there in his underwear, whilst her mother prophesied rheumatism, pneumonia and other ills, the younger women giggled, and others just stared as if contemplating a dangerous lunatic.

By the time I had been escorted to the family matting beneath the blossoming trees, brother-in-law had arrived on his bicycle with a change of underclothes plus a pair of socks, a fine set of under and outer kimono belonging to father-in-law, and a flat type of *obi*, the tying of which consumed much time and the attention of the womenfolk.

"You are stupid, don't you know that no one swims in the lake before July 1st," scolded herself.

"You might have been poisoned by the water snakes," put in the vinegary aunt from Formosa.

"You'd no right to take that boat. Ida San, the boatman, is very angry," said Kaneko.

"But it is a fine day, the water is not so cold, and you must know that since I was able to walk I never could resist water; I either fall in, am pushed, or jump in of my own accord."

"I am sorry about Mr. Ida, or whatever his name is, and I shall be happy to apologize and pay for any damage to his boat. And I have never heard of water snakes that bite. Surely this lake does not possess a Loch Ness Monster?"

Just then a hoary old man arrived, sat down in front of me, and amid a great deal of chuckling presented me with a bottle of sake. He turned out to be none other than the allegedly angry boatman, said he hoped I'd be his friend, and furthermore, thanked me for taking out his boat, the capsizing of which had cleaned it out and saved him a job!

"Well, it seems to me that you are the only person unhappy about my swim," I observed to her ladyship.

"Oh, all right. I know it was funny and they'll talk about it for days around here. They'll probably write about it in the newspaper. But it won't please father and only make him more difficult than ever."

The sun went down like a great ripe persimmon, the lanterns

flickered amid the pink encrusted trees, the park gradually filled with the children from the schools, the men-folk started to arrive. But despite the merry group around me and the spirit of the true spring which the blossoms had brought I felt sad, and sobered by the fact that my breaking of the conventions by swimming at the wrong time of the year and so making Kaneko's family all the more conspicuous would most certainly upset her father, and that we'd better take the first train in the morning and leave them in peace.

II

Between the branches the stars twinkled and the lantern-lit park spread a shimmering glow over the still waters. Hundreds of voices seemed to be singing as many different songs. Elaborately clad geisha went from one party to another singing and dancing to the strains of samisen; there was constant laughter, and children dashed about playing touch and hide and seek. It was as joyous a scene as I had beheld anywhere and the gathering of people of all trades and classes was like one great family party. On the rough stone charcoal brazier a pan of beef, vegetables, bean curd and various strange edibles was steaming; on another smaller charcoal pot was a large kettle in which the half-pint sized bottles of sake were heated. Cup after cup of wine I exchanged with a continuous stream of well-wishing visitors, sometimes there were five or six cups in front of me to be emptied, and then to conform with custom I had to return them filled to their donors who then after having my own cup filled would hand it back at me. It was a long process which it seemed would never end for we seemed the most popular gathering in the whole park and in addition to relatives there was old Ogawa, an aged man who lived opposite, farmer Hidesaburo, the barber, the cousin of the morning suit, and One-armed Cho who seemed intent on becoming my man Friday. But there was still no sign of father-in-law, and under the influence of sake, beer, and "Buckingham Palace" whisky I had attained such stage of "don't give a damn-ness", and felt that he could go to the devil as far as I was concerned.

With some ceremony, and brushing aside of sundry womenfolk His Worship the Mayor was presented, a cheery sort of character, well-pickled, his face as red as a beetroot, who expressed the opinion that the whole town was honoured at harbouring such a distinguished English gentleman, proceeded to mumble what was apparently meant to be God Save the King! and laughed so much that I expected he'd have an apoplectic fit. He then insisted that I accompany him to his own particular camping site. I stood up, and soon realized that perhaps only a Japanese can make his kimono embrace him properly, that I was not going to look even more ridiculous by wearing shoes, like an enormous Italian prima donna I had seen singing *Butterfly*, slipped off my socks, and managed to adjust my toes in between the thongs of Cho's *geta*, and stumbled off with the mayor on one arm and the handsome geisha, Hideya, on the other.

Countless cups of sake later through stops at half a dozen parties and a further collection of name cards of Yamamotos, Itos, Ishis, Satos, Kobayashis, Nakagawas, Nakamuras, and others, we arrived at a small restaurant at the far end of the park where a convivial party of the mayor's cronies for several geisha was making merry and gave us a very noisy welcome.

I immediately decided that if I were to stay in Japan I'd have to obtain some instruction on how to wear a kimono. For on trying to sink down on my knees in proper fashion I found that the garment had a nasty habit of flying apart to expose my legs and the waistband shot up around my chest. The way in which a Japanese woman so gracefully sinks down and sweeps her kimono under her without apparent effort, so that it is a creaseless compact expanse between her obi and her knees, has never ceased to fascinate me.

But, no sooner was I seated upon a pile of cushions prepared by the very solicitous Hideya than to my great surprise I looked up to find none other than father-in-law seated before me offering a sake cup. And as the geisha filled it the company roared its approval, the old man gazed at me with a broad smile, and I wondered if this was occasioned by the sight of his kimono I was wearing, his genuine pleasure in discovering for himself that it would be better to make the best of the barbarian his daughter had had the temerity to marry against his wishes, or simply because seeing that practically the entire population was disposed to be friendly that he could not go on cold-shouldering me any longer.

I tossed back the hot sake, handed him back his cup, then Sato San proposed a toast and, late as it was, it seemed that our party had just begun.

And from a disgruntled looking old bull, father-in-law had become a great, joyful, oversized boy, laughing and joking, singing, pressing food and drink upon me and in general fussing over me and proclaiming it seemed his general pride that I was his son-in-law.

It was long after midnight when with Sato and Hideya, we staggered away from the mayor's party into a swirling flurry of pink petals swept from the trees in the rising breeze. Lanterns swayed and flickered, and a sad mess of paper, empty bottles, food boxes and cigarette packets presented a sordid contrast with the tent of pink loveliness now being slowly shorn of its splendour which flecked our hair and clothing and dusted the ground like snowflakes.

Here and there a few stalwarts were still eking out the sake and beer, others lay deep in drink and sleep.

Outside the park, Sato succeeded in bidding us adieu over the old man's protests that he accompany us home for a nightcap. We stumbled homewards with the geisha as escort, father-in-law's song echoing over the silent town and, just as we rounded a corner ran slap into diminutive mother-in-law and Kaneko, each carrying a lantern.

"You ought to be ashamed of yourself, you silly old man," scolded mother-in-law at her grinning spouse, "waking people at this hour!"

The geisha simpered, herself attempted to look severe but without any great success, but there was something of a hard glint in her eyes as she thanked Hideya for taking care of us, and as we were lighted on our way home and I glanced back at the figure of the delightful entertainer, something was muttered, about cats!

"Cherry Blossom Time in Japan." Not so very many years before a bevy of chorus girls garbed in flowery patterned kimono, such as I now realized no Japanese would be seen with in a coffin, twirling sunshades, and singing a song with this title had captivated me from the stage of a London variety theatre. Around the year I was born they used to sing "I Love you little Jappy Soldier, tra, la, la, la, la, la . . ."

And if the British and American Press now thundered about the menace of Japan, dumping, Manchuria and China, while general Western conceptions of the country and its people still bordered on images of an Eastern Lilliput so skilfully woven by Messrs Loti and Hearn, my first experience of the Japanese equivalent of a cockney Bank Holiday or a Fourth of July celebration left me enchanted beyond all measure and with the feeling that I had sensed something of the pulse of a kindly and happy people.

Satiated with happiness, and with food and drink, I was soon dreaming of my childhood, of schooldays in a town on the Thames Estuary, of the bustle of London where I had been born within the sound of Bow Bells: I was back in my seafaring days as an apprentice, *Glenshiel* plunging into the storm-tossed Bay of Biscay, licking the salt-spray from my lips and glorying in the challenge to the angry ocean, watching the stars fade into the false dawn of Eastern seas and heading into the sunrise, to be awakened to reality by the tinkle of a bell and the clapping of hands as father-in-law paid his morning tribute to his ancestors. And I sank back again into a doze of doubt that the happenings of the previous night had not after all been just a dream. A fantasy unfolded before my eyes of a youth captivated with a young nurse bandaging his injured wrist, of walks together amid gay and strange streets, in quiet shrine and temple precincts. I watched her descend the gangway of a steamer, a fatherly looking British consul in a Chinese city was giving them his blessing, they were laughing and splashing in waves, gazing hand in hand at the myriad lights sparkling like the gems of a mammoth tiara on Hong Kong's Peak . . . then I was stumbling almost naked out of the lake, and then a shake, Kaneko's smile, and the clip-clap of *geta* outside were real indeed.

III

Contrary to my suspicion, the old man's behaviour of the night before had not been the result of a rush of blood to the head, or through a general mellowness brought about by sake and the cherry blossoms, for he not only awaited me to have breakfast with him but had an iced bottle of beer on hand in case I might be suffering a hangover.

Mother-in-law beamed her satisfaction, herself was quite obviously relieved and she announced that her father had obtained a small house for us which would be more comfortable, and had, in fact, paid the first month's rent.

"Well, it is very good of him. But how on earth are we going to live? And you know I should be back in Hong Kong in a fortnight."

"He says that he has already arranged for you to give private English lessons, many of his friends have sons who want to enter the Imperial Universities, and the higher schools. The English examination is one of the most difficult obstacles. He thinks you'll have plenty of time to write and you can study and learn the language."

"But do you want to stay?"

"I did not want to, but I think you do, and father really wants us to stay."

I could not have wished for more. I had written a series of stories on the junks of the China Coast, had had several articles and stories published in England and America, but in editing a travel magazine and at the same time having to secure most of the advertisements there was little time or opportunity to write what I pleased.

That morning the town watched and grinned as we made our first appearance out of doors in daylight with father in law who whisked us away to a temple where he introduced a venerable shaven-headed priest as our future landlord, who led us to a small bungalow type house on the edge of town approached from the road by a narrow pathway alongside a paddy field, and situated in front of a small pinewood.

The garden, at the bottom of which was a clump of bamboo, was overgrown with weeds, and outside the porch was a banana tree. The front door was of the Western variety instead of the Japanese sliding one, which led directly on to a room with a floor of boards about eight feet wide which adjoined another with raised floor and matting and divided from it by wooden paper-windowed sliding panels. From a back door a sheltered path led to a shed which harboured the kitchen, and next to this was the usual, but conventional primitive offices. It was terribly dilapidated, the paper hung in strips from the doors of the closets, the *tatami* was torn and brown with age, cobwebs twined about our faces and hair, and clouds of dust arose where we walked.

Beside the porch was an alcove with a window facing the

garden, and wide, sliding windows from the room with the board floor revealed an attractive view of Mount Ibuki.

The prospect of rendering it fit for habitation was appalling to say the least, but that little house seemed to cry out to be lived in. I visualized all that might be done with the garden, saw shining *tatami,* attractive new panels on the closets, clean *shoji* paper, and, as we had lived only in apartments and boarding houses, a first real home to ourselves, and all for fifteen yen, or thirty shillings a month!

While Kaneko and her father bustled about the place noting all that had to be done, the priest informed me that he had a number of books on Buddhism in English, and that he was an admirer of Oliver Cromwell, which I thought a strange choice for a Japanese.

Leaving father-in-law with the priest, on our way home I noticed outside a shop a large, bear-like creature made of porcelain, which had enormous testicles and a pot belly.

"Good heavens! What is that?" I inquired.

"Oh, that is a *tanuki.* I don't know what you call it in English."

I hadn't the foggiest idea.

"But does it exist in the flesh?"

"Oh, many people say they have seen them. They are said to be able to bewitch you," she replied with a giggle.

Life was most certainly filled with surprises and on arrival home I sought the assistance of the dictionary.

"Tanuki—a badger; a cunning person," I read.

"I cannot remember having seen an English badger," I remarked, "but I am sure I should have done so if they are anything like the Japanese type."

Kaneko laughed and confessed that she, too, had never seen one, but on her mother being told what we were laughing about she became quite serious and maintained that the *tanuki* most certainly did exist, and indulged in all manner of wicked pranks.

"Ask your father," she advised herself.

"What, has he seen one?"

"No, he did not see one but he saw its footprints."

"Oh, please tell us about it."

"Well, one night when father was coming home he saw a bicycle at the side of a path. It seemed a strange place for anyone to leave a new machine and as he stood there wondering he heard someone singing and laughing and, outside a small hut in which farmers sometimes keep their tools, to his astonishment there was a man named Kuroda sitting up to his neck in one of these stinking pits of fertilizer in which farmers empty their honey buckets.

" 'What are you doing, Kuroda?' father shouted.

" 'Come in, come in! It's fine in here,' Kuroda replied. And so off father went to arouse people who brought a rope which they slipped over Kuroda and dragged him out to the river. But while doing so someone pointed to a large footprint and all then knew that the poor man had been bewitched by a *tanuki.*"

"Oh, then father did not see the creature?"

"No, but if Kuroda had not been bewitched why would he do such a foolish thing?"

"I expect he was boozed," scoffed Kaneko.

"Oh, I do not think so, the *tanuki* is a cunning creature. You never see them. They just lie in wait for people in lonely places. Why do you think we say *tanuki-oyaji*, for a foxy and cunning old man?"

A few minutes later when the old man arrived he confessed that Kuroda had indeed been full of booze. But that was exactly when the *tanuki* took advantage of you, he observed with a grin, and as for the footprints, well mother-in-law had stretched the long-bow a little as he had not actually seen them, but the people in the neighbourhood said they saw them the next morning.

"But never mind the *tanuki* for now," he said with a chuckle. "Later I will tell you about some other fabulous creatures and goblins like the '*kappa*' and the long-necked female demon, but we'd better get busy because I have arranged for you to move into your own home tomorrow."

Chapter Four

I

THE NEXT morning, just after the old man had said his prayers, the barber and his boys came around with a "Dunropu"-tyred cart, followed by One-armed Cho and Hidesaburo the farmer, who assisted mother-in-law turn out pots and pans, crockery, firebowls, bedding, and all manner of other house-setting-up paraphernalia with which they set off to our new abode.

When I arrived there after breakfast accompanied by half-a-dozen very small children a host of friends and relatives were washing and scrubbing, fixing new *shoji* paper, cleaning the garden, patching the roof, and an electrician was fixing the wiring.

I tried to make myself useful and picked up a window to slide into its groove but, after wrestling with it for a minute or so was about to give up when a boy about as big as sixpence came along, took it from me, and calmly fitted it in place. And the chuckle from everyone as good as said: "Now you just keep out of the way, for the mysteries of a Japanese house are beyond your poor Western comprehension."

I then tried filling buckets and wringing out wash cloths. But I could not even do this properly. For Japanese wring cloths or clothes toward them, just as they strike a match away from them, use a saw toward them and pull boats up on a beach stern first. And so I became a miserable looker-on until Kaneko took pity on me and suggested that I'd be doing all a favour by taking the children who were enjoying making nuisances of themselves, to the lakeside, adding with a chuckle, "But don't go swimming!"

I started out with five children, but when we arrived at the park there were ten. We fed the wretched monkeys in the small zoo, threw stones in the water, helped a fisherman haul up his boat, watched a gang of men digging a canal, and each child contrived to become smothered with a mass of chocolate and other stickiness. There was little chance of my looking after them, in fact they took charge of me; for was I not an ignorant foreigner, unable to speak a civilized language, and with strange ideas about running noses and how Japanese toddlers should behave?

By noon when I returned it seemed the house cleaning and removing was nearly complete and all, including the priest and two of his acolytes, were scoffing large bowls of chicken noodles. It was a different house. The woodwork glistened, windows had been cleaned, there was new *shoji* paper, the board floor gleamed, there was new matting, the kitchen had been distempered, and

34

father-in-law had bought us a table, four rush-bottomed chairs, a small desk, a book-case, and a chest of drawers.

On top of the cupboard in the alcove next to the front door stood the old couple of Takasago, and in the place of honour in the matted room hung a scroll depicting Kwannon—Goddess of Mercy, seated at the edge of a cliff, which the priest said was very pretty but a bad painting because according to Buddhist belief Kwannon is without sex and should be depicted as such.

As Hidesaburo was about to start out to obtain rocks with which to construct as a small Japanese garden, father-in-law proceeded to fill two small bottles with sake and the farmer sat down again. But to his disappointment and my amazement the old man then proceeded to douse the house with the precious fluid.

"He is purifying the house. He should have done it before you started drinking," said Kaneko answering my inquiring glance, "because first wine is dedicated to the gods."

It was, after all, no different to our custom of christening a ship with a bottle of champagne.

What remained in the second bottle the old man rubbed into his hair. He said it promoted growth. I was to find that he always did this when filling bottles just as he would eat a single grain of rice which one of the children had left on its chopsticks. But if Japanese are most particular about waste in their home life, yet outside on excursions and picnics no more profligate people can be found anywhere and they litter the parks and beauty spots with half-eaten lunch boxes, fruit and other food.

During the afternoon a nice little rock garden took shape, complete with a pool lined with pebbles and fashioned chiefly by the priest and the barber. But it seemed that Hidesaburo who brought in the materials together with plants and shrubs could not bear questioning concerning where these had been obtained.

With sunset, and everything in shipshape and Bristol fashion, slippers in the porch, a kettle hissing away on a firebowl, curtains on the side windows, a letter box affixed to the gate and, even a pole provided on which to hang out a flag on national days, who should arrive but aunt from Formosa and Kimi bearing a large bundle from which were produced a kimono, under-kimono, *haori, obi,* even Japanese socks and clogs, all made specially for me.

On the table lay several packages done up in white paper and bound with the red and white cords used for gifts, and packets of stamped postcards.

"Being master of the house," said herself, "you must now go around to the neighbours with these gifts to introduce yourself and ask them to be neighbourly."

"Oh, no, you are not going to make an exhibition of me! You'll have to go, tell them that your husband is shy, tell them he is ill, tell them anything, but I am not going."

However, father-in-law decided otherwise and I was soon dressed in my Japanese finery during which there was much debate how my *obi* and the two short cords which fasten the *haori* in front must be tied, mother-in-law had me squatting so she might arrange the collar of my *haori* and I was turned around, stretched and bent like a puppet on strings.

The *tabi*—socks with a socket for the big toe—came in for much comment and were compared with those of a certain wrestler named Dewagatake who weighed some six hundred pounds and whose feet were two feet long and ten inches wide!

The barber, who was president of the district barber's association, was to accompany mother-in-law and myself on our expedition as he had to introduce me to the street master, who happened also to be a barber, and he returned shaved, pomaded and attired in such splendour as seen only on important ceremonial occasions.

After some difficulty in fitting my toes into the clogs, we set out, probably the queerest looking trio the town had ever beheld, accompanied by the usual crowd of children and creating much opening of windows and doors of the curious as we passed by.

The street master was in the midst of shaving a customer whose face was covered with lather, but he dropped everything, we went into our bowing act, requested him to be kind to us, presented him with our gifts, while the half-lathered customer bobbed up and down in his chair quite unconcerned and obviously enjoying the performance as did what seemed half the populace in the doorway and out in the road.

Then off we went with an admiring crowd at our heels to bob and bow at near neighbours to whom we took a bag of sugar or a box of soap, and a packet of postcards to those not so near.

My feet ached, my head sang from sheer bewilderment and self-consciousness at the sensation I had provided; but it was not over yet; for our home lacked a bath and, as I would have to get used to it sooner or later father-in-law decided there was no time like the present, and whisked me away to the public bath-house which I was to find such an interesting and jolly place.

II

That bath-house was to become my favourite haunt, and it was there that I met so many kind and jolly folk who seemed to go out of their way to extend me their friendship and who eventually accepted me as just another patron.

It was only some two minutes' walk from home and approached from a narrow lane; smoke was belching forth from a tall iron chimney, and the windows were covered with steam which contrived to make the lights within appear like great pearls.

Father-in-law slid aside the door to the men's section and I heard a female voice bid him welcome and, as I stepped over the threshold, a young woman sitting in a kind of box between the male and female departments put her hand to her mouth to check an exclamation of surprise, then politely gave me the usual greeting.

As the old man fumbled for his money I stood behind him

extremely embarrassed and unable to control my eyes from wandering to where on the other side of the pay box ivory bodies contrasted with sleek black tresses, one of which was that of a buxom middle-aged woman who turned, and holding a small towel in front of her, started a chat with the old man as carefree as though they might be meeting at a social function.

After slipping off our footwear we stepped onto the matting of the dressing from where old man Ogawa and two other elderly men sat around a firebowl clad only in their *"fundoshi"*—literally, an "arse clout", chatting and smoking. Father-in-law handed me a basket for my clothes and chatted to his friends while I stripped off and stood there with the small towel clutched before me to hide my credentials, conscious of the fact that not only was the girl in the pay box watching me with interest but heads were craned around the partition from the female section whence giggles and whispers proclaimed that I was indeed hot news.

To add to my embarrassment there was also a sudden influx of customers whom the old man greeted one by one and introduced to me, and in making my bow with that towel clutched over my privates I must have been enough to make a cat laugh. So when he slid aside the bathroom door and motioned me to follow him into the steam I needed no second bidding and slid in sideways as I did not like the idea of exposing my rear end to the interested company. I must have looked stupid; like a bashful virgin about to be deflowered.

Years later I was to bow bollicky naked, without benefit of towel, to no less a personage than the late General Tojo.

In the centre of the large bath-room was one bath, about fifteen to twenty feet square in which several men, one holding a small boy, were relaxing; others sat outside on the tiles on wooden stools soaping and washing themselves, rinsing off from wooden buckets which they filled from taps in the wall, one was shaving by the aid of a mottled mirror, and two others were immersed in a small bath in the corner which contained greeny-grey water and in the middle of which a balloon-like bag floated.

Father-in-law pushed a wooden bucket and stool towards me, sat down before the line of taps, filled his bucket and commenced to rinse himself. The change which had come over him in his attitude towards me was almost unbelievable; for now it seemed that he was anxious to show me off wherever possible. I followed his movements very carefully; when he got up I did likewise, and then followed him into the soupy looking medicine bath with the floating bag. There we sat for perhaps five minutes while he conversed with our fellow inmates, and then stepped out for the real business of washing.

But in making for a stool and bucket I came to grief over a stray piece of soap and went slithering across the tiles on my back. This brought forth expressions of alarm, but when it was seen that no bones were broken a hearty laugh all round. There now appeared a stocky individual wearing a *fundoshi* and a towel tied round his head, who I was given to understand was a sort of major-domo around the place, and commenced to massage and slap around an old gentleman who'd just left the big bath. Called the *sansuké*, he turned out to be a general back-washer, massager, and stoker of the furnace, performed in both male and female sections, was a fund of information on every conceivable subject and a very jolly fellow.

The old man certainly took his bath seriously, lathering every part of his anatomy, rinsing off, and then soaping up and scrubbing away all over again. I meticulously followed whatever he did until my body was like that of a prize porker preened up for a cattle show. Then over he went to the taps to sluice himself with cold water and wash out his small towel.

We then joined a half a dozen others in the large bath, the temperature of which it seemed to me would have boiled lobsters. The old fellow just got his neck on the edge and appeared to be intent on a sleep and I sweated and clenched my teeth in an effort to demonstrate that contrary to the opinions of the rabble raisers in the Japanese Press that the British Empire was decadent one of its sons was still sticking his chin out and maintaining the jolly old stiff upper lip. However, when an old man started clapping and shouting and I expected that, he too, objected to being boiled alive, and instead of a refreshing injection of cold a jet of boiling water scalded my tenderest parts, I decided that "mad dogs and Englishmen" were just not in the race and skipped out leaving that inferno to the hardy sons of the samurai. Father-in-law seemed still asleep, and so not knowing what to do with myself I sat down again before the taps and did some more burnishing of my toenails until he finally joined me and gave himself another dose of the cold water treatment and dried himself with the damp, wrung-out small towel, a process which takes a lot of getting used to.

The dressing room was filled to capacity and several women who had finished their ablutions were sprawling over the pay-box chatting with the custodian as pa-in-law and I, towels clutched before us, entered from the bath room.

I was dressed in a jiffy, but the old fellow just stood there talking and stroking his now rosy red body with his towel, while a sort of running commentary, obviously about me, was being maintained by the women for the benefit of others still bathing in the section next door.

"The Japanese wash their bodies, Koreans wash their clothes—and the Barbarians do not wash at all."

Influenced no doubt by the Shinto emphasis on purification, the bodily cleanliness of Japanese is a characteristic which has been praised by many writers since the first Europeans, the Portuguese, visited the country in the middle of the sixteenth century.

"For the Japanese a bath is a necessity, for the Chinese a luxury."

"Cleanliness is one of the few original items of Japanese civilization. Almost all other Japanese institutions have their roots in

China, but not tubs," wrote Professor Basil Hall Chamberlain some seventy years ago. He also remarked on the sweetness of a Japanese crowd and this is still to a great extent true.

Pierre Loti found the people of Nagasaki in the eighties quite fanatical about bathing which according to him they practised in tubs in the street. There was at one time a bath which used to be wheeled about from house to house.

Three hundred or so years ago the bath-houses of the great cities were nothing more than glorified whore-houses until authority clamped down on them. Promiscuous bathing continued until the early part of this century, the sexes being separated in some houses only by a rope; but even when this was forbidden by law they continued to bathe together in the country and still do in some places. It was the West with its prudish ideas about nudity which hastened to rob the heathen of the benefit of sunshine and clothe him in Mother Hubbards, and made the Japanese aware of nakedness. For in Japan the "nude was to be seen but not looked at", until strip-tease and the art photo salons came along with the so-called post-war re-orientation and democratization.

"Well, what did you think of the bath-house?" inquired Kaneko.

To her great amusement I related in detail my first impressions.

"It is a great place, and I think I shall soon get used to it and like it once I cease to feel like a performing monkey in a circus."

Chapter Five

I

IT WAS a delightful lotus-eating existence.

I was up with the dawn, sometimes scribbling until the small hours of the morning, and armed with books on phonetics which I had procured from Kobe, spent a couple of hours each day ministering to the needs of a varied assortment of scholars introduced by father-in-law, from two tiny boy sons of a doctor who was convinced that they'd get nowhere without a knowledge of English; serious lads who talked of John Stuart Mill and Adam Smith, even *Sartor Resartus,* giggling high-school girls, one of whom would endeavour to play tickle toe under the table, the priest, a policeman who was probably only keeping an eye on me, a dazzlingly beautiful young miss, sister of my wealthy friend who was so popular with the local geisha, and who was to marry a businessman who expected to be sent to Calcutta; to a very serious farmer, and a flighty middle-aged widow with plenty of money and nothing to do who when herself was absent seemed bent on more attractive studies.

One-armed Cho with a baby on his back was seldom far away and old man Ogawa called round at least once a day. A rugged, white haired old fellow, he reminded me of my paternal grandfather who was never without his black bowler hat, I believe he even slept in it, who hated socialists as instruments of the devil, who'd have allowed lords, dukes and such to walk over him and who believed in "God bless the squire and all his relations, and keep us in our proper stations".

Old Ogawa seemed to have a weak bladder, for invariably when out in the town I'd come upon him making water, in a stream, against a tree, or against someone's house, and he'd turn his head, toggle in hand, to greet me. He was said to have been very wealthy, had buried five wives, and been mayor of the town; but wine and women to which he was still partial despite his three score years and ten, had brought about his downfall and he was now dependent on sons and daughters concerning whom he never ceased to complain.

True to his promise Hidesaburo had started us a small vegetable garden and, as herself had protested that she did not like the fertilizer he used, would appear with his rubber-tyred cart to which he'd draw her attention: "You see, pure horse dung only!"

One morning, as just after sunrise I sat at the open window with my English language newspaper which the boy had just delivered, enjoying a smoke and my first morning cup of tea and the sight of Mount Ibuki clad in a rosy mystery, my reverie was brought to an end by a most revolting smell as a farmer started to spread the field outside with the contents of a cartload of honey-buckets.

"I suppose that when I was a child I did not notice it," said Kaneko, "but now I find it perfectly disgusting; there ought to be a law against it."

"Oh! And then how are the farmers going to get along? What comes out of the soil must go back to the soil, you know."

"Well, do they use that horrible stuff in England?"

"Many farmers do. Probably they're the people who win all the prizes at the agricultural shows—giant pumpkins, melons, and you know they say there's nothing like it for roses. But most such valuable fertilizer, instead of being processed so that it is inoffensive to the nose and non-productive of disease goes down the sewers or is dumped out at sea where the fish eat it—fish which eventually appear on the table. All that is wrong here is the method, and particularly the way those buckets slop over in transit along the roads."

We closed up the house and went to the family for the day.

Hidesaburo thought it a great joke. "It is just a country smell that's all, and better than all that stink of motor cars and sweat of the cities; if you'd let me use the real stuff for your garden I'd grow you the finest tomatoes you've ever seen."

Kaneko wouldn't have him in the house in his working clothes, he'd loll on the window sill while I gave lessons to my pupils, when we were eating, bring us all the local news, talk about his military service in Siberia, and became immensely proud of his ability to greet me in English.

"Goo' moaning, ticher!" he'd say, with a chuckle.

"Good morning, Honourable Best of Three Young Sons of the Mountain Field," I'd reply, giving the literal translation of his name.

"*Ohayo Yabu Sensei,*" he'd counter, giving me the Japanese equivalent of mine.

"What's 'My Dear'?" he once asked Kaneko. "Your husband always says 'My Dear'." And so she became Mrs. My Dear, and as Hide progressed and amazed his friends he soon became known as the English-Speaking Farmer, a title of which he was vastly proud.

Father-in-law dropped in at all times of the day, and although professing to be very busy always had time enough to proudly boast of various incidents in the lives of his ancestors, never tired of re-telling how a rascally priest had swindled the family out of great wealth, and never failed to cap it all by prophesying that very soon the pot of gold coins said to have been buried by a great-great-grandmother under a pine-tree would turn up to revive the family splendour.

I was unable to make very much of a show for, as far as I know, my ancestors were humble Essex yeomen, not a trace of aristocracy, no admirals, generals, even members of parliament, highwaymen, pickpockets; not even an O.B.E. have I been able to trace among relatives; but I did relate with pride how one of my forbears constructed a village fire-engine and also slipped in the rather remote relationship to a Lord Mayor of London through the husband's brother of a great-aunt.

However, when I gave a short talk to the students of the local middle school I was dumbfounded to learn that I had been introduced as the son of a millionaire who owned some sort of a railway terminal in New York.

The old man adored his family, spoilt the sons to an extreme so that they behaved as though heirs to the Mitsui or Iwasaki fortunes, and I never witnessed better food or clothing, even in the homes of the very wealthy, than he provided.

According to Kaneko and mother-in-law he had been a proper old roué, had gone off one night to Tokyo with a geisha during an iron and steel boom, and although he sent funds home regularly they saw nothing of him until four or five years later when he just walked in one evening with a *Tadaima!*—"Now I'm back!" just as if he had only been across the road for a haircut, and sat down and shouted for sake and food.

II

In July I decided that I could no longer delay my return to Hong Kong to settle our affairs and bring back our few possessions. Sailing from Kobe in a Blue Funnel liner and returning in an NYK vessel I was back before the end of the month and, after a hold-up at the customs house where they insisted on inspecting a case of some two hundred books for prohibited literature, and especially the works of Karl Marx, took the first train to my new home buoyed up with happiness and the conviction that for me it was the best place in the whole wide world.

Kaneko was waiting, clad in a lovely summer kimono. Father-in-law had often intimated that her sophisticated Western clothes were not suited to the country, he'd taken great exception to a red rubber raincoat, for in those days only children wore red, and I liked the change. The sight of a Japanese woman wrapping herself in kimono is a joy to behold and makes the slipping and wriggling into a dress an eyesore in any comparison.

During my absence Kaneko had made me several *yukata*, the light cotton kimono used in summer and to the bath, and this became my daily wear in the hot weather.

In our area firewatchers used to go around each night beating a drum, slapping the wooden blocks together, and trailing the iron rod. Once every hour you'd hear Bong—Bong—bong, bong, clack-clack-clack, clack, and the clanketty, clank of the rod.

Every now and then a neighbour used to deposit a black lacquer box with us which would contain some notice of local importance, a subscription list for some cause or other, perhaps a local shrine festival, roadmending, or even a party for some young man called up for military service, which Kaneko would deal with and then pass on to the next house. This was one of the ramifications of the *tonari gumi* or neighbourhood association.

One day after the box arrived, herself announced: "You will have to do fire-watch duty for three nights starting tomorrow."

"Now look dear, you surely do not expect me to go around banging a drum. That is your job, or get your brother over to do it for me."

"Oh no, you'll have to do it. The Emperor is going to Fukui for the general manœuvres and the policemen are being taken away for special duties, so law and order must depend on the neighbourhood associations. It will be a great experience for you, and it is your duty as a householder."

"Oh, well, then I hope they let me play that drum and I'll put in a little less monotonous beat to cheer up the neighbours."

The next day the whole town was bedecked with flags to honour the passage of the Imperial train and outside our gate were the Rising Sun flag of Japan and a St. George's Cross, which was easier to make than a Union Jack, and which brought round the policeman to inquire whether we were starting a hospital, and who went away quite unconvinced that this was indeed the original flag of the land of my birth.

That evening I reported to the fire-watch H.Q., in the shop of a matmaker. Here were assembled an old woman, an ancient man, and the master of the shop, sitting round the fire-bowl drinking tea.

At ten o'clock we went into action. Led by the mat-maker who carried a lantern, I followed with the drum, the ancient man with the wooden blocks, and the old woman brought up the rear with the iron rod. Bang, tiddy bang, bang—bang, bang! Bang tiddy, hang, hang—hang hang! My strictly unorthodox drum beat startled my fellow fire-watchers and then they chuckled. This was a novel beat and the old man followed it up with the wooden blocks. Clack, clack-a, clack, clack—clack, clack! Shutters and windows opened, dogs barked, and children left their beds to follow us around the area; for never had such a strange drum beat been heard in that town, even in the prefecture, and never perhaps had they seen such an extraordinary firewatcher and, as we trooped past my home an extra vigorous beating of my drum was quite unnecessary as there was herself standing at the window vastly enjoying watching me perform my duties as a householder.

For three nights I paraded with the drum, and the matmaker's shop became quite a popular meeting place for the neighbours, friends from the bath-house who brought along sake and beer, and many of whom sat smoking, talking and drinking with us until the early hours of the morning. It was a fine and jolly experience, my drum beat became accepted in the area and was even taken up in other parts of the town.

III

The time came when we could no longer put off our visit to
Hidesaburo, whose mother, aged ninety-two, was most anxious to
see us. One fine afternoon we set out across narrow paths between
the paddy-fields where the rice was in fine shape, streams rippling
with an abundance of water, their banks covered with wild-flowers,
nettles and reeds.

Just after passing a water-mill we came upon several children
who announced that they were Hide's offspring come to show us
the way, then three mongrel dogs greeted us, and before a ramshackle farmhouse whose moss-clad thatch sprouted iris, stood
our friend.

"Ha! You'd hardly recognize me would you?" he said with a
chuckle. It was the first time I had seen him properly shaved and
wearing kimono.

In the middle of a large room was a square fire-pit. The rafters
were blackened with smoke and age, and from which hung all
manner of dried herbs and fruits, and on the walls hung straw
capes, large wide-brimmed hats, as well as oilskin and rubber
rainwear, and on a ledge the Shinto god-shelf, below which were
full-length pictures of the Emperor and Empress of Japan. In a
corner stood a hand-loom on which was a half-finished piece of
red velvet.

Mrs. Hide turned out to be a careworn, pleasant woman whose
tired eyes reflected the strain of bearing and raising nine children.
And seated on the clean, though patched and worn *tatami*, was
Hide's famous mother, ninety-two years of age, who had borne
fourteen children of which he was the youngest, and had been
unable to walk since her mid-seventies. Her face was like a piece of
polished leather, her eyes bright, and she had every one of her
teeth which were enamelled black, so that when she opened her
mouth in the half-light it appeared that she had no teeth at all.
She had been born in 1841, married in 1857 when the feudal
practice of blackening the teeth on marriage was still observed,
and had never known toothache.

She spoke in a very high-pitched voice and as she eyed me up
and down with what I thought was not disapproval said to
Kaneko, "Tell me, what is it like to be married to a foreigner?"
Herself blushed and mumbled, much to the old lady's amusement,
who then announced that should she be born again she'd marry
a foreigner for a change.

"He looks a lucky man," she observed, "and he has a fortunate
name. You are to be envied O'Kane, for your family name is at
present unlucky and now you have taken your husband's name I
see good fortune in store. But you will never have children."

"No, mother, they'll have lots of children," protested her son.

She shook her head. "No, they'll never have children of their
own."

"Beware when you are twenty-nine," she told me. "Never travel on the twenty-ninth of the month. And this year you should not journey towards the north or north-east."

By this time the house had gradually filled with Hide's relatives and neighbours, homely folk, all of whom by their washed and brushed appearance seemed to have been invited to the party which by all the preparations being made promised to be quite a banquet. But the old lady held the floor, asking Kaneko what kind of food we ate, what it cost to feed me, did my country have an emperor, how often did I bath, to queries concerning our married life which caused herself to blush and brought chuckles all round.

Just as we sat down to eat and the sake started flowing a gaunt man entered, accompanied by several children, who was introduced as Nakayama San, a farmer but also a tile-maker, who seemed to be trying to grow a beard but whose hair sprouted from his cheeks, from his neck and even from his ears and from the deference paid him I gathered he was the village master.

It was obvious that much trouble had been taken in preparing the meal for the raw fish had to be brought from town; there were all manner of vegetables, grilled eels, and finally legs and wings of chickens dipped in soy and grilled over the charcoal fire. Kaneko protested that they should not have gone to so much trouble.

"We eat simply," said Nakayama San, "but we know how to nourish ourselves and our children—and this is indeed a very special occasion, for never have we been honoured with such an interesting guest whose wife is the daughter of Tomosaburo, our friend."

Mrs. Hide had now started work at her loom and said that she had to finish the velvet by the next day for one of the factories which gave her piece work. It seemed strenuous labour and the threads were woven over pieces of copper wire and driven home with a bar with handles at each end. Withdrawing the wires with pliers is very difficult because the cloth must be held over the fire at just the right temperature.

Hidesaburo had been trying without much success to prise the cork from a bottle of what looked to me suspiciously like "Buckingham Palace" whisky which was at length passed to Nakayama San who surveyed it, gave an order to one of his children, who ran off and reappeared with a glass cutter with which he soon cut off the neck.

It was not "Buckingham Palace" though it tasted just the same, and according to the label was Prime Highland Whisky, bottled in *Skotland*.

"Who wouldn't be a farmer?" exclaimed Hide when I remarked that it must be a hard life.

"It's the best life, and my family have been farmers for centuries. Yes, we suffer at times from drought, from insect pests, from shortage of fertilizers, and from corrupt officials and rice speculators, but I grow and store enough for time of need, and my pond is always filled against drought. In the winter evenings when the snow lies deep we make straw sandals and bamboo ware, the material for which is to be had for the taking; my wife makes velvet and reels silk to pay for the children's clothes and other needs, and I go to the mountains and cut wood for our own charcoal.

"Often I go to the mountains for roots and shrubs, clip them up a bit, put them in pots and sell them on market day to the foolish townsfolk who are either too lazy or stupid to go and get them for themselves."

"The gods have given us what we need," broke in the straggly bearded one, "even the glow-worms which the children gather on summer evenings and sell in bamboo cages."

"Go to Manchuria, some say. My brother went there to find it bitterly cold, barren soil, things difficult to buy. He said he'd sooner starve at home."

"Yes, all my folk have been farmers, I'll always be a farmer, and I hope my sons will continue to take their living from the soil."

The thump of the loom ceased as Mrs. Hide observed: "Yes, you are content with anything, aren't you? I want something better for our sons."

"Oh, you would have them policemen like your fine brother with his brass buttons and his little sword, walking about as if he owned everybody, picking up old men for piddling in the city streets, arresting boys for riding two on a bicycle. I am a free man, I want them to be free and not to worry how they speak to a factory boss or a pissy official."

"My brother's an educated, decent young man," retorted his spouse.

"Yes, he doesn't get his hands dirty, he does not smell of manure, he doesn't get drunk—unless someone else pays for it!"

The tile-maker started to sing.

Hide's baby girl was fashioning a crane out of silver paper, her sister sat by Kaneko showing her drawing book, and the old crone was nursing a baby.

"I want to hear a foreign song," said the old woman. Loud applause greeted this suggestion and so after taking another slug of the fiery Osaka *Skottish* whisky I burst into the "Farmers Boy", the meaning of which herself translated for their benefit. Then for an encore "So fare thee well my bonnie young gel, for we're bound for the Rio Grande". But my final number brought the house down and to the thump of the hand loom all joined me in "What shall we do with the drunken sailor?"

"Washara duwara dunka sayra
Washara duwara dunka sayra . . ."

Hide looked at the tile-maker and round the company as if to inquire: "Well, what did I tell you about my foreign friend! He's a knockout isn't he?"

Twilight had now set in and after a great deal of delay in

taking our leave and promises to come again we finally set out with a motley throng to set us on the road.

At the crossing of two paths stood a gaunt, dead looking tree, leafless and eerie in the twilight, at the foot of which was a wooden shelter in which resided a stone Jizo clothed in a red apron and at whose feet reposed dishes of stale rice, stumps of candles and half burnt sticks of incense.

The simple stone figure of the Buddhist saviour, patron of little children, of pregnant women, and guardian of travellers whose wayside shrines are to be seen throughout the length and breadth of the country, seemed to exude compassion and invited confidence in his powers of kindness, and Hide said quite gravely: "At one time, before the Jizo was placed here, many unhappy folk hanged themselves from that tree which exerted an evil influence on all who passed this way and around which all manner of fearsome ghosts and evil goblins gathered after sunset. When I was a boy none ever came near this place after nightfall if they could possibly avoid doing so."

Kaneko shuddered. She was most susceptible to ghosts and has always claimed that she saw the spirit of her grandfather floating away from his body in a faint blue light.

With Hide leading we trudged in single file along the narrow path towards the water-mill, whose thumping, creaking and groaning added a somewhat creepy note to the singing of insects and the croaking of frogs.

"What a lonely place!" observed Kaneko as we drew abreast of the water-wheel. "And what an uncanny noise at night!"

"You know the story, don't you?" inquired Hide. She nodded.

"Of course, they say that many years ago the owner of the mill killed his wife and three children in a fit of madness, then sliced open his stomach and threw himself in the stream," she explained.

"Yes, and until a famous Shinto priest exorcized the evil it is said that on the anniversary of that terrible day the mill turned blood during one whole night," added the farmer.

We hurried on to the highway where we said goodbye to our kind friends, and as we neared our little home, from out the small pine-wood came the "Too-whit-too-whoo!" of an owl.

"Oh, dear! What with that tree and the water-mill, and now that hooting of the owl, I am goose-pimples all over," said Kaneko with a shudder. And, as I opened our door a bullfrog gave out a great full-throated bellow to add full measure to the somewhat spooky ending to a happy and memorable day.

Chapter Six

I

O'BON, THE Feast of All Souls, when the spirits of ancestors are escorted from their graves to be honoured and feasted in the homes, had passed, the cicada's strident note rent the air, and dragonflies made love and swooped gracefully above the pools and streams.

Now I was no longer any novelty in the neighbourhood, I could walk abroad without acquiring an escort of children, and local interest in the English language had dwindled to a point where my only students were the serious-minded Endo, son of the brewer of sake, and the two tiny sons of the doctor.

Poems, essays, short stories poured into the local post-box, ninety-five per cent of which came back with the usual "editor's regrets", and finances were indeed at a very low ebb. And that early September morning my newspaper seemed packed from back to front with dire forebodings for mankind in general, what with the mouthings of a bull-necked braggart in Rome, the bombast of a brown-shirted fanatic named Schikelgruber in Germany, be-whiskered Japanese generals whipping up the ultra-nationalists with their periodic warnings of crises and a very able old journalist and historian indulging in his usual hate against Great Britain and the United States, well-spiced with much horror stories of their greed and brutality to impress the gullible of the need to liberate the masses of Asia from their foul clutches.

Disappointed lovers were casting themselves into the craters of active volcanoes, a youth had cut off his finger and sent it to a liberal minded statesman, another had written a letter in his own blood. There was an article by a noted philosopher on the need to revive "the true Japanese spirit", extolling the fine spiritual qualities and, the altruistic intentions of Japan towards all her brothers and sisters of down-hearted Asia as opposed to the hard materialism of the West. Indignation poured from the editorial pen concerning the insult to national honour arising from the accusations made by certain foreign manufacturers of textiles that Japanese had pirated their designs; a student had again invented a silent aeroplane engine, the authorities were deeply concerned over the contaminating influences upon Japanese youth of Western jazz and dancing, and an actress was in the pillory for having a permanent wave.

There was also a warning about the activities of foreign spies and particularly the missionaries who cloaked their real purpose of undermining the Japanese spirit in ostensible good deeds towards lepers and the poor.

After breakfast who should appear but Ishii, the policeman, a jolly fellow, patron of the same bath-house, and who I suspect had been appointed chief of the foreign section of the local police station to keep an eye on me. Usually I quite enjoyed Ishii's visits, despite the stupid questions he'd put to me concerning the age of my great-aunt, when and where my grandfather had been born or the colour of my mother's eyes; but on this occasion he was as welcome as the plague and, after he had badgered me with questions concerning the situation in Abyssinia, my opinion of Hitler and Mussolini, which I gave him without pulling punches, I became downright indignant.

"Why do you continue to ask me such stupid questions, Ishii San?" I inquired with some heat.

"Oh, it is my duty," he replied. "We do not always believe the newspapers and we like to know what a foreigner thinks about world affairs."

I picked up my paper. "Well, I hope you do not believe this rag then, and its highly respected oracle Mr. Tokutomi which is no doubt poisoning the minds of millions of your people who cannot think for themselves?"

He seemed shocked and turned to Kaneko.

"Oh, but your husband is wrong about Tokutomi Sensei, he is a very great Japanese and a learned man."

"Well, I agree with my husband that he does not write as if he is learned," she replied.

"Oh, but you see, he has to follow a policy," countered the policeman, "because Japanese are likely to forget their duty and are too easy-going. They must be educated and reminded to be true Japanese."

"And this is to be accomplished with lies and hate? You do not read such rubbish in the *Asahi*," she replied.

"Oh, but the *Asahi* is read by the more intellectual type of people. Some think it is far too liberal."

"Well, but it does make an effort to respect the truth," she countered.

"Oh, but why does your husband get angry? Are we not all kind to him, is he not happy here?"

"Of course I am happy! I have never been among nicer and kinder people, including you, Ishii San. However, I cannot but feel indignant at the constant efforts to spread hatred through a pack of lies in imitation of the methods of Hitler and Mussolini."

"Don't take things too seriously," remarked Kaneko. "There's nothing you can do about it, so why worry?"

"Well, if more people would worry and express themselves freely there wouldn't be Hitlers and Mussolinis and Stalins and Francos."

Just then the postman appeared at the window, but instead of tossing the mail on to my table he waved a piece of paper which he wanted signing for a registered letter.

And the woes of the world disappeared immediately when to my great joy, and astonishment, I opened that letter to find a cheque for no less than seventy U.S. dollars, the largest sum I had ever earned for a single article.

"What did you write?" inquired the policeman, greatly interested.

"Oh, a piece about a chap named Bill Adams!"

"Biru Adamusu?"

"The Japanese called him Anjin Miura—he was from a place called Gillingham, in England, and he came here in 1600 and built some of the first ocean-going ships for the Shogun."

Ishii seemed dumbfounded that anyone should pay so much for such a story but left with, I felt, some satisfaction in that he was now able to give an interesting report to whoever was supervising my movements, interests, opinions and sources of income.

"Well, thank goodness he's gone—and you should not be rude to him. And now we can pay our bills," sighed Kaneko.

"Rude! Next time he'll be coming round to inquire if my bowels are open."

"Don't be silly. You should know by now that Japanese are a little bit inquisitive."

"Little bit! It's a disease. How old are you, your mother, grandfather ... they're age crazy! I think we'd better go off to Kyoto and Tokyo for a few days."

"Oh, and spend everything and come back to a diet of eggs, eggs, eggs and potatoes!" Eggs, were strange to say, the cheapest form of nourishment in those days and the poultry merchant threw away livers, kidneys and gizzards!

"It won't cost so much and I can collect for three articles which have been published in Tokyo."

"I think we ought to wait till you sell something else before we go away on pleasure."

"Pleasure! What do you mean? I've got to find outlets for my work and besides I will not learn much staying here all the time."

"Good morning," interrupted father-in-law. "Ishii San tells me that you've published a book in America and received a lot of money!"

"Oh, it's a book already! Probably be the secret plans of the mosquito-net factory by lunch time."

"I'll come with you to the bank. If you go alone they'll cheat you on the rate of exchange. These Goshu people are too shrewd."

Outside the stonemason's was One-armed Cho, with a canary in a bamboo cage, surrounded by a group of small children and, as usual, a baby on his back.

By the way father acted in the bank one would have thought I was Mr. J. D. Rockefeller, for he would deal with none but the manager and in that personage's private office made quite sure that my cheque was exchanged for the last sen which represented

100th part of one shilling and twopence, and even *rin*, which was 100th part of that.

Outside our door a bird chirped away in its bamboo cage.

"Cho brought it," said Kaneko.

"Well, that was kind of him, and this is turning out to be a very nice day after all."

"But I wonder where Cho got it? He has a habit of buying things and sending the bill to his brother or to father. I suspect he found it before it was lost. You know he can do anything with bird. He once had one which used to go about with him perched on his shoulder, he also taught a crow to talk."

Within half-an-hour back came father-in-law, with Cho, and a fishmonger who claimed the bird which he said had escaped when his daughter was cleaning the cage.

"But you could not catch it," said Cho San. "You gave up getting it back. I did not go out and catch it with a net, I called to it and it came to me, so I think that it is mine by right."

"Fool!" exclaimed father-in-law. "Giving away things which do not belong to you. One day you'll do something which will land you in prison."

"Oh, but I am most grateful to Cho San," said the fishmonger, "for getting back our bird. And I must apologize for giving him so much trouble. He is quite right, we have no right to keep a bird if we cannot look after it properly, but you see my wife is very fond of it and so I hope you'll excuse me for causing so much trouble."

Cho San was now beaming and looking very important and magnanimous, but when the fishmonger departed with his bird became somewhat indignant. "What a mean fellow! Always asking me to mind their baby, run errands, find homes for their kittens, and takes away from you the bird they could not catch and which I had given you."

Cho San was a funny chap. He'd borrow something, once a coat belonging to father-in-law, which he'd sell or pawn to buy presents for children. The previous winter he'd sold all his blankets for this purpose and disappeared for days until mother-in-law found him blue with the cold and sleeping under newspapers.

II

That evening herself went off with her family to five or six hours of "country theatre" provided by a barnstorming group, and although I had already enjoyed a performance yet I did not feel that I could cope with another long session of sitting on the *tatami* of the flea-bitten and dilapidated hall. Going to the play was like a regular picnic; a family would hire two or three mats, according to their needs and take along food, sake, and even a charcoal stove on which to cook, and so what with the aroma of food, children running up and down the "flowery way"—a raised platform leading from the rear of the hall to the stage on which the performers made their entrances and exits—it was an interesting and colourful experience.

One melodrama, and the way it had been received by the audience, had intrigued me. The scene had opened on a lonely moor, a lonesome pine-tree centre stage, in front of which was a low embankment and on the back drop were a few angry clouds between which was the great, golden harvest moon.

Along the "flowery way" tripped a maiden dressed for travelling with wide-brimmed straw hat, her legs encased in a kind of cloth puttees, wearing straw sandals, and grasping a stout staff. On stage she peered to right and left and announced she was looking for her dear, old blind father, but finding he was not around made her exit amid the commiserations of the audience.

She was followed by a homeless type of fellow, bamboo basket over his head and playing a mournful dirge on a flute, and when he could find none to keep him company he, too, departed. Then came a poor old blind pilgrim calling his daughter's name. "Grandpa! Grandpa!" cried the excitable and kind-hearted members of the audience. "She was here just a few moments ago." But the old fellow did not appear to hear them and just hung about the stage muttering the story of his life until suddenly, from below the embankment, there leapt out a nasty looking customer, a black cloth concealing the lower half of his face, a great scar running down one cheek, and with sword in hand. "Look out, grandpa!" screamed the audience. "Look out!" But, alas, to our horror the wretched old pilgrim was foully done to death, and his assassin then calmly proceeded to wipe his bloody sword on his kimono and then went through his victim's belongings. The audience roared its indignation. "Beast! Monster!" they shouted. And as the villain made his exit small boys tried to grab his legs and pelted him with pieces of charcoal and any rubbish they could lay their hands on.

But no sooner had this rascal gone than back came the maiden, still calling for her dear old dad. And when she discovered the corpse her grief, and that of the tender-hearted audience, knew no bounds, and there was great rustling of nosepaper, deep sighs, and other expressions of pity.

Then the wandering flute player returned, commiserated with the poor girl, and in a dramatic gesture in which he removed the basket from his head and disclosed a handsome, strong countenance, to loud cheers vowed that he'd wreak swift vengeance upon the wretch who had committed such a gruesome deed.

Then, when the heroic minstrel fellow had led away the father-less girl, the villain actually had the temerity to return to the scene of his crime and judging by the anger of the audience, I expected that he might be lynched. By the way he searched about the stage it appeared that he'd mislaid some valuable object or else some highly incriminating document. And just as he seemed to have given up his quest there appeared before him the spirit of his victim in the form of a fiery, bobbing luminosity. Horror-struck at first, he recoiled from the ghostly object, but when it bobbed close to his face he drew his sword and attacked it; but every time he made a cut it flitted away and hovered in space bobbing up and down to infuriate him so greatly that he seemed on the point of madness. He was panting for breath, mopping his brow, and uttering terrible oaths when down the "flowery way" charged the flute player, sword in hand like some knight of old and in a moment they were at it hammer and tongs, thrusting, cutting, and the audience making as much noise as a crowd at a baseball game. At one period it seemed that the hero was getting the worst of the encounter and the audience seemed somewhat downhearted, but of course their favourite could not possibly lose and at last the villain was disposed of and amid great rejoicing the hero and maiden took their leave to live happy ever after. Shades of *Sweeney Todd, the Demon Barber,* and *The Murder in the Red Barn!*

III

That evening after entering the bath-house I was just taking off my clothes and talking to old Ogawa and policeman Ishii who'd finished bathing when there was a commotion in the women's section next door. Then the *sansuké* entered leading a red-faced, middle-aged man who apparently wished to take his bath with the women.

"If you can go in there, why can't I?" he protested.

"It is my business," replied the *sansuké*.

"Business! You dirty old devil! And you like it, eh?"

"Fool! To me naked women mean no more than dolls, or potatoes, or anything."

"Who are you calling fool?"

At that moment the door to the men's bath slid open and in came a naked, shrivelled and aged woman, supported on the arm of a fine, handsome young man.

"Oh, and what is this? Women in the men's side," cried the unruly fellow.

The old woman bowed low to the company, and said. "Please excuse me, but there is none to bring me except my grandson."

"Please do not trouble yourself," replied old Ogawa. "You come as often as you please, and you are fortunate in having such a devoted young man to look after you."

I hurried into the bathroom but when I had finished my friends were still in the dressing room discussing the individual who had disturbed the tranquillity of the place.

"Yes, and if you did your duty you would have arrested that fellow or thrown him out," said old Ogawa to the policeman.

"Oh, but I am off duty and it was a small matter, the man was drunk," replied Ishii.

"Oh, but on duty or off you make yourself a nuisance on all

manner of petty affairs, no lights on bicycles, and worry folk with questions about what is not your concern."

"Especially the age of their grandmothers," I prodded as I slipped on my *geta* and wished them goodnight.

I had not gone more than a few paces when a woman called my name and I turned to find Hideya, the geisha, behind me.

"We expected you were at the bath-house. I came to tell you that Kato San is having a party and wishes you will join him."

The night was young, herself at the play, and the willowy creature simply could not be denied. I said I'd go home and change.

"Oh, no, you look so nice as you are," she urged. My rich friend Kato, several of his cronies and a number of geisha were already quite merry, the portable gramophone was grinding out popular tunes, and geisha were dancing with geisha on the soft, matted floor. For despite the frowns of authority and the rules and regulations which had been promulgated for dancing establishments, many of which had been forced to operate much like speakeasies, the craze for Western dancing had spread even to the country and any desiring to be thought sophisticated just had to learn to fox-trot, waltz and tango.

That evening it seemed every geisha in the town plus maids and even their mistresses just had to have me trot them around the *tatami* and with most of them it was hard work, their tight *obi* restricting their movements, their sticky hair and ornaments scratching and oiling my chin. With the tall, graceful Hideya I never tired for she was not only the most charming of the town geisha but was a natural dancer. Great pains had been taken by her to teach me Japanese songs, the more popular and more modern type which I found little difficulty in mastering, and some I had learned parrot fashion from the records made by the popular tenor, Fujiwara Yoshie. But the *nagauta* type which often sounded to me a little different than a dog in pain required such vocal contortions as were quite beyond me. Father and mother-in-law were both fond of this type of song and could produce what to me seemed to be the most unearthly sounds.

When it came time to leave it was raining and, despite my protests Hideya and two of her charming friends insisted on escorting me home with umbrellas, and as if sensing my thoughts she said, "Don't worry about your missus. The play won't be finished for another hour."

But my attractive escorts were not content to leave me at my gate, they came to the porch and when I opened the door were soon inside and had my gramophone going. Then one perched one of Kaneko's hats atop her elaborate coiffure, and then to my horror started to disrobe. Hideya and the other girl could only stand and giggle while I almost went on my bended knees in my pleadings to them to get out of the place lest Kaneko find them there. But kimono and *obi* and various strings and accessories soon littered the floor and that impish creature was then striding about and preening in one of my spouse's dresses. My pleadings only seemed to aggravate their impish mood and terrified lest Kaneko should appear I told Hideya to get herself and friends out of the place while I went up the road to meet my wife.

When I arrived at the corner there was no one in sight, and I stood there for what seemed ages before the three geisha came out of the house, had difficulty in stopping them from joining me in my interception tactics and, when they were out of sight heaved a great sigh of relief, dashed into the house, tidied things up and threw open all the windows to rid the place of what seemed an overpowering smell of women.

"I am so sorry to keep you waiting up, the play started late," herself apologized in a most contrite manner. "And what have you been doing?"

My visit to what she scathingly referred to as "Cat Street" could not be withheld, for butcher, baker, candlestick maker, or her father would convey the good news in due course.

"I suspected you'd be out with that good-for-nothing Kato once my back was turned," was her reaction. "It's disgusting the way you men can find amusement with those powdered and painted dolls."

"Oh, but how can I refuse his kindness. I could not say I was busy."

"You could say you had work to do, and anyway you should have come with us, it looks so bad to people."

However, when on the following day mother-in-law came round to report that the geisha association and that of a neighbouring town had approached father-in-law with the request that he ask me to start a dancing class for them, she behaved as if I had been propositioned to start a house of ill-fame.

"Oh, dear, what a wonderful job, spreading Western culture among the geisha of Omi!" I chuckled.

"It's not funny, it's an insulting suggestion and it just goes to show what a laughing stock you've made of yourself," she replied with some heat.

"Good lord! And what about teachers of Japanese dancing, aren't they highly respected?" I jested.

"Don't talk nonsense. You said we should go on a trip to Kyoto and Tokyo, and now I agree that the sooner we go the better," she replied.

"Ah! Now you are talking. First you said we couldn't afford it, and it has taken the geisha and talk of giving me a job as a dancing master to make you change your mind!"

Preparations for our journey soon had her as affable once again as a well-bred cocker spaniel, but I could not help wincing in considering what her reaction might have been had she returned from that play just forty minutes or so earlier?

Chapter Seven

I

FOR TWO days we browsed amid the temple courtyards, shrines, gardens and palaces of Kyoto, the ancient capital and a city rich in beauty and the charm of the traditional, whose peaceful old world streets, side by side with all the bustle of the modern age seem to exercise an almost irresistible appeal upon all who have time to "stand and stare".

Pagodas, pavilions, hoary moss-clad rocks, aged trees, wide avenues and narrow lanes, the River Kamo and the canals lined with willows, even the lilting speech of its people exude echoes of its heyday which fostered and developed all the arts and sciences introduced from Korea and Cathay under the tutorship of the civilizing influences of Buddhism.

But if Kyoto is no place for comfort when the wintry winds whistle through its streets from the surrounding hills, in summer and early autumn it is too stuffy for comfort, and as I felt that I had been too long away from the sea we decided to make for Kamakura en route to Tokyo to see the Great Buddha and might be lucky enough to sample the views of Fuji-no-yama from the shores of the Pacific Ocean.

At one stage of the journey a large woman got in with a boy child of perhaps five or six years of age and sat opposite us. We exchanged polite conversation, and then the boy started howling and grabbed his mother's kimono near her breast. After trying to pacify the child she gave a sigh, which was also perhaps intended as an apology to us, heaved out a large breast for the boy and continued conversation with Kaneko.

"Fancy giving the breast to a boy of that age," I remarked.

"Well, there's still a lot of prejudice towards cow's milk," she replied. "My cousin used to howl for the breast when he was almost eight years of age. Many say that this is the reason so many Japanese have protruding teeth."

"Yes, and as far as I can see there are more men with rabbit teeth than women."

"Because they are always fussed more as children." I started to laugh.

"Don't laugh, she'll think you are laughing at her!"

"Oh, but I was reminded of a story my father used to tell. It seems that a young man was on his way to a wedding, all dressed up in morning suit with lavender gloves and silk hat. He was only a poor clerk so he had to use a tramcar and, just as the car started, in came a large Cockney woman with a baby, sat down opposite

56

the self-conscious young fellow, and pulled out her breast to suckle
the child. But her baby did not want any part of it and the young
chap was crimson with embarrassment when she said in a loud
voice; 'Nar, kerm on, tike it, you little bleeder, tike it, or I'll give
it ter the gent oppersit!'

"But I'm sure he did not want her breast," she said, with a
puzzled frown.

"Ha, ha! He was just longing for it!—Of course he did not
want it, imagine how he felt with the woman saying that to him in
a tramcar filled with people!"

"Oh, you mean it would have been all right if none had been
there?"

"Kaneko! Please imagine the situation—silly as it is!"

"Well, that is what I thought, for how could a young man want
the breast of a strange woman?"

Further discussion on this subject was prevented by the end
of the suckling opposite and the announcement by the conductor
that we changed for Kamakura at the next stop.

II

Kamakura, where in the Middle Ages the great Yoritomo
Minamoto established his "tent government", was at one time a city
of a million people. Now the veritable lung of Tokyo whose
citizens throng its beaches in the summer away from the petrol
fumes and stuffiness, yet it retains a wealth of historic buildings—
temples, pavilions, shrines, and above all the great image of the
Buddha seated on lotus petals, cast in bronze in the fourteenth
century, which is visited by thousands throughout the year from all
parts of Japan and from abroad.

As I stood for the first time before that mighty figure, with its
background of low hills and trees, its calm and benign expression
seemed to epitomize all the truths of the gentle Gautama's
teachings.

> "Be heedful when the heathen pray
>   To Buddha at Kamakura,"

wrote Rudyard Kipling, and I wondered how a heathen could
contrive such beautiful image and how Kipling could so term
the followers of the "Light of Asia". A group of tourists, Americans
by their clothes, were climbing up into the lap of Buddha to have
their photographs taken by a Japanese photographer who was
posing them, watched by a couple of obvious 'tecs whose interest
was further engaged by the appearance of Kaneko and myself. A
group of elderly Japanese with the somewhat slow shifting gait of
farmer folk, two or three of the women bent with a lifetime of
stooping in the fields, seemed to find as much to interest them in
the Americans and myself as in the great image. Pigeons perched
over the Daibutsu and stalked about the courtyard with an air

of ownership. For five sen one could climb up inside the Buddha and view the hillside from a window in His back. A stall was doing good business in charms, picture postcards, and a deal of rubbish reminiscent of the "Present from Southend-On-Mud".

At the rear of the great statue are large ornamented bronze plates, aged to a dark sage hue and polished with the passage of time, on which are inscribed the names of those who contributed towards its repair and resetting after the Great Earthquake in 1923.

The Americans were on their way out followed by one of the 'tecs, the photographer posing the farmer group, and as we made signs that we had seen enough the other 'tec adjusted his straw hat and sauntered after us.

At the gateway of the compound, between the two huge and grotesque demon guardian kings, the first 'tec was making water in a gully at the side of the road whilst regarding the tourists as they climbed into two cars. And now that I had seen, admired, and wondered, the call of the salty tang in the south-east breeze could no longer be denied. And, still tailed by the straw-hatted gent in the black suit, and led by our noses, a few minutes later we came out of a narrow lane on to the coast road and before us was the deep green, wind-lashed Pacific Ocean, roaring into Sagami Bay in serried white-capped seas and pounding on the grey, volcanic ash-impregnated sands in a foaming climax to their passage from perhaps the shores of California or whence a seaman once gazed upon the great waters from a peak in Darien. For me it overshadowed all the charm and mystery of temple, shrine and sacred image. Here was salt wind and the scents of seaweed, the seabirds wheeling and keening and all the sights and sounds I loved so well.

Fishermen were hauling out their boats stern first, in contrast to the Western practice of beaching with the bow, and securing them soundly up on the road; a sure sign of dirty weather in store.

Low down on the horizon was a smoky patch denoting the active volcano, Mount Mihara, on the island of Oshima, and all the land between us and the coast of America.

Eastwards the Miura Peninsula with its undulating pine-clad hills, its coves and bays and rock strewn shores, seemed to melt away into the green-grey of the sea as if nature had conspired with the security conscious guardians of the great naval establishments at Yokosuka and Kurihama and a few yards away from us stood our shadow to make sure that I did not perform with some super-telescopic camera.

Strolling along the coast road to the south-east, our faces flecked with the salt-spray, before us was a verdant promontory, its lower slopes of sandstone lashed by the crashing waves which cascaded spume high up among the pines and, as a cut between the cliffs opened out, there in a dark, rose-tinted and overpowering beauty, was peerless Fuji-no-yama.

As we came over the rise in the cutting between the hill and the point, the mountain seemed to rise from out of the bay behind the narrow bridge connecting Enoshima—"Picture Island," and the pine-clad mainland, its slopes merging into the lesser peaks to the south which undulated into the horizon beyond which was the tip of the Izu Peninsula.

Seated on a stone at the neck of the point with the rising wind in our hair we watched the changing hues of sunset o'er mountain and sea until Fuji-no-yama became a clear dark purple cone.

"This is where we must live someday," I whispered to Kaneko. "For never have I come across such combination of ocean, picturesque coastline, and with such views of that mountain whose beauty today I don't think I could even attempt to describe."

"Inamuragasaki is famous in history. It is here that Nitta Yoshisada threw his sword into the water and prayed that the tide might ebb so that his armies could approach Kamakura from the sea," she observed.

"Oh, when was that, and did the tide respond to his prayer?"

"It was a long time ago ... perhaps the eleventh or twelfth century. Yes, the tide went out and Nitta Yoshisada caught his enemies by surprise. They thought he must cross the hills where they were prepared for him. He won a great victory."

"It is a beautiful scene, isn't it," remarked someone, and I turned to find the plain-clothesman at my elbow.

"My husband says it is the most beautiful place he has seen," replied Kaneko.

"Your husband?"

"Yes."

"Well, where do you come from?"

"Please tell him our ages, the colour of my mother's eyes, about the scar on my wrist, and how many hairs I have on my chest," I broke in impatiently, furious that we could not sit and admire the scenery without such pests bothering us, and walked out on the headland leaving herself to deal with him.

She joined me a few moments later and tugged at my arm. "Don't be so sharp with people," she reprimanded. "He is quite a nice man, says it his job to watch foreigners to see they do not get into trouble, and to assist them. He was most apologetic and only wants to help. Says there is quite a cheap hotel where he'll introduce us if we wish to stay tonight."

"I do not blame your husband for getting annoyed," said the detective when we joined him, "nearly all foreigners do, but I have to report who has been here because this is on the edge of an important fortified zone. I wish I could speak English, it would be so much easier."

"Why do not the authorities arrange for English-speaking policemen to deal with foreigners," I inquired, by this time quite liking the frank friendliness of the man.

"Who could they keep once they'd taught him English or French? He'd get a better job, he'd be a fool to waste his talents being a policeman," he replied with a chuckle. We decided that we just could not afford a night in Kamakura and then a couple of days in Tokyo, and the policeman kindly led us through the charming coast village of thatched houses to a tramway station where we thanked him and boarded a car for Kamakura.

Outside Kamakura Station, Kaneko whispered, "Look there's the famous writer!"

"Which famous writer, and where?" I inquired looking about me.

"Why over there, underneath W.C."

And sure enough the famous European writer of what in those days were considered very dreadful sexy stories, and who after a week in the country had started a series on Japanese Womanhood in one of the English language papers was, to my great amusement, standing posing for flash photographs underneath the sign which proclaimed the station water-closet, which on later investigation proved one of the most filthy I had ever experienced.

"Well, I do hope those photographs come out, complete with that sign," I chuckled, "they'll delight his many critics and probably boost the sales of his books."

Chapter Eight

I

THE Tokyo hotel, recommended by a kindly taxi driver to whom we had confided the extent of our penury, was a modest establishment to say the least. It lacked all the virtues of Western style hostelries and even the usual courtesy of Japanese inns. Perhaps this was because I was the first barbarian to be accommodated, and the fear of what strange behaviour might be expected from me; there had in fact been a great deal of indecision concerning whether there was a room vacant although we were to find the place more than half empty. Japonica made strange contrast with stuffed chairs upholstered in dusty looking velvet, antimacassars, brass spittoons, iron beds with knobs on, and in what was intended as the lounge a passable flower arrangement stood cheek by jowl with the inevitable picture of Mount Fuji, shipping line calendars, and a lithograph from Leipzig in a heavy frame of a handsome well-proportioned nude chained to a tree and no doubt anticipating the imminent arrival of Frankenstein or a dragon.

Aside from the shy but willing room maid, the rest of the morose hotel staff might have been recruited from some penal establishment. Outside, the street-cars jangled and hooted their way in competition with the trains in and out of nearby Tokyo Station, while nondescript boats plied their mysterious ways amid the grey sewage of the canal.

My introduction to the city I was to come to know and love so well was a long and sleepless night; and to cheer things up a bit, after a most unsatisfactory breakfast the law arrived to be satisfied as usual concerning our ages, etc., and that we were not living in sin.

Finding a number in the complicated Japanese telephone directory had Kaneko almost at the end of her tether, and getting it through what passed as the hotel switchboard a major operation. But our adventures with the telephone must have delighted the policeman to whom of course all was reported. A magazine publisher, a newspaper, a Buddhist priest, a doctor, the Siamese minister, an iron merchant and the son of a wealthy financier, no doubt constituted an excellent bag for his notebook and got my dossier at Metropolitan Police Headquarters off to a fine start.

Prospects of immediate payments seemed dim. Buddhist priest was in Burma, iron merchant, friend of father-in-law, in hospital, doctor had taken to the sea as a ship's surgeon, son of financier was out of town but expected back any moment, and Siamese minister in Bangkok.

61

Tokyo provided a wealth of colourful contrasts. There were plenty of highwheeled private rickshaws, horse-drawn carts piled with honey-buckets, bicycles by the thousands, many drawing two-wheeled trailers, Cadillacs, Rolls-Royces, Tin Lizzies, and Chevs and the taxis kept abreast of possible fares while negotiating the price of the ride. And while clothing was mainly Western with the menfolk, yet intermingled with the din of traffic was the clack, clack, of *geta* and probably half of the women wore kimono.

The red-brick buildings designed by Josiah Condor and his imitators made striking contrast with the concrete and stone edifices in the business section and Kasumigaseki.

The Imperial Palace with its fine wide moats, its stone ramparts and green slopes presents such a pleasant scene as is found in few places within a stone's throw of a great main railway station. Droves of folk of all ages, mostly from the country by their clothing and manners, were paying their respects with proper awe and dread before the Nijubashi or Double Bridge. Duck and other water-fowl swam and gambolled unconcerned in the sanctuary of the moat, and the tiled towers with their classic curves which are also contrived so exquisitely in the stone ramparts made vivid contrast with the white walls and the wealth of pine and other trees.

To circle the moat seemed one of the best ways of seeing part of Tokyo. Years later a British Ambassador made this an almost daily constitutional, but he'd started life in the Grenadier Guards. By the time we were half-way round herself was complaining bitterly that if we completed the circuit she'd need a new pair of shoes.

We paid our respects to Japan's heroes at the Yasukuni Shrine at top of Kudan Hill, then browsed about the fantastic area of new and second-hand bookshops in Kanda, surely one of the most wide embracing in the world, where students by the courtesy of indulgent booksellers spend hours day after day reading books they cannot afford to buy.

At Kanda, Kaneko decided that as we were near the residence of Mr. Suzuki, the iron merchant, she would take a taxi and inquire after his health and that I could spend as long as I wished in the bookshops and meet her at our hotel.

When she'd gone I felt that bookshops might wait and entered a beer-hall, and for the equivalent of about 8d. obtained a large jug of excellent draught lager and surveyed my fellow imbibers. Most were students, there were also two or three who looked like university professors, thumbing through their secondhand book purchases. Then I noticed a gaunt, red-faced foreigner who as our eyes met, exclaimed, "And the top of the morning to ye!" joined me at my table with his almost empty jug, and introduced himself as Kevin O'Reilly, descendant of kings, professor of the English language, philosopher. "And a dabbler in every trade and profession ye could lay your tongue to; even a doctor in a gold mine." Kevin proved to be possessed of a prodigious thirst and after I had paid for a jug, when this was quickly emptied he said, with a merry twinkle in his eyes:

"Me bhoy, you couldn't have met Kevin on a more unfortunate occasion and it is to me shame that I cannot today return your compliment; but seeing as you are a stranger and I perceive a scholar and student of this fair land well then I'll have no further compunction in requesting that you fill her up again and bide awhile for the time when I shall be the host."

So I pushed out the boat once again, thankful that we had our return tickets to Nagahama, my acquaintance took a mighty pull of beer, stuck a hoary looking finger and thumb into one of his cavernous nostrils from which with a wince he picked some offending hair, and observed: "Now, for your great courtesy, and for the fact that I can see what a fine fellah y'are I'll reveal something of the mysteries of this fabulous land and its charming, industrious, sometimes aggravating, bloody-minded, yet for all that, lovable people."

"How long have ye been in these parts?" he inquired, and when I had told him that I had resided in the country for only six months observed, "Ah, then now's the time to write a book, though three or four months is just right, and begorra, ye might make millions like all these ladies and gents who without a snigger of the language, after wining and dining with the sons and daughters of the samurai, nigh deforming themselves sittin' drinking tea according to what they're told are mysterious and ancient rituals, probin' on a month tour into temple and shrine, and for the gents, of course, into the social conditions in the Yoshiwara, get back aboard their steamer, and whisht! Before the vessel docks in London, San Francisco or where have you, complete the masterpiece of revelation into the charm and glory of this ancient land."

He accepted a cigarette, looked at the empty jug, smacked his lips, and I took the hint and called the waitress.

"Aye, it's thirsty work is talking, me son, but what I am about to confide is worth more than gold, for it's the result of years of observance and study. And I'll tell ye a secret; for ye see that shortly I shall release upon this troubled world a work of such scope to shatter all preconceived notions and the pretty theories of a man whose father was a countryman of mine by the name of Hearn which his forefathers must have bastardized from O'Hearn, or Ahearne, aye and even those of Basil Chamberlain, greatest scholar of this beanstalk of them all."

"Beanstalk?" I queried.

"Ha, ha! And here's the secret, my bhoy. For me masterpiece will be known most appropriately as 'The Jap in the Beanstalk'."
I pointed out that the Japanese were very touchy about being called Japs. "Ah, but that is part of my scheme in educatin' them to developin' a better sense of humour. Ye see, they all know Kevin. Why, I teach at the Police School, I've taught barons and dukes and the like, financiers, cabinet ministers and I tell them I'm a Mick, an Irisher, a son of the Ould Sod. They know Kevin

O'Reilly, aye and when me book is published they'll realize the love, the pure love that's in his Irish heart in teaching them to laugh at themselves and savin' them from ruin. Ye see all the world's a beanstalk, y've got yours, I've got mine, and the Japanese have their own particular kind from which from more than half way up they're liable to topple with an awful bump unless they listen to the words of wisdom from such as meself."

"Come to Tokyo, me bhoy," he'd urged. "Here's where history is in the makin'. Join the motley crew of barbarians in the salubrious capital of the Mikado. Good men and true, bums, charlatans, scholars, those versed in the arts of scientific lying that call themselves diplomats, prosperous peddlers of fertilizers, oil, and weapons of destruction. Their lesser brethren dabblin' in a hotch-potch of merchandise and services from pots and pans, and whisky and Spanish Fly, to life insurance; the foreign teacher like meself, down at the fag end of the scale with the scallywag journalists, in contrast with the professors from Dublin and Oxford and Cambridge, and the gentlemen correspondents of *The Times* of London and New York. God-botherers by the score, spies, sycophants, and withal as interesting a bunch as the Nipponese themselves can show."

But it was not the picture drawn by old O'Reilly which was to lure me away from Nagahama, for the glory of Fuji-no-yama, seen from the picturesque Sagami Bay at Inamura, and the smell and sight and sounds of the billowing rollers crashing in from the Pacific, had set "a wind in the heart of me and fire at my heels".

When I returned to our hotel I found herself engaged in conversation with a very personable young Japanese, most apologetic over being out of town when we telephoned, who indeed brought a gleam of sunshine and welcome to the great city which we could have hardly expected seeing that I had simply been asked to telephone him the good wishes of a friend.

I doubt that Yoshi had ever visited other than the Imperial Hotel to greet strangers with letters of introduction, and after a few minutes of idle chatter he urged us to accompany him out of that depressing hostelry and do him the honour of visiting his "humble home, meet his stupid, unattractive wife, where there was no food but which he hoped we would do him the honour of eating".

Even today not so many Japanese take even old friends into their homes, let alone a mere acquaintance; but perhaps the fact that I was from that part of Essex where Yoshi had spent some time at a vicarage near Benfleet, being prepared for Cambridge, was some sort of a very special bond between us.

His "humble" home proved to be a handsome residence situated on the rise of Kojimachi just below the Yasukuni Shrine, combining all the charming simplicity of the Japanese traditional with the better forms of practical and tasteful Occidental modes of living.

Here we met Aiko, the charming Mrs. Yoshi, daughter of a

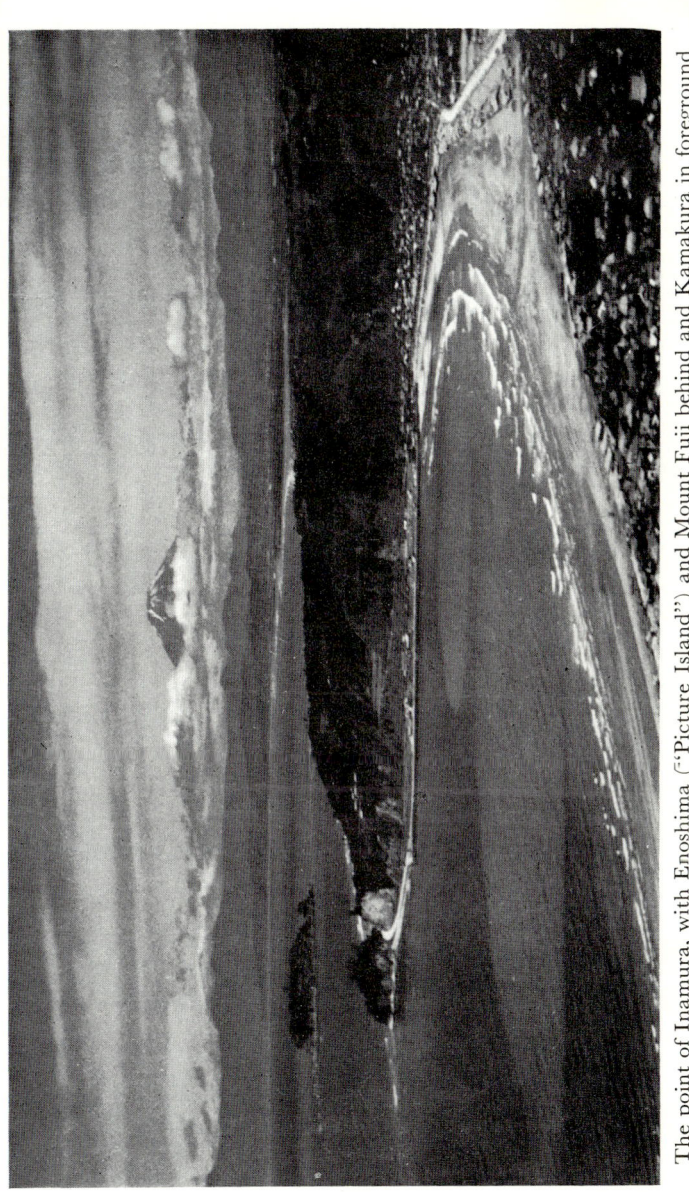

The point of Inamura, with Enoshima ("Picture Island") and Mount Fuji behind and Kamakura in foreground

(*Above*) The author (second left) with Hideya, the geisha and friends at Nagahama, 1934

(*Left*) The author (left) holding a conger eel after spear-fishing at Oshima, 1935

diplomat and former ambassador at Rome, talented, fluent in English, French, and Italian, and who, unlike most of her country-women of those days was not a mere yes-woman to the male but asserted her own opinions without in any way losing the essential femininity which the Japanese woman, despite democracy and the space age, still manages to maintain to a high degree.

Yoshi was passionately fond of ski-ing and had represented Cambridge University in championships in Switzerland. Japan is the ideal ski-ing country, but it was not until an Austrian army officer instructed the Japanese army in ski-ing that this was realized, and it was Yoshi and other such enthusiasts who virtually created many of the popular ski-ing resorts. Well and truly were we dined that evening, and as our newfound friends seemed to keep a sort of open house we met Japanese engaged in banking, shipping, two Cambridge graduates who'd gone into partnership as architects and had both been at Cambridge with Yoshi, students he was assisting through university, as well as Max, a jolly and energetic young American lawyer who was to become a firm friend until his death in 1958, and Thomas, a kindly English professor who was later to launch me into a new career, and his delightful French wife.

This was a new kind of Japanese world in contrast with that of the country, my friends of the bath-house, One-armed Cho, and all the charm of Nagahama which I had come to love. But I realized that I had been lotus-eating far too long, and if I were to dwell by the side of Sagami Bay, the key to that dream could perhaps be found only in Tokyo.

Fuji-no-yama, who'd hidden herself in cloud on our journey from Shiga, smiled upon us for the greater part of our journey home. Her snow-crested summit was visible from between the chimney stacks soon after leaving Tokyo, sometimes to the right but mostly to the left of the railway, rearing up it seemed almost above us in some parts of Shizuoka, her conical form presenting varied aspects until when near Nagoya she faded from sight below a screen of lesser peaks. Long, long ago a certain Hokkusai, perhaps the greatest Japanese wood-block print artist of all, had trudged the Tokaido and Nakesendo trunk roads, put to sea in fishing craft in Suruga and Sagami bays, in order to depict Mount Fuji in all seasons and from all aspects to create his immortal "Hundred Views", prints of which are so eagerly sought by collectors all over the world.

Yet even if Hokkusai, together with countless other poets and artists of all ages, left such testaments of admiration for Fuji-no-yama, none perhaps exceeded in intensity of sentiment the poet Sokan, who wrote:

> "Mount Fuji should be
> Preserved a special sight
> For New Year's Day."

Chapter Nine

I

NUMBER 50 Sendagicho was one of perhaps a hundred houses bearing the same number in a narrow street to the rear of Tokyo Imperial University. This archaic numbering system, which still persists, makes tough going for the stranger in search of Mr. Sato Jiro, or Saburo, who may be located from the map in a nearby police box—but if he doesn't know the personal name and how it is written, then he may be due to perambulate through all the Satos in the block which may mean from twenty to a hundred.

Father-in-law, who but a few months before probably would have paid us to leave, seemed quite disconsolate, talked of how much he'd done, what plans he had for the future and made me feel quite ungrateful. Mother-in-law was really upset, poor One-armed Cho on the verge of tears when we told him of our departure, and friends of the bath-house, with the exception of old Ogawa, begged me to stay. The old man said that no good could come in remaining in such a dead-end of a place and that he'd still be a rich man if he'd have gone away when he'd had the chance. At a farewell party given for me by my playboy friend, my geisha acquaintances, and especially Hideya of the long classic face and the willowy figure, seemed to act as if they would really miss me, but I fancied it would be the dancing they'd remember.

Our first two days in Tokyo were spent with my ship's surgeon friend, Nagasawa Yutaka, and his hospitable parents, brothers and sisters, at their home in "Black Gate Street". And it was during those two days that I sensed the essential warmheartedness of the Edokko, and first came to understand their affection for their native city in which the literature, the theatre, and other arts had developed by and for the common people, in contrast to those hitherto practised and developed by the court nobles, the priests, and military caste.

When I'd first met this young doctor he'd confessed that he hated white people, and at the same time apologized for giving me offence.

"Have you known many?" I inquired. He confessed that he hadn't but he'd read enough about their lack of culture, their brutality towards the helpless people they'd enslaved in many lands, and from what he'd seen of them they were overbearing and lacked delicacy.

"Well, you know there are many in London, New York and other places who consider your people cruel, hypocritical, dishonest, mere imitators and wholly unmoral, and like yourself the majority would have to admit they'd never known any Japanese."

We had become close and devoted friends, and the one-time hater of the white man and his family treated us with such consideration and genuine kindness as if we'd been cherished friends or relatives.

I had marvelled at the manner in which the country had received me, but the great city conceded nothing in the genuine warm-heartedness of its welcome.

Yet, as I lay down to sleep for the first time in our Tokyo home, all the tender memories of the country town beside Lake Biwa crept softly one by one before my eyes, and I knew that those first impressions would be with me forever.

No longer would I hear the owl in the clump of cryptomeria, instead of the banana tree outside the door there was a telegraph pole. But the asphalt road accentuated the clip-clop or clack, clack, of *geta*, at night the silence was broken by the haunting pipe of the seller of Chinese noodles, and much too early in the morning the cry of the vendor of *natto*—the gooey mess of fermented soybeans which I still find quite uneatable but which is much esteemed by many Tokyoites.

Our new home was modest to an extreme. There were really two small rooms, one of which could be partitioned with sliding screens, a tiny kitchen, a sort of closet which held a wooden bath, and the usual primitive office.

Yoshi lived up to his promise, and not only introduced me to the editor of a travel magazine who gave me commissions, but also helped out with some part time work in assisting him compile a guide book for tourists. Within a week of our arrival the little house received all manner of newfound friends, students who wished to practise their English and stayed on and on to try my patience to a breaking point, and one afternoon a large car blocked the street outside to disgorge a smartly dressed swarthy gentleman who in a pronounced Oxford accent introduced himself as the Siamese Minister. He apologized for not being in when I had called at the Legation, and to Kaneko's chagrin stepped in without removing his shoes, and then entertained us for an hour with his witty and interesting conversation while the policeman redirected the traffic seeking to pass and the neighbours no doubt marvelled that we boasted a nodding acquaintance with the diplomatic corps.

Life became interesting, to say the least. At every opportunity we took the fast and excellent train service to Kamakura, explored the coast around Inamura and the island of Enoshima, and I marvelled that nothing was being done to preserve the scenic beauties and improve this lovely area.

Each day brought new acquaintances, some to remain firm friends, as well as all manner of surprises, and I ranged far and wide in trying to recapture the spirit of the great city of days gone by. Asakusa, the amusement quarter, chock-a-block with cinemas, restaurants, the various traditional Japanese entertainments centred around its great Kwannon temple, was always fascinating. The nearby Yoshiwara, where any in search of the delights of Venus might choose a partner from the photographs displayed outside or in the entrances of the very clean and well-decorated houses to assist forget his cares and rid himself of excess energy was free of pimps and panderers where the visitor was left alone to decide his pleasure. And if he were not particularly interested in the specialities of the quarter might sit and drink a cup of tea, beer or sake in one of the many houses of pleasure without being pestered to go the whole hog.

The majority of my newfound Japanese friends were interested in literature, the arts, drinking, dancing and other laudable pursuits and, of course, in making money. The newspapers warned of crises, denounced treaties with foreign powers as subtle weapons designed to hamstring Japan and prevent her proceeding forward to "carry out her lofty aspirations to bring about world brotherhood" etc., etc., and often featured gushing accounts of the sincerity of youths who'd written letters in their own blood and sent their own pickled fingers to politicians in protest against so-called materialism and mismanagement of the nation's affairs. But most of my friends seemed quite embarrassed when I asked their opinions on such manufactured attempts to create alarm. Sometimes I'd meet queer characters whose business seemed to be to probe the foreign mind who would scrape up an acquaintance, buy you drinks, and if you were British denounce the Americans, if you were American denounce the British, and press on with theories concerning the "Japanese Spirit", lack of understanding of Japan's just aspirations and all manner of boring poppycock concerning culture—a new fad which their friend Hitler had succeeded in propagating in a big way, and seldom failed to insert a lecture on Bushido! In the lounge of the Imperial Hotel I was introduced to a gentle-mannered American gentleman who to an admiring coterie of Japanese and foreign satellites would hold forth on the beauties of Shinto, and its superiority over all other known forms of religion.

In the lobby of this quaint and famous hotel, much over-rated concerning its earthquake-proof qualities, because other much larger buildings not designed by the late Mr. Wright had stood up very well indeed to the terrible 'quakes of September 1st, 1923, were to be found such interesting hotch-potch of personalities as had to be spoken with to be believed.

Snoopers from the Home Office, the gendarmerie, the navy, the military, infested the place and were soon to be reinforced by their counterparts from Hitler Germany, and Italy. It was a great resort for newspapermen and one American put me right into the picture of how the great world Press operated in Tokyo and at the same time gave me sound advice concerning whom I might or might not cultivate without getting involved or pinpointed in some way or other.

Herbert was a gaunt individual with a prodigious memory, boasted an acquaintanceship with almost every Japanese who was anybody at all, smoked a foul-pipe which was usually held together with a piece of adhesive tape, invariably wore a garment which appeared to be a cross between an overcoat and a jacket and from the cavernous pockets of which he could produce anything from aspirins and adhesive plaster, scissors, safety-pins, nails and screws, nose-paper, memo pads, to spark-plugs (he was an ardent motor-cyclist), railway time-tables, knives, complete with instruments for removing stones from horses' hoofs, bottle openers, magnifying glasses and a variety of stomach, energy and other pills. Aside from fast motor-bikes, poker and poking, Herbert was a terrific trencherman, but this did not fill out his gaunt frame but only seemed to make his moustache more straggly. His friends swore that he harboured an enormous worm. Among Herbert's poker playing friends was a once world-famous violinist who'd dropped in to Tokyo on a concert tour, got mixed up in a poker game with a bunch of newspapermen, and had been paying for that experience ever since.

Much of my early insight into the life of Tokyo—the mobile restaurants which dispense noodles, small establishments famous for certain kinds of *sushi*—rice rolled in paper-thin seaweed and stuffed with ginger, or capped with slices of raw fish—grilled eels shops, and others, as well as bars, beer halls, one establishment which dispensed what was known as *denki*—electric—whisky, at about twopence a shot, various coffee shops, some of which insisted on silence to enable their customers, mostly students, to enjoy the music of Brahms, Beethoven, Mozart and other composers from gramophone records, was provided by a host of new friends; and particularly the Watanabe brothers, who'd put their all into a publishing business and just about bankrupted themselves over a very handsome biography of Admiral Togo, in English.

Most of the Watanabe's business seemed to be transacted in a coffee shop named *Koichiro* which was presided over by the foremost Japanese authority on coffee who'd written books on the subject. And it was here over a cup of Mocha or Java, even Kenya or Persian coffee, that I met young and struggling artists, musicians, architects, writers and others.

When one sold a painting or a story, or was otherwise in the money then we'd sample a beer-hall, a *sushi* establishment, or one of the hundreds of small bars of the Ginza area.

II

Kaneko insisted that it was time I obtained a permanent job to ensure there were no more brain bashing and embarrassment at the end of each month when the butcher, baker, landlord, our maid Tatsu and others had to be paid. Tatsu was a jolly buxom wench, with a well-developed sense of humour, and when the butcher's boy found himself flat on his back after trying to take a certain liberty with her, we realized that she also knew something about judo.

There was one excursion in search of a pawn-shop which we decided must be some distance away and in a quiet place with a bundle containing Kaneko's best kimono and obi. In the tramcar the parcel seemed to scream its destination to fellow passengers. We walked around all evening but every pawn-shop seemed to have a reception committee waiting outside to receive us, so we gave up the project and I was compelled to sell for paltry sums many of my precious books.

An international scenario writing contest had been announced in the newspapers, sponsored by a well-known Japanese film company. I sat up all one night producing my entry which was a corny affair entitled "The Son of Madame Butterfly", which called for the visit to Japan of the son of Lieutenant Pinkerton, and his discovery of his step-brother in the person of a handsome chap who is in training for the Japanese swimming team for the Olympic Games, and also a fine singer. I visualized a perfect role for the popular singer who at the time was the particular heart-throb of all young Japanese womanhood. And, to our great surprise, one morning the newspaper announced that my scenario had won the first prize! But there was a snag in this as the prize money of some 1,000 yen was not to be paid until the picture should go into production.

One thousand yen was a small fortune in those days. Down at the coffee house my friends showered me with their congratulations and quite obviously expected a celebration, and when I told them that no cash would be forthcoming until production of the masterpiece one and all expressed the opinion that a down payment must be made by the producer. It ended with my 'phoning Yoshi and as the producer happened to be one of his personal friends inside an hour I had received 300 yen on account, took off with my friends to celebrate, and anticipated the great happiness this would bring to No. 50 Sendagicho. But it was well past ten o'clock when I managed to disentangle myself from all but Kanzawa, who perhaps guessed from his own experience that there might be stormclouds brewing on my hearth and insisted that he accompany me home just to pay his respects to my better half.

The Ginza night-stalls, now no more, but a colourful feature of Tokyo night life where everything from the most fantastic Japanese toys, haberdashery, hardware, and all manner of knick-knacks could be purchased, provided me with a number of peace offerings, and among them I saw the pup, a liver and white pointer secured by a miserable frayed piece of string to one of the willow-trees, panting with thirst, while its scruffy owner was engaged in demonstrating the virtues of a tortoise which was secured by a cord inserted in a hole in its shell. The little dog simply could not be resisted and despite my friend's insistence that I should buy a pooch from a reputable dealer, I settled for 5 yen, we got a taxi, and the little animal, possibly about six weeks old, licked my face until we arrived at my doorstep.

And if there had been a minor typhoon in the offing it subsided when Kaneko saw that I was accompanied by a friend, and it positively blew itself out as soon as she set eyes on the pup which I had already christened Nick after a childhood pet.

The arrival of our first pet required a celebration, and while we fed little Nick, and Kanzawa and I toasted him and congratulated ourselves on our foresight, he lapped up a couple of bowls of milk, explored the house thoroughly, barked his approval and then deposited his visiting card on the *tatami*. This was soon removed by Tatsu who thought it was a huge joke, but she then disappeared and returned with a wooden box filled with sand, and nearly went into convulsions when it was pointed out that Nick was a dog, not a cat!

For a couple of days, with the bills all paid and the antics of our pet to delight us, there seemed not a care in the world to bother us, and the rantings of Hitler and the jackal Mussolini failed even to raise a laugh. And then poor little Nick suddenly went completely off his food, his eyes became watery, his nose was dry, and we summoned the local vet. He wagged his head, gave the little chap an injection which perked him up a bit, but only for a few hours, came back next day and gave him another shot, and the next night the little fellow died with a sort of look in his lovely brown eyes which seemed to imply that he was so sorry he could not stay.

The next morning the animal undertaker arrived bright and early with a wooden coffin into which our short-lived little pointer was placed wrapped in a white cloth, together with his new leash and collar, and a coin with which to pay the ferry across the River Sanzu—the Japanese Styx. Then Kaneko and Tatsu took the little coffin to a temple where the priest said a mass for Nick, thence to the animal cemetery outside Tokyo which had been founded by the admirable wife of a former American military attaché. Aside from the grief his short stay with us had engendered Nick had proved a rather expensive purchase. He was the first of our many dogs, and although as each one died from old age or disease, two victims of war, and we pledged never again "to give our hearts for dogs to tear", yet after each parting, we soon realized the awful gap which a pet and friend's passing created, and suddenly there would be the sounds of barking and a new pup would be with us to ease the loss of his or her predecessor and brighten the home once more.

III

My friend, the Viscount, a jovial middle-aged aristocrat, was extremely fond of animals, kept several dogs and cats, and a large aviary containing hundreds of exotic-looking birds which he'd imported from various parts of the world.

He was also a dabbler in languages, had a fair knowledge of French and a smattering of half a dozen others including Russian, Portuguese and Chinese.

The Viscount was also passionately fond of music and musical instruments. He thumped his fine grand piano and unfortunate listeners into near insensibility, positively rendered one speechless and hypnotized in his painful renderings on violin and cello, and set all the dogs in the neighbourhood howling for mercy when he got out his trumpet, trombone or clarinet; and when I first met him was taking instruction from an Italian for piano accordion.

The Viscount was president of a dozen Japan-Calathumpia or other such societies devoted to the promotion of mutual goodwill and understanding, as well as a national association of hairdressers, and in this connection hunted foreign decorations with the enthusiasm of a philatelist after a misprinted Victorian Mauritius penny-black.

Descendant of a branch of one of the great feudal clans in Kyushu he was truly one of nature's gentlemen. None ever sought in vain for his assistance in a needy cause, and his home was an ever open door to the sons and daughters of any from his native place seeking employment, or studying in the capital to whom he behaved like a benevolent foster father.

Powerfully built, unlike the usual patrician type of Japanese, his jet black eyebrows contrasted sharply with his almost white hair and his merry twinkling eyes. He radiated good humour and inspired affection in all who had the good fortune to know him, but I suspected that many regarded his quite un-Japanese candour as the hallmark of a fool.

One afternoon the Viscount called for me in his car, which no doubt gave us added prestige with the neighbours as the vehicle bore his well-known family crest, and whisked me off to his favourite *machiai*. This was an unpretentious establishment in a narrow road in the Akasaka district, but entered through an exquisite rock garden.

The Viscount was expected, and when we were greeted by the mistress of the place I realized that he had just as keen taste in women as in music, decorations, and exotic birds.

Soon my friend was divested of his smart striped-trousers and black jacket, refused to don the light kimono which was held up for him by our lady host, and sat down in his underpants to sip tea and a sweet cake, while I was swathed in a striped cotton kimono so short for me that I looked like the fool in a stage play, and during which his chauffeur and a couple of maids brought in a suitcase and several bundles of packages from his car. When tea drinking was ended beer was brought in and when he had quenched his thirst with an enormous draught he stuck his large chin in his hands, grinned and said: "Now you make yourself at home. I brought you here today because I would like to show you my decorations. I have to go to a reception at the French Embassy and this will be the first chance to wear my wonderful Grand Cross. Count X has angled for this order for years and when he sees me wearing it he'll be just green with envy."

While he had a bath I enjoyed myself watching the sun fade over Tokyo in the company of a particularly attractive maid who seemed to be charged to see that at no moment should my teeth be other than awash with beer.

And when "His Excellency" returned, amid an aroma of scented soap and talcum powder, the serious business of dressing him for the French ambassadorial function began.

His uniform was in black and gold with a broad green stripe down the trousers. There was lots of gold lace around the high-buttoned collar and large epaulettes drooped down on his arms.

"Ha, ha! I suppose you think I look like a *chindon-ya**," he chuckled. "But just wait till I am ready, for this is only the beginning."

From out of ornate and important looking boxes came a succession of medals, stars, crosses, attached to ribbons of every colour of the rainbow until but one box remained unopened. As each was fastened or hung upon him he dwelt at length on its merits, its history, and the reasons for which it had been awarded him, and when he looked like the veritable Christmas tree and there seemed no more room for the colourful baubles, at any rate on his front-side, he opened the remaining box and held up the most magnificent of all. This was a sort of heavy St. John's type of cross in gold, in the centre of which appeared to be a ruby worth a king's ransom and about the size of a pigeon's egg, suspended from a ribbon of heavy, turquoise coloured, silk brocade.

"Now what do you think of that!" he exclaimed with glee. "The finest of the lot don't you think, and from the smallest country of all." He named a Baltic State, long since swallowed up by the Soviet Union.

I gazed and I marvelled, and when he put on his hat which resembled the French kepi but which had what appeared to be a feather duster stuck in front, I almost exploded with laughter.

"Well, my young friend," he announced, "you now see before you the most handsomely decorated major in the Japanese Army."

"Major in the Army?"

"Well, I retired as a major, but I am still on the reserve and also the president of the reserve association in my district. But I do not like wars,—only a madman does, and all these decorations, barring the Tsingtao medal for an expedition in which I did not take part—have been gained in my gentle pursuits of peace, goodwill and understanding—yes, and of course, the interests of culture."

The mistress, the maids, and the chauffeur fussed around him, flecking off imaginary specks of dust from his person, there were Ahs and Ohs of admiration, and then a clock downstairs struck six.

---

* *Chindon-ya* are people who dress in all manner of costumes, paint their faces, play musical instruments and parade the streets to advertise a product, a show, or the opening of a shop.

"Oh, I must be off," he exclaimed. "But you wait here, ask for anything you want, and I'll be back in an hour or perhaps an hour and a half and then we'll go out and have a fine party."

I could not imagine that the Viscount could have possibly enjoyed himself as much as I did that evening; I had a good bath, my back washed for me, ate and drank, had songs sung for me and sang back in return, learned a few new parlour games and forgot all about the return of my eccentric and jolly friend until I found that it was already nine o'clock.

The mistress suggested that he'd probably gone off from the reception with some crony and was probably in a Ginza bar, but I could not credit that he would do so in all his regalia, although it would no doubt have made him extremely popular. And then just before nine thirty the chauffeur arrived and I was told to get ready to accompany him to where the Viscount was waiting.

Some ten minutes later we drew up in front of a bicycle dealer's and the chauffeur got out, opened the door, and bade me follow him. As we entered an alleyway alongside the shop I heard loud laughter, and then from an open doorway spied my friend seated on the *tatami*, his jacket unbuttoned, his feather duster hat stuck on the head of a young woman, half a dozen children around him all wearing one of his decorations, the smallest of all with the grand cross with the pigeon-egg sized ruby dangling round about its waist, and several admiring adults, including a mournful looking fellow with a bandage round his head.

"Ha, ha! Come in and meet my friends!" cried His Excellency when he spotted me. I entered, somewhat bewildered, and as soon as I was seated a sake cup was placed in my hand and filled from an enormous bottle.

"Oh you look so surprised," chuckled the Viscount. "I am sorry to have kept you waiting. As a matter of fact I confess that I forgot you, but you see things happened so suddenly. The poor fellow there with the bandage shot out of a side street on his bicycle just as we were passing. And so I took him to the hospital, fixed him up and I had to bring him back here to his master to explain matters, for it was our fault for getting in his way."

I nodded and marvelled; bicycles shooting out of side streets across main roads without warning having always struck me as being ridden by people bent on suicide.

"I had to put things right for the poor fellow," he continued, "because you see he had been drinking and his good master here might have given him the sack! Oh, but everything is now fine, and what do you think? It seems that this family came to Tokyo from our place in Kyushu only five years ago. The world is small isn't it."

An hour later we left the cheery bicycle dealer and his family and friends and for the amusement to which they were treated that evening the unfortunate assistant who elected to be run down by my bemedalled and decorated friend, was no doubt the hero of the family, who was probably counselled to be careful in future to try conclusions with a marquis, count, or even an Imperial Prince—just to see how that might turn out!

A few days later I called on the Viscount at his home to find him with a much bewhiskered old gentleman who was introduced as a general. "Now, here you have a real soldier, not like me," he said, as he introduced us, "He would start a war tomorrow if he could." And turning to the general said with a chuckle, "Yes, you would start a war, but you wouldn't have to fight it, would you!"

The general thought this remark a huge joke, they both laughed and laughed, and in a few minutes the old soldier was enjoying immensely the story of how Count X burned with envy over the Viscount's Grand Cross of Calathumpia, and how the reception ended in the home of the bicycle dealer.

Chapter Ten

I

ONE day in the early spring of 1935, when there was considerable sabre rattling taking place in various parts of the world and Mussolini was bombing Ethiopians, Hitler forcing elderly Jews to scrub the pavements of Berlin, and the Japanese getting more and more involved in China, Manchuria and Mongolia, much to Kaneko's relief I obtained a permanent job.

"There's a vacancy for an English teacher at a higher school in North Japan," Professor Alfred Thomas had informed me, "and I have taken the liberty of putting your name forward. I feel sure you will fill the bill."

I was interviewed by a very fatherly professor at the Tokyo School of Foreign Languages, a hive of shack-like buildings across the road from the moat of the Imperial Palace, who was the foremost Japanese authority on phonetics, and one of the finest Japanese speakers of English I had met. He received me in a study cluttered up with various recording machines and charts illustrating phonetics of all the major languages and completely incomprehensible as far as I was concerned, showed me his latest work on his pet subject, and then talked at length on Thomas Hardy. A swarthy, thick-set gentleman was then shown in and introduced as the head of the English department of the Hirosaki Higher School who immediately put me at ease with some conversation about the Tower of London and Harrison Ainsworth, John Masefield, Galsworthy, and spoke with pride of the privilege he'd had in being received by Thomas Hardy at Max Gate. It seemed ages before any mention was made of the job, and then as if it was simply an afterthought of no consequence, he intimated that the school term would start on April 10th but that if I was unable to settle my affairs in Tokyo by then that I could arrive up to a week later.

"Oh, and I must tell you," he said, "that we are not favourably disposed towards the tendency of some foreign teachers to promote Basic English; it may be all right for shop boys and clerks, but it will not help our students in their entrance examinations to the Universities."

I assured him that such artificial guide to the English tongue was absolute anathema to me, we shook hands all round, he told me they would send me travelling expenses, that I would sign my contract on arrival at Hirosaki, and I left to report back to friend Thomas that, thanks to him, I was hired.

"Well, now you are on the way. You have one of the plum

teaching jobs, away in the cold North it is true, but by and by you can get a school in a warmer part of the country, or a university in Tokyo.

"You are succeeding an eccentric character who is very popular with his students, has a collection of medals and decorations earned for his derring-do, was with Shackleton in the Antarctic, is a parachutist, gunnery expert, has a mania for motor-cars, doesn't drink or smoke, eats enormous quantities of boiled sweets, drives the police and the gendarmerie frantic with his brand of Irish humour, but is withal a first-class teacher. But I expect you'll hear from him as soon as he knows you've been appointed his successor."

Kaneko was overjoyed, but Tatsu felt that Hirosaki was too far from Tokyo and that she was afraid she'd not be able to understand the local dialect. The Viscount gave me a party to celebrate my good fortune and promised to write to his niece, an Imperial Princess whose Prince was attached to the local Army Divisional headquarters, Yoshi promised to come up in the winter and teach me to ski, and friends down at the coffee establishment vowed they'd come and stay from time to time to alleviate my loneliness.

Lieut.-Col. T. Orde-Lees, D.S.O., A.F.C., O.B.E., Royal Marines, retired, wrote to congratulate me on succeeding him, offered me a pair of skii, a pressure cooker and other odds and ends at a bargain price, hoped that I would take over their dog and maid-servant, and announced that he and his wife would call on us within a few days on their way through Tokyo en route to England.

Orde-Lees was in his mid-sixties, a wiry, blue-eyed six-footer, who looked as tough as steel, gave one the impression that any time he gave you was holding up some matter of earth-shattering importance, but positively exuded a chisel-like Irish humour.

His wife, the second Mrs. Orde-Lees, was a charming Japanese lady half his age who seemed to speak only when spoken to, and was almost crippled with arthritis which her husband attributed to the Hirosaki winter.

Having been warned about his sweet-tooth we had prepared a regular feast of sickly pastries, and whilst stuffing himself with half-a-dozen of these, he endeavoured to put me in the picture concerning my school, the city, the students and my colleagues.

"Can you juggle? You know, perform with a few eggs, tennis balls, knives and forks?" he inquired.

"No? Well then I'd advise you to learn. Best way of livening up the second year classes in the middle of term.

"Don't ever let them get you down. They'll try hard. And never, never complain of their behaviour or laziness to your colleagues or the principal. Do that and you might as well call it a day.

"You'll find certain characters don't wash, don't shave, don't study, just grovel in what they call 'higher school spirit'. Don't mind them, they turn out all right, and especially if you can get them to like you. Be firm, don't allow them to pull your leg too much, and don't allow them to visit you or you'll never be rid of the pests.

"If you have not a morning suit, then you'd better buy one, any second-hand garment will do, no matter if it is green with age, and with it you may wear brown boots if you wish, and a green tie.

"The dog is a scavenging little rascal, the maid has some kind of religious mania. The school refused to decorate the house so I have painted all the walls myself. You may find they look a little queer. The colours occurred to me in a dream. And so if you'll let me have the fifteen yen for the skii and odds and ends then I think we'll have to be on our way."

There was so much more I wished to learn but as he was quite obviously not prepared to give me another moment I handed over the money, he wished us good luck, took another cake which he munched whilst putting on his shoes, and I then offered to show him the way to the bus, which was the quickest route to his hotel.

"I'll thank you to mind your own business concerning our transportation!" he snapped. And then, seeing my surprise grinned and said: "Yes, I know the bus may be quicker, but you don't know that I have been keeping a book of Tokyo tram coupons for the past year or so and if it takes all night and I circumnavigate the entire city we'll reach our hotel by tramcar."

I was not to see this fantastic character again until 1941 when he passed through Hong Kong with his wife and baby daughter with the last British evacuees from Japan before Pearl Harbour. But I was soon to learn a deal about him and perhaps it was only recently in a new book on Shackleton's expedition and the open boat voyage to Elephant Island, that I fully realized what a privilege it had been to boast a slight acquaintance and to have succeeded him in my first teaching job in Japan.

II

A few days before our departure for the frozen North we spent a day beside the Pacific Ocean where from Inamura which had attracted me away from Lake Biwa, Mount Fuji reared into the cloudless blue heavens in full white mantle.

"We left Nagahama for all this. Tokyo was a stepping stone, and now, instead of a step closer we are off in the opposite direction," I remarked.

"Well, there's plenty of time. And from Hirosaki you'll be able to see the Tsugaru Fuji—Mount Iwaki," Kaneko replied.

"Yes, but there's no sea, no Sagami Bay, no fishing boats in the sunset . . ."

"Oh, you want too much. You have a fine job to go to, no more worry about bills, and you are not satisfied. Do you think you're likely to get a job here on the beach. Gazing at the sea and Fuji-San won't pay the grocer and the rent, you know."

And so in the first week of April we left Tokyo for Hirosaki, seen off by a tearful Tatsu, and many friends, including Jack Brinkley who arrived with a tiny Airedale puppy, which in spite of all the regulations against animals travelling on the railway unless in a special box, I smuggled under my coat until Kaneko was safely ensconced in her sleeping berth and able to hide the pup behind the curtains.

"I'll call him John," she said.

"John, my foot! It's a she-male. You'd better compromise with Joan," I retorted. And Joan she became before we were twenty minutes out of Tokyo. The pup seemed satisfied and quiet enough and so I went off to the dining car in search of a beer. But when I came back to the compartment, to my horror there were sounds of yelping, and the guard was close on my heels bent on inspecting tickets.

As I popped my head between the curtains to find Joan joyfully climbing around Kaneko's head and licking at her face while yelping her glee, to his amazement I burst into song, and continued with "Old Man River", as I handed him our tickets. He broke into a grin, bent down, pulled aside the curtain of Kaneko's sleeper, dropped it, smiled and wagged his head, and then went on his way. I imagined what a fuss would have been made in similar circumstances when breaking regulations in certain other lands—especially the bother which a German official would have made, and felt that if it is often true that lack of careful attention to keeping to the letter of the law merits criticism of the Japanese, yet that railway official showed not only a sense of humour, but also a kindly discretion.

The cherry blossoms had been in flower when we left Tokyo, but the next morning at Aomori carts were removing great blocks of ice which had been cut from the streets to be dumped in the sea. All around the mountains were still covered in snow, but the air was crisp and the sun shone out of a clear blue sky.

There seemed no further need to conceal Joan under my coat on the local train down to Hirosaki and the station officials even debated her qualities and were vastly interested to learn that her forebears came from Yorkshire across the world and of which they'd never heard.

The local dialect seemed almost a foreign tongue to Kaneko who found it difficult to converse with the friendly farmer women who got in and out and seemed so very interested in us and our strange little dog. Two old women took turns in delousing each other's hair and both obviously suffered with trachoma, a disease which I was to learn was more prevalent in Aomori than in any other part of the world!

Here it was early spring and even on the lowlands patches of snow and ice contrasted with the dark fields in which the farmers were busy hauling out and spreading compost, above which Tsugaru Fuji—Mount Iwaki, one of the many conical shaped mountains designated local Fuji-Sans, reared 5,392 feet into the heavens.

But although I could not shake Sagami Bay and the coast at Inamura from my mind, yet all prospects from the window of that slow local train seemed pleasing enough, our companions friendly, and so we arrived at Hirosaki to start a new life.

III

We were met at the station by the kindly Professor Kuno who'd engaged me at Tokyo, together with other members of the English department who conducted us to our home, a not unattractive two-storied house in Western style painted in two shades of grey which I was to learn was the official colour for all government buildings, standing in quite a spacious garden and next door to a similar house, the residence of the German teacher, and opposite that of the principal.

A neat little woman dressed in blue serge Western clothes opened the door and announced that she was our maid. Joan nipped in behind her, ignored a black and white mongrel, sat down and faced about and by her attitude proclaimed: "Well here I am and if you don't like me then it is just too bad; because from now on I'm the boss as far as dogs, or for that matter even humans, are concerned."

As I stepped over the threshold I must have shuddered at the sight which met my eyes for Professor Kuno said apologetically, "I am afraid Professor Orde-Lees had strange ideas about decoration." "He told me he saw it all in a dream." I replied, "but I would prefer to call it a nightmare."

The maid started to titter and Kaneko followed suit.

The closest I had experienced to such abomination in interior decoration had been a fourth-rate night club in Shanghai. Black and salmon pink stripes formed the chief motive, interspersed with triangles, globes, and wavy lines and all laid on as with a trowel, as if to make sure it should remain for all time. "Whew!" I exclaimed. "It'll take a dozen coats to paint that lot out." But we'd seen only a sample, for in every room, excepting one upstairs in Japanese style, and the kitchen, Orde-Lees had given more than full expression to his dream and had I not known him to be a teetotaller would have put it all down to a shocking case of D.T.s. Green, blue, pink, yellow, more salmon as in the hallway, and always the black stripes and triangles and globes and squares. It conjured up visions of buckets of blood, celebrations of the Black Mass, and the Chamber of Horrors at Madame Tussaud's. The house was spotless, there were several items of school furniture, chairs with velvet seats, a desk, a bookshelf, and a cupboard was bursting with British and American magazines dealing with motor cars, aviation and diesel engines.

Ominous were long metal handles fastened into the brass knobs on all doors which the maid explained had been fitted so that Mrs. Orde-Lees could open them with her elbows. And because of her chronic arthritis, which had been with her ever

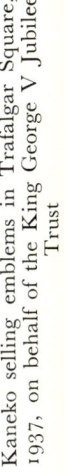

Kaneko selling emblems in Trafalgar Square, 1937, on behalf of the King George V Jubilee Trust

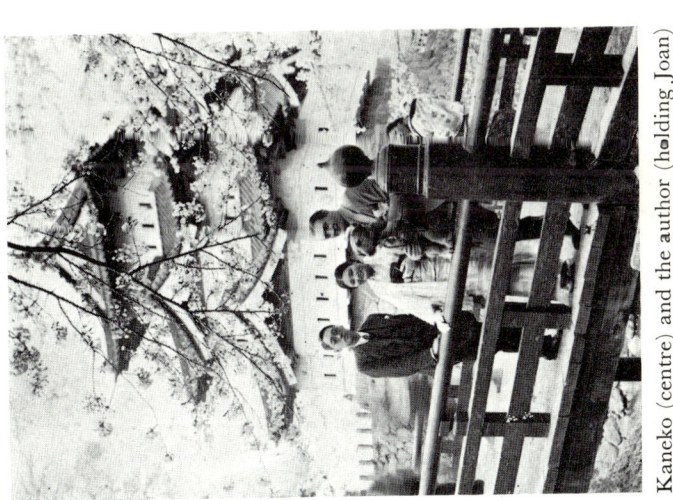

Kaneko (centre) and the author (holding Joan) with Professor Urhan (left) at blossomtime in Hirosaki, 1936

(*Above*) Hirosaki school picnic at Maya, 1936

(*Left*) The author at Yamagata, 1938

since they'd come North from Tokyo, for the greater part of the year they'd occupied only one room upstairs. Kaneko looked a little sheepish at hearing this, but I reminded her that Nagahama in winter with its snow and damp had surely hardened her against such ills.

The little mongrel, a very pretty little creature much like a Japanese Chin, was named Ponchan. She followed us around greatly interested but whenever she came too near Kaneko or myself the little Airedale gave a bark and showed her teeth.

An early visitor was a distinguished looking gentleman dressed in kimono and *hakama* who introduced himself as Professor Yatomi, head of the department of Japanese literature, to whom it seemed the Viscount had written, and told me that he had been a tutor to the Emperor and Prince Chichibu as well as to Naokuni Matsudaira, the Viscount's nephew. He recoiled in amazement and then laughed heartily at Orde-Lees's interior decoration which he said he'd heard about but having seen it considered that rumour had if anything been somewhat conservative, and promised to get the painters to work immediately.

This gentleman then sent the maid out to telephone for a taxi, took us around the straggling city, during which we were able to order some furniture, saw the famous Hirosaki Castle, and then entertained us at a restaurant.

The air was warm and the sun shone out of a clear sky, but snow and ice were still much in evidence; yet many of what in the distance had at first seemed patches of snow turned out to be the apple blossom in the orchards for which the district is famous. On the roof of every house were traps to prevent the snow from piling too high. The speech of the people was generally incomprehensible, even to Kaneko. The professor said that many of the local expressions originated in Kyoto whence the feudal lords had come in ancient times with their families and retainers to establish an outpost of the Empire and to guard the northern marches.

The majority of the women wore *mompei*, the baggy, trouser-like and practical garment into which the lower part of the kimono is tucked, and nearly everyone wore rubber boots, which were very necessary judging by the state of the roads, and I decided I should have to get a pair without delay. A dilapidated looking cinema advertised, "Blue Angel" with Marlene Dietrich, "Man of Aran," and a super-colossal Hollywood spectacle starring John Gilbert, plus newsreels, and all for 20 sen, about twopence.

"That's the most popular cinema with the students," explained Yatomi Sensei. "A regular fire-trap. Always sit near the exit. Always use plenty of flea powder before and after going there, wash your hands in disinfectant, and keep them away from your eyes until you have done so."

The city simply teemed with students; primary, middle, those from the private academy which had been established in the latter part of the nineteenth century by Protestant missionaries, and of course those from the higher school wearing capes of dog-skins, and invariably wooden clogs and without socks, all of whom regarded us with interest but raised their caps or even bowed smartly to Yatomi Sensei. Some appeared about my own age and I thought looked tough customers.

Back at our new home we found flowers and fruit and other expressions of goodwill from the principal and other colleagues, the maid impatient to get away to an important church meeting, Joan delirious with delight, the painters already at work in the hallway, and a wood fire roaring in the simple but effective galvanized iron stove.

With sundown the temperature dropped sharply, soon the stars were glittering overhead, and we retired to rest, both well content at the reception accorded us and what showed promise of being a very pleasant home.

Chapter Eleven

I

THE next morning I paid my official call on the school principal, Dr. Nakayama, an elderly, whimsical man, who immediately put me at my ease, announced that he was being transferred and that his successor would arrive in a few days, and proceeded to entertain me with tales of the extraordinary idiosyncrasies of my predecessor which he seemed to have thoroughly enjoyed, and especially in telling how Orde-Lees would go into the town, buy a potted plant and walk home balancing it on the top of his head followed by a throng of admiring school children. "I do not mind a man expressing himself," he said, "but he must not try to make fools of the authorities. One day I had a very worried gendarmerie officer here who told me that Orde-Lees had informed one of the students that the reason he was so interested in climbing Mount Iwaki was to survey for suitable sites on which guns might be dropped by parachute in case of war between Japan and Great Britain. When I asked Orde-Lees if he had made such a statement he simply roared with laughter and said, 'If people ask stupid questions they must expect stupid answers!' But what a man! No wonder your countrymen have exerted such influence upon mankind. He once told me that he had tried to persuade Captain Scott to let him take an aeroplane to the South Pole in the expedition of 1910 and claimed that had Scott agreed they'd have reached the Pole before Amundsen and Scott would not have lost his life."

Dr. Nakayama then advised me as to how I might succeed with my students and colleagues, and I left him saddened at the thought that he would be leaving in a few days and succeeded by a scholar of German literature and language, who Kuno informed me was a strict disciplinarian of stern, unyielding character. As Kuno and I left for the school three military officers on horseback were approaching and as the leader drew near my colleague bowed low, and when the officer saluted I recognized him as Prince Chichibu, brother of the Emperor and to whose Princess I had a letter of introduction from the Viscount.

The school, painted the usual grey, consisted of several two- and one-storied buildings situated by the side of the main road to the Army Divisional Headquarters, with spacious grounds and playing fields enclosed by fine, tall cryptomeria. Just inside the front gate was the small stone structure with bronze doors in which reposed the picture of the Emperor.

In the common room I was introduced to my colleagues of the English department, the Japanese teachers of German—the new

German lecturer had not arrived from Berlin—Chinese and Japanese literature, mathematics, physics, etc., then presented to the office staff, and finally drank tea with the army officer in charge of military training, a red-faced cherubic little man who told me that he had been brought back from retirement.

I then followed Kuno into every class-room where the lesson in hand was interrupted whilst I was introduced, when all stood up and bowed and I bowed back at them. All students were dressed in the black, high collared, brass buttoned uniform, standard from middle school to university but distinction made in the one white band round the cap for middle schools, two white bands for higher schools, plain for universities, but all having their distinctive cap badges. The new boys seemed shy and conscious of the newness of their uniforms, stood up and bowed very correctly, whilst the second year lads surveyed me with half smiles as if wondering what sort of devilment they might be able to get away with during my lesson, had greasy looking uniforms, seemed unwashed, and many even sported a moustache, or a straggly beard or side-burns. One class in particular looked like a bunch of brigands and I fancied that Kuno gave a shudder as we left the room. The third year classes appeared quiet, no doubt all conscious of the fact that it was going to be tough to make up for the time wasted in the second year, graduate, and then hurdle the stiff examination for an Imperial University.

"You'll find the first year boys very shy to begin with," said Kuno. "You see they have been studying English in middle school from Japanese teachers only and most of them have never heard an Englishman or American speak, so you'll need a great deal of patience. With the others it will be easier; the second year literature crowd will try your patience to the limit, they'll be testing you for a while just to see if you can stand up to their pranks. Orde-Lees was a good teacher, played up to them a great deal, but would stand no insolence. Perhaps you may know that he had to leave the Peers' School because he boxed the ears of a cheeky young Imperial prince. The third year students will for the most part have got over their general laziness which most go through in second year and realize that they have to work hard even to graduate, so please help and encourage them all you can. Orde-Lees did not encourage the students to visit him at his home, although he did sometimes take them for rides in his little Austin 7. But the boys will want to visit you and if you agree I'd suggest you stipulate a fixed visiting day. You'll find the students from Tokyo, Osaka and other large cities quite sharp and inclined to be cheeky, in comparison with those from this district and other country places who are generally rather slow but very studious and sincere."

II

I entered a second year class, register in hand, with a certain amount of trepidation, having been informed that it was the most unruly in the school and that the toughest characters had been there for a couple of years. On the blackboard was a caricature of myself, Kaneko and Joan, which I pretended not to see and in a small jar on the desk was a single dandelion. I called the roll. Then a villainous looking rascal with hair around his shoulders, moustache and a goatee beard stood up and said, "Sir, may I ask a question?"

"Why, certainly," I replied.

"Then please tell us how teachers call the roll in an English school."

"In exactly the same manner as here in Japan," I replied.

"Do they not call out Mr. Brown, Mr. Smith?"

"No they do not, Mori Shigeru," I countered with a smile. The rascal grinned and sat down and the class roared with laughter which was repeated when I thanked them for the floral decoration and without turning my back rubbed the caricature off the blackboard and then set about exploring the extent of their knowledge of spoken English. Fifty per cent. seemed downright hopeless, a few announced that they had no interest in English, one tall lad seemed almost fluent, and the rest were just passable.

"Do you like tunnels, sir?" inquired one lad.

"Tunnels are very useful especially in a mountainous country like Japan."

"But do you love tunnels, sir?"

"No I cannot say that I love them."

"Professor Orde-Lees was a Tunnelophile."

"A what?"

"A tunnelophile; he loved tunnels."

"Oh, really, that is a new word to me."

"Yes, sir. When new tunnel was opened near here our teacher, Professor Orde-Lees, took four of us through tunnel in his car. We passed through, he turned round and passed back, we passed through again, we traversed tunnel incessantly, dozens of passing through were made. All of us were surprised. We asked our teacher, 'Sir, why do you pass through tunnel so much?' and he said sharply. 'That is my business, for I love driving through tunnels.' And all of us believed him to be a great man."

The first year classes gave no trouble, all were still basking in the great glory of having passed the difficult entrance examination to the school, were no doubt having to sing small in the presence of their seniors who apparently subjected them to all manner of uncomfortable penances just for being new, and I warmed to my task of making them speak and understand during the first two terms. To my amazement I found that with their Japanese English teacher they were using Carlyle's *Sartor Resartus* as a text book, enough I thought to sour any English boy, let alone a Japanese. Other classes were studying Galsworthy's *Man of Property*, which was one rainy day responsible for a lad remarking to me that it was raining "elephants and tigers".

"Galsworthy writes that it was raining cats and dogs, sir, and so for a change I thought that other animals may be employed."

With the third year students I was asked to discuss and explain the editorials from the London *Times*, which were far above the heads of the majority, as well as conduct readings from the works of Shakespeare to prepare them for the entrance examination of the Imperial Universities. The work was pleasant, the hours of teaching amounted to only 16 per week, with perhaps another four spent in assisting my colleagues with their text-book work.

In the common room were such periodicals as *The Times*, the *Times Literary Supplement*, *London Mercury*, *Atlantic Monthly*, and the library contained quite an extensive collection of works on English and American literature, biography, and other subjects. I took to playing tennis with the students and my colleagues, as well as *Kendo*, the Japanese fencing, in which swords of split-bamboo are used, but because of my size, mask, breastplate, short jacket and *hakama* had to be ordered from Kyto. At first I found this a gruelling sport, my feet suffered greatly from splinters in the board floor of the exercise hall, after a few minutes the mask almost suffocated me, and my instructor's wrists seemed made of iron.

III

The new principal who relieved the easy-going Dr. Nakayama proved a strict disciplinarian which it seemed the school badly needed, and his first act was to make the long-haired scruffy students visit the barber and spruce up a bit. A serious student of German language and literature, Professor Anzai was also extremely fond of music, an admirer of British political institutions and detested Hitler and Mussolini and all they represented.

Finally the new German professor arrived with his wife from Germany and proved to be a victim of Hitler persecution simply because his mother was Japanese. He'd been in Germany since infancy, and had inherited all his racial characteristics from his mother. His wife was the Nordic type, and like himself a mathematician. Forced out of his position as an assistant professor at Berlin University his future appeared gloomy when on hearing of his plight the benevolent Suzuki family which had built up a great business from their "Ajinomoto"—"Essence of Taste"— paid their expenses to Japan and found him the position at Hirosaki.

Certain sections of the Press gave the impression that Japan was wholeheartedly with Hitler and his policies, but educational circles did not appear to subscribe to these views. Before very long a well-respected German professor at Tokyo Imperial University who would have no part of the Nazi movement, was to be persecuted by the Nazis who endeavoured to persuade the Japanese authorities to relieve him of his position at the university, but met with a flat refusal and aroused the indignation of academic circles.

Apart from myself and the German neighbours, the foreign community consisted of two middle-aged American lady missionaries, a Canadian missionary and his wife and children who were extremely nice but frowned on the cinema as an instrument of the devil, and seemed intent upon having me join the Band of Hope and sign the Pledge, and the hearty, huge, and energetic Father Cornelius who presided over the local Catholic Church and its kindergarten who was to become a regular visitor and our closest foreign friend.

The Father, I learned, had earned for himself the nickname of Father Piss. This had come about when on his return from a visit to his bishop he had informed his surprised congregation in church one Sunday that he had been away on *"shonben"*—to make water, instead of *"shobai"*—on business.

Father Cornelius was typical of the priests of his faith I'd met in all parts of the Far East. Men truly dedicated, often spending the greater part of their lives away from home. The Father's church had been almost entirely rebuilt with contributions, mostly from his own family in Holland, and in the busy season the kindergarten cared for the infants of the farmers while they and their womenfolk toiled in the fields and orchards, a social service which the Protestants also provided.

The 29th April was a National Holiday to celebrate the Emperor's birthday. In the morning we assembled at the school auditorium, bowed before the portrait of His Majesty, sang the *Kimigayo* and then Yatomi Sensei took me off to the residence of Prince Chichibu where, although well wined by His Highness's aides we were not permitted to see him or Princess Setsuko. However, the aftermath was a visit from the manager of the Kaikosha—perhaps the Japanese equivalent of a PX or NAAFI, who extended us all the privileges of the establishment which was almost a universal provider, would order anything not in stock, and for which we paid about 15 per cent. less than the retail prices.

I had heard a great deal about the cherry-blossoms around Hirosaki Castle, but when they blossomed, I realized that their beauty had not been by any means exaggerated. Bowed and twisted by the heavy snows so that their branches swept down to just above the waters of the castle moat the tightly packed profusion of double flowers presented a scene unsurpassed even by the blossoms of Yoshino. The country folk as well as students made merry under the flowering trees till late into the night and the litter they left behind remained an eyesore for weeks.

Kaneko engaged wholeheartedly in gardening and, in spite of warnings from many that Hybrid tea roses would not succeed because of insects, we ordered a selection from Yokohama, including "Daily Mail Scented" and "Killarney" which were to prove the most successful, and set about confounding the pessimists. In the back garden we sowed spinach, lettuce, beetroot, radish, tomatoes, mustard and cress, and celery.

I made no attempt to prevent the students calling on us and did not even stipulate a visiting day and soon hardly an evening passed without callers. But if they enjoyed listening to my records, practising their conversation, or engaging in idle chatter, I too found such visits most rewarding. One very serious-minded youth, the shortest boy in the school and for this reason nicknamed "Monster", never came with a fellow student or would leave if one arrived. So enamoured of the English language had this lad become that he attended the Protestant churches, visited the missionaries' homes, and Father Cornelius was instructing him in the Faith just as the Baptists and Methodists were in their particular brands of Christianity. On Monday mornings "Monster" looked a wreck. For on Sunday from crack of dawn till late at night he was in and out of churches and then had to burn the midnight oil swotting for Monday's lessons.

There were several Korean students and these were without exception quite brilliant, which no doubt they had to be in order to gain entry to the school. Boku was a handsome lad with a good command of English and a passionate interest in law. "But what is the use of studying," he'd complain, "when there is no chance of becoming more than a clerk so long as the Japanese rule our country and give all the best positions to their own people." Kim, another Korean lad, had only one ambition which was to go to the United States before, as he put it, the Japanese could use him for cannon fodder in their war which they'd be bound to start, and after which he'd be able to return to an independent Korea. I wonder if he did? And if he is now north or south of the 49th Parallel?

Joan, and Ponchan, loved to accompany us on long walks into the countryside when the Waterside Terriers of Wharfedale, ancestors of the Airedale, seemed to spur Joan into behaving more like a seal than a dog. For she would leap joyfully into ponds, bark for sticks to be thrown, dive into rivers and streams for rocks which she'd bring ashore to build into a cairn, while Ponchan who could not stand water yelped her glee at the antics of this strange creature. Soon Joan was counting up to five, to the holding up of the required numbers of fingers, or speaking them in English or Japanese, and coaxed with a stick she wanted to retrieve or a titbit.

It was the wily Ponchan who led the Airedale into bad habits and especially into lifting fish when the fishmonger was not looking. This led to Joan doing so quite brazenly and the cost of her clandestine snacks started to appear on the fishmonger's bill.

At school I experienced annoyances and much frustration, particularly with the second year literature classes. Cheekiness, which a teacher in England would have dealt with in no uncertain manner, cutting classes, and what I considered downright rudeness. These often made me bad tempered and moody but it was

Kaneko's sound advice and the knowledge that she was nearly always right which prevented me from handing out a thrashing and thereby most certainly losing my job. But at *kendo* I gave one of the cockiest students a welter of clouts with my sword-stick not strictly in the places allowed by the rules, but which proved highly effective. When a class failed to appear within five minutes I'd mark all absent and then go home or else go out and play tennis. Suddenly there was a change for the better, attendance improved, and one evening Mori Shigeru, considered the most intractable of all, and who'd been at the school for a record period, turned up at our house with two or three classmates, became a regular visitor, and a good friend.

My German colleague was soon in trouble. At his first lesson they'd tried on the dodge of asking him how teachers called the roll in Germany, convinced him that the suffix San was customary and so he came to labour through the register ... Kato San, Suzuki San ... much to the delight of his tormentors, and when I expressed amazement that he should have fallen for it, lacked the courage to cease the practice. But his big *faux pas* had been in reporting bad behaviour and laziness to the Principal. One morning when we set out for school together I noticed that he was carrying a portable gramophone. "They are getting better, my friend," he remarked, "and I am happy to teach them German folk-songs. Already some are singing *Der Lindenbaum* and today one of the boys is bringing some records of our fine German songs which I do not possess."

It happened that he was teaching that morning in the class next door to mine. But my class seemed restless and very quiet and I sensed that there was something in the wind. Suddenly from next door came the throaty, sex-laden voice of Marlene Dietrich, a roar of applause in which my lads joined, and demands to know why we did not have such interesting English folk-songs.

The general exuberance of the students reached its peak in the annual "storm" which took place on the anniversary of the school's foundation, and on which occasion the unfortunate teacher who'd rubbed his lads the wrong way might expect to hear all about it.

With sundown a procession left the dormitory carrying lanterns on bamboos, flags and banners, and sometimes placards bearing caricatures, all bawling out the school song and the "Dekansho".

Descartes, Kant and Schopenhauer, the bane of Japanese students in the first two decades of the present century, had not as is commonly supposed anything to do with "Dekansho", for it was originally a wrestler's song and the title comes from "Dekashita!" —Well Done!

The road between our house and the principal's was jam-packed with laughing, singing students who shouted "Banzai Anzai!", serenaded him when he appeared and then began calling my name. There was much good-natured banter, I learned that my nicknames were "Broom" and "Blue Shirt", and after failing to get my German colleague out of doors, to our great relief and the alarm of many of the devoted subjects of the Emperor living down in the town they went on their boisterous way. They had no quarrel with discipline, which Anzai wielded with no holds barred; but they had no use for any teacher who could not handle them without resort to the assistance of the Principal. One such unfortunate had his fence broken down and his windows smashed, and fled through his back door in fear they might do him violence.

The majority were carefree, healthy young men but some embraced a morbid nihilism, took little part in sports or other amusements and when they caught me alone would astound with outpourings concerning what they considered their own uselessness, and the futility of life. One handsome lad was to commit suicide, after having broken up the happy home of his landlady with whom he had an affair, aroused her jealousy by carrying on with her daughter and then left the girl with a fatherless child.

All were submitted to a form of military training which few except perhaps the Germans would have tolerated. Route marches over rugged terrain in the depth of winter or the blazing heat of summer often rendered the less robust in such shape that they had to leave school. A forced march over the mountains in snow and ice soon weeded out the many susceptible to tuberculosis and often resulted in their deaths. Some years before over a hundred young soldiers had died in a gruelling march through a blizzard on the slopes of Mount Hakkoda.

IV

When school broke up for the summer holidays my friend Capt. A. B. Millar, 2/13 Frontier Force Rifles, Indian Army (ret'd), came up from Numazu with his Japanese wife to spend a week or so and accompany us on a trip to Hokkaido. Abe had a gammy leg, result of a Turkish bullet in the knee received one night in 1918 in the Mesopotamian desert; but in 1942, though well over age, he was to walk out of Burma into India and in 1944 trek back in again.

Knowing that his military career would invite much questioning and suspicion of the local police and gendarmerie I took the precaution of informing them of his coming, provided all the information I could about him and begged that he not be pestered during his stay.

The authorities thanked me for my information, promised to let my guest alone but suggested that an officer pay a courtesy call during which he would endeavour to assist us with advice on our trip to Hokkaido.

However, if Abe was not pestered at Hirosaki, when we arrived at Aomori to take the ferry across the Tsugaru Straits, a deputation of detectives and gendarmes was waiting and pestered us even on the boat. But while awaiting our train at Hakodate when we sampled what seemed a vast quantity of the excellent Sapporo draught beer, incidentally the finest in Japan, our wives took care of the plain-clothes men who'd exhausted our patience and with whom we'd decided to hold no further conversation.

It was our first visit to Japan's northern island. One might have been in northern Europe, for instead of the pine-trees and the paddy fields, were pasturelands, cows, horses and sheep grazing, the silver birch, oak and poplar, silos beside the log farmhouses, and all set in rugged, magnificent scenery.

Soon after leaving Hakodate the rains came and, after making a wrong change, instead of arriving at Noboribetsu hot-spring resort, at midnight we found ourselves at a lonely station with the impossible name of Oshamambe from which it seemed we could not escape until dawn. And when a kindly station master showed us to what appeared to be the only hotel a drove of police and gendarmerie arrived to complete our misery. What mysterious military secrets Oshamambe harboured I'll never know, but we could not convince our questioners that we'd arrived there by mistake, and they appeared quite relieved when they'd got us safely aboard the first train out.

Noboribetsu was enveloped in mist and rain and in the sulphur vapours arising from the numerous springs and geysers. The hotel was a massive wooden affair of several storeys. Rivulets streaked the roads of red mud, dappled with patches of sulphur, and it was a relief to relax in a large room which could be partitioned into four separate compartments if required.

Our wives preferring to bathe in privacy Abe and I donned *yukata* provided by the hotel and set off in search of the famous "One Thousand Persons Bath". This was of swimming pool dimensions about two feet deep and surrounded by a tiled floor on which people of both sexes, young and old, sat on low stools soaping themselves. Men were engaged in shaving and women rinsing their hair. None except children showed any unusual curiosity on seeing two tall foreigners, but greeted us with friendly smiles. This made up for everything, even the depressing memory of Oshamambe.

Clad only in singlet and trousers I clambered up the hillside in the torrential rain to see the boiling "hells"—a series of geysers shrouded in mist and vapours which gurgled and boiled to present a truly awe-inspiring sight. But a quick look was enough in such weather and after filling my pockets with lumps of rock sulphur for the dog's drinking water I hurried back to the monster bath and after having doused myself stepped into the hot and vapour-shrouded water to be greeted with:

"*Sensei, konnichiwa!*" from three students in one of my science classes who expressed their surprise at meeting me, and in of all places a communal bath. They offered to guide us to the Ainu village at Shiraoi, a short bus ride away, but we decided that this would have to wait for more pleasant conditions and with the rain still coming down in buckets set out to return to the mainland.

The same squad of policemen and gendarmes saw us off their premises at Hakodate and did not appear convinced with our reason for staying a night at that confounded Oshamambe. As the ferry neared Aomori the skies cleared and the sun came out as if a veil, spread over Hokkaido for our benefit, had been lifted now we were out of the way.

We returned to Hirosaki by way of Lake Towada, a vast volcanic crater perhaps dating back to before the birth of time, and surely one of the most charming of its kind in the world, whose turquoise-blue waters and rocky banks are studded with birch and hardy pine-trees of every conceivable shape.

The remainder of our holiday was spent at Nagahama, Kaneko travelling there with Joan after a few hours in Tokyo to enable our beloved Airedale to stretch her legs after the ordeal in the dog box from Hirosaki, whilst I renewed Tokyo friendships for a few days, was wined and dined by the Viscount, Yoshi and others, and before going down to Lake Biwa just had to swim at Inamura and bask in the salty sunshine of Sagami Bay.

There was bathing in the lake with Joan, who soon established herself in the affections of the populace, excepting those of a priest after she dived into his temple pool bent on devouring his carp and goldfish, excursions to see my old friend Hidesaburo and his aged mother, and a terrific session with my friend the brewer of sake, and Mishimaya, the restaurateur.

Chapter Twelve

I

THE autumn, when the "sky is high and the horse is fat" was a season of great activity with the harvest, and particularly in the orchards where men, women and children gathered the crops of "Golden Delicious", "Indo" and other species of fine apples. The most common brand was a large rosy type which had been introduced from Canada to start this industry some forty years before.

The children and the students were expert scrumpers, and none paid the slightest attention to the special trees which the farmers labelled with an invitation to any to help themselves, and preferred to select their fruit.

Kaneko bought a barrow load from a farmer woman for about one shilling and for days devoted herself to the making of apple jelly to send to our friends in the South. She also put up some two hundred beer bottles of tomato juice, and prepared excellent green tomato pickles from a recipe given her by our Canadian missionary friends.

We had been in the habit of ordering brown bread from a German bakery in Tokyo. One day the baker arrived with a dark, reddish loaf, to announce that knowing our preference for this type of bread he was now making it to save us the trouble of sending to Tokyo. After taking one bite I realized that all he'd done was to mix cocoa in the flour.

Our garden had turned out a great success, the roses, especially "Daily Mail Scented," were admired by all, and we had more than enough lettuce, kale, radishes, and beetroot.

Our only problem was the maid inherited from Orde-Lees whose so-called religious activities became a positive nuisance. She was an awful scandal-monger, had not a good word for any one, even the pastor of her church, was never around when you really wanted her but always begging leave to attend some god-bothering meeting, and it was a great relief when jolly, good-natured Tatsu agreed to come up from Tokyo.

We met her on the day of the first heavy snow and had no sooner got her out of the train than she exclaimed: "What a lot of Korean people in these parts!" She was quite alarmed when told that she was only listening to the local dialect.

Soon, the horse-drawn carts and carriages gave way to sleds, even the tiny tots started going to school on skii, snow-ball fights occupied the school-boys, and before Christmas our whole world was white, with blue, sunny skies by day, and the temperature sinking to below zero at night.

It was a fine, bracing climate, and we enjoyed long walks into the snow-clad countryside with Joan and Ponchan who revelled in plunging into the snow-drifts.

Classrooms were stuffy, to say the least, and the students clad in dog-skin backwarmers and mufflers, appeared to have taken the vow not to wash again till spring came round. After calling the roll I would freshen things up by opening all the windows. One morning there was a huge snowman on my desk which I ignored while calling the roll, and then heaved it into the class with the remark that thanks to their foresight for once the floor would enjoy a little fresh water.

The Christmases at Hirosaki were certainly the whitest I had experienced and among the very small foreign community gifts were exchanged, carol-singing sessions were held to remind me of my childhood, and I enjoyed the celebrations of Catholic and the various Protestant denominations represented in the district.

It was during our first winter that the old professor of archaeology brought me a bottle of sake frozen solid, heated the end of a wire in our stove until it was red hot, inserted this in the neck of the bottle and probed around until he'd melted a small chamber of liquid in the centre of the bottle, called for two wine glasses and invited me to drink what he described as the true nectar of the gods. It was indeed a superb drink, though expensive, for he explained that the cream of the entire bottle was concentrated in the melted liquid, and the remainder would be weak. This old man who spent his holidays with a party of student enthusiasts digging in the beds of dried-up rivers, chiefly in Akita prefecture, had an extensive collection of primitive pottery, axes, arrow-heads and other objects, and it was his theory that the Ainu were not the Japanese aborigines but a race they had eliminated called the *Koro-pok-guru*. In those long winter evenings it was such kind and interesting old scholars like him and Yatomi, as well as our student friends and Father Cornelius, who made life so very pleasant. Another great favourite was the aged professor of Chinese classics, a typical philosopher, who on ceremonial occasions donned a frock coat, green with age and with silken lapels, combined with brown elastic-sided boots and perhaps a striped shirt and red necktie. The students were very fond of the old man and I could not imagine he had ever uttered an unkind word.

In striking contrast to my worthy colleagues was the industrialist father of one of my students who on a visit to his son stalked around the school as though he owned it, invited himself to our home, and during the best meal we were able to put up for him at short notice delivered a pompous oration on the superiority of Japan and things Japanese and the impending doom of the British Empire. I thought he was the rudest, most arrogant Japanese I had met compared with whom the most obnoxious pettifogging officials one encountered were gentlemen. His son, too, was a rarity among the students in that he was a snob; he was also rather stupid in his work but was much envied for his splendid Leica camera.

II

On February 26th, 1936, just before the end of the school year, occurred the mutiny of a regiment in Tokyo, when former prime minister Admiral Viscount Saito, the financial wizard Takahashi Korekiyo, and many others were killed or wounded. The Prime Minister Admiral Okada managed to hide, but his brother-in-law who strikingly resembled the premier was mistaken for him and slain. The rebels seized control of the area around parliament which they barricaded and the entire nation waited with bated breath concerning the outcome.

Rumours were rife, and the fact that it was Prince Chichibu's own regiment which had mutinied gave rise to conjectures that he personally was involved. This was, of course, untrue, but the Prince left immediately for Tokyo and it was then considered by some that his influence had been even stronger than that of the Emperor, his brother, in persuading the mutineers to lay down their arms and surrender to the loyal troops which of course comprised the bulk of the Army. It was a difficult period and I kept my own counsel and refused to be drawn into discussing the mutiny. There was little doubt, however, that the sympathies of some students and teachers were with the misguided young officers who led the revolt against what they considered harmful influences upon the Throne. Political assassinations had continued to plague the Showa Era and, as has been pointed out by my friend and veteran newspaperman Kimpei Shiba, if the occupant of No. 10 Downing Street is perhaps safer from violence than any prime minister in the world, in those days the premier of Japan occupied the most dangerous position of any statesman.

Examinations were a source of headaches and much heart-searching for those who hoped to pass out of the school and enter one of the Imperial Universities, or technical colleges. The students were overloaded with subjects and I stretched things as far as possible to ensure they obtained the 60 per cent. necessary in my exam. One who'd failed to pass out the previous year, to every written question I had given him wrote, "I regret, my teacher that I have not been diligent and cannot answer your question, please forgive me," or "The answer is in my mind but it will not transfer itself to my pen," and "Shameful it is indeed that here again I am unable to clarify the situation," and followed up by leaving a note at my house in which he implored me to be kind to him, pointed out that he knew he had been lazy, and ended by stating that if he did not pass the examination he would be shamed before his parents who had endured much in sending him to high school, and would be compelled to commit honourable suicide. I gave him 61, but he did not pass, and he did not disembowel himself on my doorstep.

Some of the students just would not or could not speak English; in many cases this was due to a natural shyness and often the same lads would turn in written examination papers which would have done credit to British or American youths. But a few, and particularly "Monster", would hold the floor if given the chance and treat you to a discourse on Adam Smith, John Stuart Mill, even André Gide. Those who came to our house were forbidden to speak Japanese; this was also very good for Kaneko, but she invariably broke the rule out of sympathy with a lad struggling to put something across. On winter's nights with the snow piled up six feet outside, six or seven students often gathered in the warmth of our home when Kaneko produced an enormous pot of curry and another of rice. Their appetites were a wonder to behold and they'd often cap it all with lashings of bread and cheese. We'd discuss the state of the world, complex problems would crop up such as the moral attitude of Hamlet, the merits of popular film stars, Somerset Maugham and Galsworthy and Thomas Hardy, and for enthusiasts I'd play records of Mr. Ramsay MacDonald speaking to the Burns Society, Stanley Baldwin "On England", a recitation of Gray's *Elegy* in the churchyard at Stoke Poges, my favourite Debussy recordings, Bach, Beethoven, down to Gracie Fields, Al Jolson and Dixieland jazz.

Few seemed to have any clear idea of what they wished to be. The majority in the literature course were apparently content to pass out from higher school into law or economics at one of the Imperial Universities and let the future take care of itself. The son of our grocer, a brilliant lad who spoke excellent English and was, according to my colleague, first class at German, was determined to enter the diplomatic service. Many were destined for ready-made jobs in family businesses; the sons of farmers slaved at their studies in their efforts to get away from the hard life of their ancestors and carve out something for themselves in government service, business or the professions, while those in the science course, quiet, confident and most studious of all, were ear-marked for the medical colleges or university courses in civil, mechanical or electrical engineering.

Very often one would remark that the future did not matter as they'd all have to go into the Army or Navy. These thoughtful types sensed the stormclouds rising, knew that once the Army had eliminated opponents to its expansionist ambitions on the Continent, with Hitler and Mussolini keeping Great Britain on tenterhooks in Europe and the smug isolationist policy of the United States there was nothing to prevent it becoming hopelessly enmeshed with Chiang Kai-shek and, more dangerous still, with Russia.

The previous year when the news was received of the death of King George V, a stream of students and teachers called on me to express their condolences. The abdication of King Edward VIII over Mrs. Wallis Warfield Simpson had me badgered from all angles including the local Press, and even brought visits from inquisitive giggling students of the girls' higher school. By and large the majority sympathized with Edward; it was an ideal young person's romance like that many years later between Captain Townsend and Princess Margaret. But to my question as to whether they would approve a similar action by an unmarried Emperor of Japan they replied that it was impossible, unthinkable, and furthermore it was inconceivable that a Japanese sovereign would still be single on his accession to the Throne.

Chapter Thirteen

I

THE two years at Hirosaki were indeed happy for both of us; we made solid friendships, many of which endured all the trials and tribulations of the difficult years which were to follow, and I gained an insight into the yearnings, frustrations and joys of young men who differed little from those of other lands in work, in play, and in their hopes for their future.

In Aomori Prefecture, too, I had seen rural poverty at its worst; people compelled to eke out a near-starvation existence through the long winters, their crops in summer always at the mercy of the early cold spells, their children terribly undernourished, ridden with tuberculosis, trachoma and other diseases, but who calmly accepted their lot while their leaders, and especially the military expansionists, pressed on with their guns before rice, clothing and social welfare policy. In such conditions it was natural for them to clutch at any straw, however flimsy, which might hold out promise of salvation in some form and every type of crack-pot religion thrived among the simple, honest northern folk. The only practical good seemed to be done by the Christians.

When my contract with the school was about to expire the Principal offered me another engagement for three years; but the prospect of an immediate free passage to England could not be denied. It was ten years since I had left home, I longed to see my parents and they were entitled to see the differences which time had wrought in their offspring and something of their daughter-in-law. It was time, too, that Kaneko saw the land which she had adopted through marriage.

To allow for more to spend at home we booked passage via Siberia "hard class", and second class from Tokyo to Manchouli, and Stolpce in Poland, to Harwich. Because of the unsettled state of affairs in Manchuria and North China, I bought one return ticket with the idea that Kaneko should return via the Suez Canal and see a little more of the world than the wastes of Manchuria, Siberia and Russia, Poland and Germany and Holland from the window of a railway carriage. Professor Anzai promised to use his influence to secure me a new post on my return, he and other colleagues simply loaded us with gifts, and I was wined and dined to such extent that I felt something like an ingrate for going away.

On the day of departure with Joan, who was to be cared for by our friends the Millars, then living at a hot-spring resort in the Izu Peninsula, Ponchan having been adopted by the good Catholic Father, the snow was a good six feet deep and spring still seemed far away in that cold northern clime. At the railway station I was presented with a watch, suitably inscribed and which a few years later was to provide me and my comrades at a Tokyo prisoner-of-war camp with a few delicacies, and as the train bore us south and our friends on the platform faded from sight our eyes were indeed wet with tears of great happiness and gratitude for all the joys which Hirosaki had brought us.

Advice concerning the nine days' travel across the Soviet Union was conflicting to say the least. Some told me that the food was terrible, uneatable in fact, and that the meal tickets which might be purchased from Intourist for the nine days' meals were a waste of money.

"You have to stock up with cold meats and sausages and tinned stuffs at Harbin," they advised. "Be sure to take a tea pot and powdered coffee, and at every station hop out quick so as to head the line for the 'kiapitok'—hot water."

We spent a day or so in Tokyo, shopping for the essentials, and in bidding good-bye to the Viscount who had prepared Kaneko a vocabulary of Russian words and phrases, had a heartbreaking farewell with Joan in the sunshine of Izu, almost within the shadow of Fuji San, a couple of days at Nagahama with my in-laws and Cho and Hidesaburo and friends of the bath-house, and early in March 1937 set out from Maibara, loaded down with bags and packs for England by the then fastest and cheapest route.

II

At nearly every stop en route to Shimonoseki where we embarked for Fusan, in Korea, groups of people were gathered to see young men off for their military service. Town, village and street associations, men, women and children bearing flags and banners sang patriotic songs whilst the conscript stood awkwardly, red faced from the many toasts he'd been given, and no doubt wishing that the train would soon start and get the business over. It was a sight that was to become only too common as were, too, the ceremonies of receiving the small boxes of ashes wrapped in white cotton— all that remained of many a once proud, sturdy youth.

There was less bother from the gendarmerie and police than I had expected, the few hours' trip across the Straits in the well-appointed railways steamer was most pleasant, and we made the acquaintance of a young Japanese couple going through to London but of course travelling Pullman de luxe through Russia.

The Korean Government Railways used a broader gauge than the Japanese. The coaches were most comfortable and dining car service excellent. All officials were Japanese and at the stations, towns and cities through which we passed there was that certain orderliness and pattern of administration which I had observed in Taiwan.

Manchuria was grey, bitterly cold, uninteresting; but the South Manchuria Railway most efficient and comfortable. At Harbin where we had to change trains with a wait of several hours the cold froze one's breath and the garlic-laden air was almost overpowering. Here the sturdy, swarthy people seemed sewn up in their clothing against the bitter cold. Our passports were examined by a White Russian, there were even Russian porters on hand, all supervised by Japanese, and we handed over our numerous bags and packages to one and set off across the station square to the Yamato Hotel to enjoy what would undoubtedly be our last bath before reaching Europe and to see about our final provisioning for Siberia.

The hotel was just a piece of Japan but during our shopping expedition the Chinese, Manchurian and Russian aspects of Harbin were soon revealed in the Cyrillic shop signs, Russian churches, the droskies, the blue-clad Manchurian peasants, the Chinese eating-houses and shops, amid which strutted the Japanese advisers and officers of the Manchukuo Army of Japanese puppet Emperor Henry Pu-Yi.

During the journey to Manchouli across country more bleak and inhospitable than ever, many walled settlements were seen with their outpost towers, and Japanese armed guards accompanied the train as precaution against attack by roving bands, some of which were carrying on resistance against the Japanese and their puppet state.

A talkative gendarme confessed that he pitied people being lured from Nippon to this hard life with promises of milk and honey and, pointing to Kaneko's silk stockings, warned her that she'd better put on woollen ones before arriving at Manchouli where the cold could soon cripple her. He was vastly intrigued that we were travelling "hard class" in Russia, predicted it would be unbearable and as good as told me that I should not subject my wife to such an ordeal. Like most Japanese he seemed to labour under the impression that all Europeans or Americans are rotten rich.

The gendarme had not exaggerated; for never have I experienced such a gripping, aching cold as assailed us at the depressing wind-swept border town.

We crossed No Man's Land and passed under an archway bearing hammer and sickle flags, a large portrait of Stalin with which we were soon to be most familiar, and into Otpor and the USSR.

Uniforms were in evidence, the ill-fitting green great-coats and pointed hats of the Tartar soldiers of Stalin, the smartly turned out officials in blue with their fine, soft leather high boots, and greatcoats which swept almost to their heels; there were prosperous looking commissars with fur coats and caps, shivering ill-clothed porters, ragged men and women beggars. In the customs office were a German diplomatic courier with a briefcase chained to his wrist, a toffee-nosed Englishwoman trying to be as overbearing as possible to the obvious discomfort of her seedy-looking husband, the two young Japanese we'd met on the boat, a Czech whom the Russians seemed greatly interested in, and several Chinese. I protested at our passports being taken from us. The idea of being in the USSR of all places without a passport was disconcerting to say the least.

As we proceeded to our coach I could not but envy those entering the ornate, old-fashioned Pullman cars; but "hard class" proved not so bad as its name implied. The coach contained about a dozen four-berth compartments and each bed was well padded and covered with oil-cloth, the two uppers folding up when not in use.

There was also plenty of room for our luggage. Sheets, pillows, pillow-slips and blankets were supplied for the equivalent of about thirty shillings, there were double windows, and the heating seemed adequate.

We were the only foreigners travelling "hard" and our berth companions proved to be a young air force officer and his well-pregnant blonde wife with whom Kaneko, with the aid of the Viscount's vocabulary, engaged in an extraordinary mixture of speech and mime, to inform me that they were on their way to a sanatorium on the Black Sea after having spent two or three years in Siberia.

The train just crawled along. Outside were only snow and ice and seemingly endless forests of silver birch. Nearly all the passengers in our coach were military officers with their wives and children, the men very well uniformed, the women bundled up in shapeless dresses, but all well-shod in fine, fur-lined boots. All were extremely jolly, no doubt glad to be leaving that bleak climate, and soon the coach was filled with song and laughter. We were the centre of interest, our clothes, watches, food—Bovril, Ovaltine, powdered George Washington coffee, cocoa, Kaneko's face-powder and lipstick, and above all our portable gramophone and records, mostly Japanese songs, Western style Japanese orchestral works, plus a few modern popular songs. Great disappointment was expressed that we had no jazz—at that time castigated by *Izvestia* as decadent, capitalistic rubbish.

At the first major stop I learned the hot water drill and thereafter was prepared as the train slowed to a snail's pace to leap out and get to the head of the queue with our thermos bottle and tea-pot.

What struck us both was the smell of Russia and the Russians. It was as all-pervading as curry being cooked in a small house, but not of course so strong or to my mind so unpleasant. At first we thought it was a peculiar type of disinfectant, or a strong washing soap, a musty but not altogether bad smell which seemed to be with us until we arrived at the German border, but there was even a hint of it in Poland. At one time I was always aware of the Japanese smell of '*takuwan*', a pickled turnip, the smell of open toilets mingled with the fumes of disinfectant or incense, or that of the public bath-house or barber shop saturated with that somewhat sickly perfume so truly Japanese. The Russian smell was rather more subdued but a sort of cross between the two; at best it was musky, leathery, and at worst musty and mouldy.

The train guide, a middle-aged serious type, spoke Cockney English and informed me that he had been born in London where he had lived for thirty years and had been employed as a glass-blower. When I finished my stock of reading material he provided me with *Quiet Flows the Don*, which I thoroughly enjoyed, *The Jungle* by Upton Sinclair, some short stories by Jack London, and a lot of pamphlets written by expatriates from Britain and the USA. We passed much of the time playing German Whist and our playing cards, the backs of which showed "Johnnie Walker—Still Going Strong", were greatly admired by all, especially the Intourist guide from London. The Russian cards were of pitifully cheap paper which absorbed every particle of dirt and dust as well as grease and perspiration.

By the time we reached Svedlovsk, where the Czar and his family were done away with in 1917, we were bored to distraction and our companions talked of nothing else but the delights of Moscow and especially their marvellous underground railway.

Just before our arrival at Moscow we decided to risk a meal in the dining car. Sitting with the well-nourished, opulent looking commissars and their ladies, the young Japanese couple and the stuffy Englishwoman and her weedy spouse, we enjoyed a splendid borsch, some grilled chicken and a bottle of excellent wine from the Caspian. I cursed inwardly when told that the same meal was provided to holders of meal tickets which worked out at a tenth of what I paid.

The Kremlin, with its battlements and towers, is surely one of the most impressive sights in the world. But the Red Square in early March 1937 was no place to loiter, for the wind cut like a knife and not being wrapped up like the faithful queueing up to gaze upon Lenin in his tomb we satisfied ourselves with a visit to the superb cathedral of St. Basil, a glance at the Great Bell, the largest ever cast, a peep into the famed and really splendid under-ground but which resembled a museum of modern art rather than a public transportation facility. We left the streets with their dirty grey snow and ice for the comfort of the Lenin Museum, at the portals of which the guards, on confirming that we were foreigners, ushered us to the head of the queue awaiting entrance and provided us with an English-speaking guide. In that hand-some well-appointed building, amid the orderly almost starry-eyed worshippers of the father of their country, we gazed upon Lenin in oils and water-colours, in bronze, in stone, haranguing the masses, encouraging them, bestowing awards, fondling chil-dren. Interesting were Lenin's English books: *Tom Brown's Schooldays*, *Treasure Island*, alongside *The Wealth of Nations*, and the works of John Stuart Mill.

There was much building in progress, and a great number of women labourers, though in many cases it was difficult to tell their sex for they were just bundles of rags. Occasionally well-fed, opulent looking personages, with astrakhan caps and fur coats passed by lolling back in sleek cars, perhaps members of the Communist hierarchy, and perhaps even then engaged in meditating on their chances of surviving the next purge. Shops displayed the most shoddy rubbish, but through the windows of restaurants could be seen parties, mostly in uniform, enjoying meals which would have been considered lavish anywhere. On buildings and hoardings were displayed the likenesses of the "Big Brothers" presided over by Josef Stalin to whom presumably all owed even the air they breathed.

We were happy indeed to be approaching the Polish frontier. But Russia attracted me, and I hope some day to visit that country under better weather as well as political conditions, for from what I had seen of the people they are among the most warm-hearted on earth.

At Negoroloye the walls of the Customs House revealed in brilliant colours the gay and prosperous life of the Soviet proletariat; gathering in the rich harvests of corn and barley, picking luscious grapes, forging castings, revelling in their folk-dances, and underneath a slogan in several languages urged the workers of the world to unite and enjoy the benefits of Communism.

At the border the train passed under another archway with its photos and flags and banners, machine-guns pointing ominously from outpost towers towards the barbed wire of the frontier, and we sighed with relief; for we had our passports back and our spirits were indeed high as the train pulled into Stolpce with its clean and friendly porters, and its fine buffet with tables loaded with such good things at prices even we could afford.

III

The next frontier brought us face to face with the world of Adolf Hitler; cleanliness, stern efficiency and innumerable signs containing the ominous word *verboten*.

Shortly after the train started for Berlin the compartment door slid open and a very pompous looking conductor surveyed us and our baggage and then started to berate me as if I had committed some shocking crime.

A well-dressed lady in the corner explained in good English: "He says you have too much luggage and that you will have to move it and pay excess charges."

"Well, we started at Tokyo, passed through Korea, Manchuria, Russia and Poland, and this is the first time we have been bothered," I replied. She smiled, and engaged in a lengthy conversation with the irate official. Finally he gave us a last sour look, slammed the door, and left us in peace.

The German lady laughed. "Oh, we Germans are a funny people, we take everything so very seriously. That man was insulted by the mere fact that you had dared break the regulations, it was a personal affront. Now he'll brood over it and curse all ignorant foreigners."

Prior to our arrival at Berlin Kaneko changed into a kimono. I thought she looked wonderful after nearly twelve days in trains, and the pleasant German lady said she'd never realized that Japanese clothing was so very beautiful. Even the irascible old conductor gave a wry smile.

But in the few hours available between trains we attracted so much curiosity that I soon wished she'd stuck to her travelling clothes. If we entered a shop there was a crowd gathered when we emerged. When we sought shelter in a restaurant on the Unter den Linden noses pressed against the heavy glass windows. And when the no doubt well-meaning leader of the small orchestra plunged his ensemble into airs from *Madame Butterfly*, and came and serenaded her with his cat box, for the moment I felt my gorge rising; but I realized that she was, after all, the most attractive woman in the place, perhaps even in Berlin, and that all this attention was really a great tribute to me. Uniforms, young men swaggering around with dagger side-arms, the stiff German formality, cleanliness, efficiency, were almost overwhelming after the light-hearted sordidness of the USSR and I soon realized that the Germans had much in common with the Japanese in their love of uniforms and badges, saluting and bowing to each other, in regimentation and in their general inquisitiveness, bordering on rudeness with strangers.

Chapter Fourteen

I

THE North Sea was in playful mood. Under a blue sky the white-crested waves set up such motion which sent all but few passengers in the mail steamer *Queen Juliana* to cabins or the saloon and smoke room settees. But while Kaneko bathed and titivated herself for her meeting with her in-laws I gloried in the feel of a deck under my feet, the crisp wind on my cheeks, mused on my wife's coming reception, recalled my own at Nagahama, and peered into the wind and spray for the first glimpse of the low Essex shore I had not seen for nine years and seven months.

A light vessel sent me below to point it out through the porthole to herself.

"When do we see the white cliffs?" she inquired.

"Not this time. Afraid you'll only see rather flat land and a muddy estuary." She started to weep.

"Heavens! What's the matter now?"

"Oh, I am afraid. Suppose your family do not like me."

"Of course they will. They'll love you. Now you'll have to powder your face all over again." She giggled as I kissed her tears away. "Now you've lipstick on your face."

"Yes," I replied, "and take note that it is your special brand on my handkerchief—no arguments later about red marks."

Harwich is a dismal port of entry, but there were mother and father, both gone rather grey, my younger brother and my sister in-law. Kaneko simply floored the customs men. They did not open a bag. Self-conscious mother seemed a bit overwhelmed by the kimono, and suggested she might be cold; but father and brother seemed as proud as I was. And once out into the Essex countryside, with the soft rolling fields springing to life, flowers in the hedgerows, cows, sheep and horses grazing, herself gasped. "Oh, it is beautiful, and what fine great trees and such neat houses!"

Colchester, which once saw the Roman legions, had never a more appreciative visitor. It seemed to fulfil all she had expected of an old English town and we drove into the courtyard of the famous "Red Lion" for her first meal on English soil.

Mother did not like the glances people gave my wife and was fidgety and talked about having to go shopping and get her some English clothes.

I pointed out that she had foreign clothes. That she did not come across Siberia in kimono, and that I had asked her to wear her native costume because I thought it the most beautiful in the world. Mother replied that she was only thinking of her daughter-in-law as she must be cold. Of course all she was really bothered about was being conspicuous and the neighbours parting the curtains.

But never had a wandering son such glorious homecoming and never had a bride from the other side of the world been received so warmly.

For herself each day brought its surprises. First was her amazement at seeing red, green and blue eggs for sale and wanting to see the hens that laid them. It was just before Easter. Then she found that English celery was red instead of white, having never before seen rhubarb.

She missed the Japanese bath as I did. You could not soap and rinse yourself outside an English bath for the water to run down a scupper. But she found it a joy to be free of the smell of open toilets and the visits of the honey-bucket man. However, I pointed out to her that Mr. Somerset Maugham had observed that in the East people were not conscious of smells and considered that democracy was doomed there as soon as people started to be able to pull a chain. She replied that democracy or not she hoped that the next house we lived in in Japan would possess modern plumbing and that she'd never really considered its great blessings until coming to England.

One day, from early morning, Kaneko stood in Trafalgar Square in kimono selling emblems for the King George V Jubilee Trust, while I watched from across the road beneath King Charles on his horse and cursed the absurd British licensing laws. She got such a crowd around her that a policeman made it his special duty to look after her. Boys and girls wanted autographs in Japanese, newspaper photographers besieged her, she received several offers to dine and dance. But at three o'clock she'd had enough, her contribution box had been changed twice and the third one was very heavy, and so she was whisked off to the BBC to give her first talk over the air, which she did very well indeed.

Shortly after the Coronation of King George VI I met Prince and Princess Chichibu who had represented the Emperor of Japan. Both apologized for not being able to see us personally at Hirosaki because of the stiff conventions. The Prince said he was having a grand time visiting old friends he'd known at Oxford, free of all formality which he said he disliked intensely.

When we attended a garden party in London in honour of the Japanese Prince and Princess and I lacked appropriate headwear an old friend who owned a wax-works took me to the end of Southend Pier and removed a grey topper from the head of King George VI. It fitted me perfectly.

John drove us to London for the garden party in his Rolls-Royce. The string band of a Guards regiment played in the splendid garden, while kimono-clad Japanese ladies, Kaneko I thought looking better than any, chatted with formal clad English men and women, sipped tea, and were presented to Japanese and

British royalty. It was a rather delightful occasion. But John, the Aberdonian, whom I had taken as my guest, took a very poor view indeed.

"Why, laddie," he said as we drove away from St. John's Wood, "if that's enjoyment give me Hampstead Heath among the Cockneys, or Southend Pier every time. Why ye'd of thought most of them were at a wake."

One day I was received by His Excellency the Japanese Ambassador to whom I had been given a letter of introduction by the Viscount. Mr. Shigeru Yoshida was the first Japanese diplomat I had met up till then who did not seek to impress but on the contrary exuded warmth and good humour. He was particularly interested in what was being taught at the Higher Schools and asked about visiting lecturers. When I told him that the students came in for regular two-hour discourses on the Japanese Spirit he burst out laughing. "Oh, yes, that's it, that's it," he chuckled.

At that time little did I think that he would be the man to lead his country out of defeat and despond and emerge as the greatest Japanese statesman of his day.

II

Taking my wife to see all the glories of my native land was a continual source of happiness and perhaps I felt much as she did when escorting me to such charming spots as the Moss Temple near Kyoto, to the greatly venerated Taga Shrine, to Amanohashi-date, or to attend the colourful Japanese festivals.

Canterbury Cathedral enthralled her even more than Westminster; the Tower of London, too, was a great success, especially as she was able to convince a Beefeater that the description of the sword presented to Lord Kitchener by the Emperor Meiji was upside down. But she would have wished to visit the Tower in fog to recapture something of the spirit of the essay on that ancient structure, perhaps among the best ever written by the late Natsume Soseki, whose writing she greatly admired.

At Cambridge where we stayed with Walter Lewis, the University printer and his family, Kaneko said that to study in such surroundings would perhaps be the Japanese student's conception of an educational paradise.

We hiked and hitch-hiked, she became expert at waving down motorists while I kept out of sight till they pulled up, or took trains or buses all over Essex and East Anglia. At Thaxted, birthplace of my forefathers, she met the famous Red Vicar, the late Rev. Conrad Noel whose banner was the Red Flag and who rallied his flock around Christ—the First Communist.

"What is this idea most foreigners have that Japan is a land of flowers?" she inquired one afternoon as we were passing a row of cottages, each with its garden bright with a variety of blossoms.

"Oh, well, so much has been made of the cherry blossom which is surely very beautiful; then there are the iris, the camellia, the plum, the hydrangea and so many other kinds of flowers, and Japanese flower arrangement."

"But you never see such a variety of flowers in the gardens of ordinary homes in Japan. Yes, we have lovely blossoms, but what about your hawthorn and plum and apple . . . and the wonderful roses. There is no need for flower arrangement, why, anyone with a little common sense can make a beautiful arrangement of your English flowers. I think that our flower arrangement is useful when there are few flowers to be had, it teaches us how to utilize even twigs and reeds and branches."

"Well, you must admit that nowhere in the world can you find such wonderful landscape gardens as in Japan. Look at those glorious temple gardens in Kyoto."

"Yes, that is true, but they are rather severe, they are not gay. The rose gardens in your parks, the great beds of flowers make people happy, and I think that Kew Gardens must be the most beautiful home of flowers and shrubs you'd find anywhere in the world. All these foreign writers who say so much about our love of nature have given the Japanese the idea that only they understand nature. It is nonsense. None respect and care for nature better than your own country-people. Look how trees grow right in the middle of fields, sometimes in the middle of the pavement, and look how people treat their fine parks; why, the Japanese would ruin such parks and that is perhaps why we have nothing like them."

"Now don't be too critical of your people. You know as well as I do that they have a delicate sense of the artistic quite unlike our own. If they have little respect for public places and lack civic pride that will come with education and better standards of living."

The less savoury side of the English scene she found in the slums, which caused her great surprise, and workmen leaving their places of employment without even washing their hands and faces and changing filthy clothes which soiled the seats of trains, buses and trams.

She thought the average Englishwoman had a nice complexion, but dressed dowdily, not nearly so well as the Americans; but considered they were unsurpassable when in evening dress. And of course, the Bobby, unlike his generally pompous Japanese counterpart who in those days expected to be bowed to, was marvellous.

After a stroll among the soap-box orators at Hyde Park, an Indian nationalist, a chap screaming hell-fire and damnation upon all winebibbers and sinners, a Mosley Fascist, a Communist, an exponent of nudism, she squeezed my arm and said: "For just this alone I am proud to be British."

One afternoon we stood in the Mall with thousands of others, to watch their Majesties the King and Queen pass by only ten feet away.

The genuine love and affection demonstrated by all watching

their new King and his Queen deeply impressed Kaneko. For in the land of her birth in those days the streets were cleared, blinds drawn and people forbidden to watch from above the street level whenever the Sovereign or any member of the Imperial Family left the Palace.

"It makes me feel sad," she said, "for I realize that our poor Emperor and Empress are just like prisoners; they can never really know their people who are taught to fear rather than love them."

III

My old school chum, George, owned the fine 9-ton Bermuda cutter *Rame* built by a certain Captain Goldsmith R.N., who had sailed her out to Malta single-handed. She was the type of craft I had always longed to possess, a real dream ship, copper fastened and sheathed, and decked with teak.

In July, we set out from Burnham-on-Crouch with George, Stella his wife, and his two cousins, to give Kaneko her first taste of little ships. She settled into things with enthusiasm and marvelled at the trim craft, its fo'c'sle which slept two, the small galley, the complicated flush heads, and main cabin which we shared with Stella and George, with its fine maple panelling.

We drifted across to Ostend, the sea like a sheet of oily glass; but ran into wind and rain on passage to Vlissingen, which sent the girls to their bunks and provided us with a splendid sail.

A foreign yacht was common in Holland, but not one carrying a lady whose shore-going clothes were kimono, and we were never without visitors from the neat, well-painted and varnished barges, with their deck gardens of potted plants and lace curtains at their cabin windows, small boys and girls, most of whom sought autographs in Japanese, lock-keepers, harbour-masters, old sailors who'd been in Eastern seas, and even a Chinese peddler of silk shawls and Oriental bric-à-brac.

Kaneko revelled in all the charm of Holland; the brightly painted homes, the well-tended gardens, the windmills, the labyrinth of waterways, the boatloads of enormous red cheeses, the lands below the sea, Frisian cows, small boys smoking pipes and cigars, but above all the extreme cleanliness of everything and everyone. Evenings usually found us in a tavern singing with the jolly Dutch people to the accompaniment of one or more accordions.

We lingered at Vere, at Dordrecht, and spent several hours on a very stubborn mud bank off Bergen op Zoom. In parts the difficult River Maas with all its ramifications, which we found almost impossible to puzzle out, was like some great shallow sea out of which here and there church steeples and clumps of trees appeared like atolls in a tropic sea.

At Rotterdam we received much hospitality from the Royal Netherlands Yacht Club, and the family of Father Cornelius, our

Hirosaki friend, overwhelmed us with great kindness at their quaint and ancient six-storey home which in 1940 was to be obliterated in one of the thousands of dastardly inhumanities of the Germans.

"Everything is so flat, yet the buildings, even the people so solid," observed herself. "It all reminds me of the Japanese artists' impressions of the Hollanders when they were the only people allowed to trade with Japan. Sturdy looking men with their great hats and smoking pipes, their flowing red whiskers and often shown with large drinking mugs in their hands."

We made an excursion to Delft, whose picturesque canals are bordered with lime trees, and saw the monuments to William of Orange, to Grotius, the great jurist, and to Admiral van Tromp, of broom at the masthead fame. Here at this delightful old-world town the Delft pottery, said to have originated in the attempts of the Dutch potters to imitate the blue and white Chinese ware, is made. But the Dutch artists were no doubt also greatly influenced by the Japanese ceramics of similar type imported by the Holland East India Company. Dutch records show that in 1664 alone no less than 44,943 items of Japanese porcelain arrived in Holland from Japan.

IV

Leaving the busy Veerhaven at Rotterdam was quite a business with such bustle of every conceivable kind of craft: the schuyts, the barges, the fussy tugs and motor launches and the passage of large tramps and ocean liners.

Schiedam, famous for its gin, looked attractive and busy but we resisted the temptation to linger as the weather report was not too promising and entered the Voorne Canal through which we were able to sail the seven miles of its monotonous straightness to the old port and fortress town of Hellevoetsluis, once a thriving place at which the steamers from Harwich used to call, but now a sleepy little town with many windmills in the neighbourhood. After we tied up the usual group of men, women and children arrived with offers of provisions. All we required was some iron, as *Rame* was underballasted, not sailing as close as she should, and it appeared that we were in for a stiff beat to windward. The ship chandler was unable to help, but after he had gone a seedy looking loafer who had been hanging about since our arrival came aboard with a heavy smooth stone, almost round, and about eight inches in diameter.

"Vell, Captin," he said to George, "und vot aboot dis vor ballast?"

George agreed to take thirty stones for five guilders, the only snag being that the man said he could not deliver until eight o'clock that night. But it seemed worth the delay and we sampled the local hostelry, which was duller than any we had come across, and at just after eight our man arrived with a barrow load of the stones which he assisted us to stow, received his five guilders, and then addressing us from the bank said: "I tink you best go soon, dose stones making to vix de vort. No matter, but maybe soldier make trouble."

"You bloody Dutch rascal," exploded George.

"It all right, you no have trouble, you go now," replied the fellow and shambled off towards the bright lights of the tavern. We were not disposed to unload our stolen stones and within a few minutes were bowling out of the harbour into the Slyk Gat and the difficult waters around Goeree island.

Rame certainly liked her new ballast and in the stiff south-wester we were soon slamming along with gunwale well under. We secured everything, the girls chocked themselves in their bunks, and then we hove to and tied in three reefs, put her under storm jib, and set about getting away from that treacherous coast and the dreaded Ooster Zand into what promised to be a very dirty night indeed.

Rame handled beautifully, her gear was sound, but George and I spent several anxious and very wet hours in getting out of soundings and that damnable lee shore and then set watches of two hours on and off. Wet and cold, aching in every limb, bruised from scrambling forward on various jobs, but cheered from time to time with a swig from a bottle of schnapps, I had, as every yachts-man, many reflections on what sort of a lunatic I was for doing this for pleasure. But I knew full well that this was the sort of sailing one really lived for and without which quiet, fine weather jaunts would soon begin to pall.

As the sun came up the wind eased a little and George bet me a fiver that I'd not be able to cook breakfast and eat it. Down below everything was chaotic; bottles, tins, face powder, books, bread, all over the place. But the girls, though a bit scarred, were content just as long as they were not required to move. I now found that *Rame*'s galley was the only fault in her design as, being on the port side, just forward of the main cabin and opposite the heads, in all but fine weather when the hatchway overhead could be opened it was a suffocating torture den for any wretched cook. The primus stoves needed pricking, the methylated spirit, pots and pans behaved like Mexican jumping beans, and plates and knives attacked me from various angles; but after exhausting my vocabulary of Billingsgate I gave George the lot—eggs, bacon, for he was the only one except myself interested in eating, even fried bread and tomatoes, which he could not finish.

By the time we picked up the Cork lightship off Harwich we were able to shake out the reefs and open things up a bit and one by one the girls began to regain confidence and prepare for the shore.

After a truly spanking passage down to the Crouch, we anchored off Creeksea as the wind died away completely, and all that was on my mind at that moment was a dream of one day sailing into Sagami Bay with the sun bathing Fuji-no-Yama in the evening glow and coming to anchor somewhere off that little point known as Inamura. George was interested. He knew that *Rame* was a real ship, that she could go anywhere; but there was his business and his family, and then too, a little matter of war clouds brewing in the East, and nearer home in the West.

Chapter Fifteen

I

AFTER a hot and dusty journey across Russia, the smoke and ash from the wood-burning locomotives penetrating even the double windows, I arrived back in Japan at the beginning of September, 1937, to substitute for friend Thomas at the head office of the Nippon Yusen Kaisha while he went to Canada for a holiday.

The bloody, unforgiving war which the Japanese referred to as the "China Incident" was in full swing, troops streaming south of the Great Wall; the commencement of hostilities which were to cover the greater part of China and up to the borders of India, even to the doorstep of Australia, and to result in Hiroshima and the unconditional surrender of Japan in August 1945.

Our friends the Millars had moved to Nishinomiya, near Kobe, and I stopped off to see them. Joan went wild with delight which turned to despair when she found her beloved mistress was not with me.

At Nagahama I found father-in-law sitting outside the house surrounded by a group to whom he was delivering some sort of an oration, but to my surprise did not appear to recognize me. He'd had an apoplectic fit and was a great trial. All day he'd sit there inviting complete strangers to take tea or a meal, grumbling about the quality of sake he was served, slightly sugared water served from a sake bottle which he was told was not up to standard because of the crisis in China. At night he'd bawl the house down whenever he awoke until mother-in-law massaged his legs. Kimi said that he had a Fox inside him and that he'd never get well until he'd made a pilgrimage to a number of shrines at which the Fox deity was said to reside. One-armed Cho had died in April of pneumonia, Hideya, the geisha, had married a tobacconist in Kyoto, and so many of the menfolk were now serving in the Army.

In England I had often longed for the pine-trees and the mountains, the clip-clop of *geta*, the Japanese speech; and now I wondered why I had left the green fields, the sounds and sights of dear old London, and the fellowship of my own people. Perhaps I was simply following my own destiny. None can prove the theory of re-incarnation; but once when climbing the steps to a shrine I recognized the scenes of a dream I'd had long before and knew what I should find at the top long before I arrived there.

Many years later I awoke with the name *Kakegawa* on my lips with no idea as to its significance. Shortly after this I was stranded at a small town in Shizuoka when my car broke down. On inquiring at the nearest house I found that I was in Kakegawa! That night I dreamt I was trudging the Tokaido highway, on which this town stands, with a vast number of people, Englishmen and Japanese, dressed in the clothes of other days. Had some remote ancestor been one of Captain Saris's company when in the early seventeenth century he'd led a mission from King James to the Shogun at Edo for the purpose of establishing trade and diplomatic relations?

I found a room in a boarding house not far from the home of my friend the Viscount. He was in his usual good form, had established a couple more societies, received another foreign order, did not take a serious view of the fighting in China and said that it would all be over when a few generals, colonels and majors got promoted.

"The only way to stop wars," he said, "is to abolish armies. For if you train people to fight then fight they must. Let them blow off a bit of steam and things will be all right." I could not share his optimism for Japan was serving to unite North and South, the Communists and the Kuomintang into a deadly and implacable foe.

A few days after Thomas left I was sitting in his office when a visitor was announced. To my surprise it was none other than the old rascal Kevin O'Reilly.

"The top of the mornin' to ye, Mr. Thomas," he said.

"Thomas is away in Canada."

"Now isn't that forgetful of me. Of course I should have come over earlier. Ye see he promised to let me have the loan of five yen, and now, what's to be done?"

"Now, O'Reilly, you surely recognize me," I replied.

"Well, I never! It must be me eyesight, and if it isn't me handsome young friend." It cost me two yen to get rid of him.

Another visitor who said Thomas always gave her a contribution of ten yen was the famous Salvation Army "Annie" who preached fire and brimstone against smokers and drinkers and haunted the bar of every vessel leaving Yokohama to relieve those departing of their Japanese change. Poor Annie, whom none could help admire, was to be mysteriously murdered some years later in New Zealand.

II

The most helpful and interesting Britons, Americans and other nationalities I had the good fortune to know were teachers, journalists, newspaper correspondents and businessmen engaged in shipping. One was a German professor, bitterly opposed to Hitler and his doctrines, a great Buddhist scholar and an abbot of the Tendai sect. Sycophants, who gushed about the soul of Japan, how the world misunderstood Japanese sincerity, abounded, and were avoided like the plague.

Often I'd spend the evening down at Yokohama where I made many foreign and Japanese friends. Occasionally I ran across old timers; men who'd known the venturesome Captain Voss, and Weston Martyr in the fur sealing days, and those who'd survived the Great Earthquake of 1923 which devastated the port city and a great part of Tokyo.

A Tokyo English language newspaper featured the most extraordinary social news written by a woman who'd apparently been weaned on Roget and one was vastly intrigued with her prattle of urbane, cultured, gifted, talented, suave, worldly, handsome members of the *corps diplomatique*; managers of banks, oil, shipping and fertilizer concerns and their charming, ravishing, beautiful, petite, brilliant, loved-by-all ladies, their wondrous hats, gowns, hair-do's, shoes, jewellery and the magnificence of their homes. I was, therefore, most disappointed when meeting a lady described so often in this newspaper as possessing all the graces to find her a bore, a shocking snob, worst of all a giggler at her own quips, who fell over backwards to hobnob with Japanese aristocracy and royalty, but never tired of criticizing the country and people. Unfortunately there were several like her, and they usually bullied their maids, shouted at shopkeepers, and would go into hysterics and take it out of their wretched husbands if they were omitted from a party list.

At Lohmeyer's, an excellent restaurant and bar operated by a well-liked German who'd been in the country since 1914 when he'd been taken prisoner at Tsingtao, and popular with Japanese and foreigners, one was nearly always sure of finding interesting and often amusing company.

An American who possessed great charm and taught dancing could, after he'd had a few drinks, be persuaded to perform the most extraordinary contortions and was known as the "Snake Charmer".

One evening I entered my favourite beer-hall to find a dozen tables placed end to end around which were about twenty-five university students listening to a first-class rendition of Hamlet's soliloquy by their English professor, who was a fine organist, a theologian, and an excellent amateur actor.

In his reminiscences a former ambassador in Tokyo expresses sympathy with the bachelor members of his embassy because of the lack of social amenities and amusements in Tokyo! His Excellency did not of course frequent the Florida and Shimbashi dance halls, such hostelries as the Cycerea and the Silver Slipper whose winsome, shapely hostesses were particularly popular with the bachelors on his staff, or other establishments which surely served to make the Japanese capital one of the most popular posts with unattached males. And the Keio Hotels down at Yokohama would have provided him an eye-opener on how the bored might really enjoy themselves.

An habitué of a certain dance hall was a tall, middle-aged courtly foreigner, always attired in striped trousers and cutaway coat who waltzed the hostesses around the floor like a duke and his debutante daughter at a royal ball. One girl told me that he was a great gentleman, never trod on her toes, but always bruised her bottom.

There was a campaign towards breeding dislike and contempt for the British in particular, and Americans. The muck sheets devoted a great deal of space to Anglo-American lack of culture and looseness of morals, while Japanese urinated on the main streets, beat up women, smashed windows, and committed any kind of nuisance under the influence of drink to be considered manly fellows.

However, the people as a whole were friendly and courteous, despite the worsening of the situation in China and the delicate relations which had been brought about with Great Britain through the actions of the military over whom the Japanese Foreign Office appeared to have no control, and when Kaneko returned via Suez, and I was offered the post of lecturer at the Yamagata Higher School, nine hours north of Tokyo, I accepted gladly, and looked forward to getting back to the country.

Chapter Sixteen

I

YAMAGATA is a pleasant, clean and prosperous city situated in the Tohoku Plain. On April 10th, 1938, the snow had cleared, except from the surrounding mountains whence numerous streams and rivers flowed through the villages and towns to provide irrigation for one of the richest granaries in North Japan, and by the end of the month the high school on a hill, just outside the city, was enclosed in a veritable bower of delicate pink cherry blossom.

Our house had been painted inside and out, herself was busy laying out the garden, and we'd acquired a bundle of amazing energy in the form of a wire-haired terrier named Peggy as a companion for Joan.

The Principal proved an extremely kind and understanding man and among my colleagues in the English faculty were Tanaka, a devout Christian, who by his patience, diligence and fine character, had broken down all barriers to rise from a dining car waiter to become one of the most widely read and respected scholars on English grammar and composition.

The foreign lecturer in German was Father Julius Holzer, a gentle and lovable Austrian from Salzburg; however, the United States had the largest foreign representation in Yamagata in Carl and Pearl Nugent, American missionaries from Altoona, Pennsylvania, and their four children, which brought the foreign community to nine.

Within easy reach were many historic and interesting places; hot-springs at Kaminoyama, and at Tendo, also famous for the production of Japanese chessmen; ancient temples at Yamadera, and one of the most popular skiing grounds in the country at Mount Zao. Three hours distant over the mountains by train is Sendai, the largest city in North Japan and gateway to Matsushima Bay with its thousands of islands, islets and rocks and considered one of the three finest scenic spots in the country.

Professor of English literature at Tohoku Imperial University at Sendai was Ralph Hodgson, then in his mid-sixties, who had been there for some thirteen years and had come out to Japan in 1924 in the same vessel as Edmund Blunden, who replaced Robert Nichols at Tokyo Imperial University. I was introduced to the author of "The Bull", "The Song of Honour", and other poems which will ensure him immortality, by one of his Japanese colleagues after Hodgson's large Akita dog I foolishly elected to stroke nearly took off a couple of my fingers, on which the poet remarked that a stranger should never touch another man's dog. When we entered the house and a friendly creature bounded up to be petted and I observed that it looked something like an Airedale I wished I'd kept a still tongue as Ralph inquired: "Don't you know a pure bred Welsh terrier when you see one?" But that genial man who had forgotten more about dogs and indeed more things than I shall ever know soon put me at my ease, told of the days when he'd judged at Cruft's Show, of Rodney Stone, the famous bull-dog, and about his own bull-terrier which he and W. H. "Super Tramp" Davies used to walk around London after dark.

He and his delightful American wife kept some hundreds of canaries whose habits they recorded in large ledger-like tomes. He described this as a life work, and the most interesting he'd ever undertaken.

Sturdy, built like a boxer, he was once an amateur champion, with a wealth of iron grey hair, fine features, inquiring eyes and perfect teeth. Ralph liked to refer to himself as the "Last of the Fancy".

There was indeed something of the Beau Brummell about him. The blue, gilt buttoned jacket, canary yellow double-breasted waistcoat, white corduroy trousers, immaculate linen and well-matched necktie.

He offered me beer or gin but said he had not touched alcohol since one day many years before when he'd come across an English billiards champion dead drunk in Charing Cross Road just before an important match.

London in the nineties, Wilde, Swinburne, Shaw, his friend who played a one man band and tootled the horn on the Brighton coach; the music-halls and magic names like Albert Chevalier, Dan Leno, and the incomparable Marie Lloyd, he spoke of with enthusiasm touched with sadness.

He was extremely popular, indeed loved by his colleagues and students, and returned their feelings with friendship and understanding. Hodgson was an inveterate pipe-smoker. Smoking a clean pipe, and he emphasized clean because he considered that most smokers never get the proper enjoyment out of a pipe because they smoke foul, was, he told me, his greatest joy. Four or five pipes, each about six inches long, were nearly always sticking out of his breast pocket. These had a small bowl underneath which were two prongs so that they'd stand upright when placed on a table. He had three hundred and sixty-five of them, made specially for him in Vienna and as he finished a pipe it would be tossed into a box, cleaned carefully by the maid and then placed at the end of the roster.

Never did I hear a harsh criticism of other poets and writers escape his lips; although he believed that poetry had declined so much because it no longer reached the hearts of men, did not move them as had the songs of all the great poets through the ages; but he wondered that perhaps his inability to understand

and appreciate some of the modern forms was simply that he was out of touch.

He left Japan towards the end of 1938, but my three or four meetings with Ralph Hodgson were rich experiences, and remain as treasured memories of a man and poet whose finest works will be read and appreciated by lovers of English poetry after many of his contemporaries are forgotten.

II

Reports of the rape of Nanking shocked everyone, but the Japanese Press countered with charges of malicious Chinese propaganda.

"What do you think?" inquired one of my students who appeared deeply concerned. "Do you believe that we are capable of such terrible behaviour as reported by British and American newspapers?"

Living among, working with them, knowing the fundamental kindness of the ordinary people, of the farmers who constituted the bulk of the Army, the charges seemed incredible. One found it hard to believe that the Japanese Army was so contemptuous of world opinion and had reverted to tactics beyond the ken of civilized peoples. But Mussolini was dosing his victims with castor oil, Hitler persecuting Jews, and probably at that time dreaming up his diabolical gas-chambers, and members of the Gestapo were reported to be advising the Japanese gendarmerie and police in the latest techniques in refined and barefaced swinery.

A British newspaper had published a photograph which showed Chinese prisoners being used by Japanese soldiers for bayonet practice, which the Japanese indignantly branded as a Chinese fake and, in spite of the treatment being meted out to British nationals in China, the lies printed in the Japanese Press about the British in India and Africa, and our role as Japan's Enemy No. 1, I simply could not imagine that they were capable of such bestialities. My opinion was shared by many Britons and Americans living in Japan. Yet, "But what else can you expect?" observed an American. "In the code of the Army the end justifies any means, a soldier must think of nothing else but death in service of the Emperor, is denied the right to be taken prisoner, must forget family ties, is forbidden even to carry photographs of his wife, and moulded as far as possible into a veritable human bullet."

But many found it difficult to square Western and Chinese reports on Nanking with Japanese pride in the discipline of their service men, with their much-vaunted Bushido, and with their record in the war with Russia in 1904–5 when even the enemy praised their humanity and treatment of prisoners. If reports were true then what had come over the Army since the passing of Nogi, Oyama, Uehara, Kuroki, and other great and humane soldiers?

An old friend who'd been in the country in 1904 observed that in those days Japan was fighting a life and death struggle with a powerful adversary; she needed the goodwill of the West and had the support of Great Britain in particular without which she could not have gained victory.

"Today," he said, "the younger military men are contemptuous of world opinion, they would welcome open conflict with Britain in the East. To recognize the rights of prisoners of war when they deny their own soldiers the right to be taken prisoner is to them unpalatable to say the least. The Chinese gave them a hard fight for Nanking, they surprised the Japanese by their stubbornness, and it's my opinion that all their pent-up emotions exploded once they'd taken the city, and before the damage was done not even the higher command could stop it. And don't forget that the Japanese military now realize that they've bitten off more than they can chew. They are in fact holding a very hot potato which is not likely to cool and which they cannot drop without losing the all-important *face*. Of course you cannot believe that the Japanese you know would act in such manner and I do not believe that my Japanese friends would either. But what happens after long indoctrination concerning their divine right to rule the East —their superiority over other races, and when they've been purged of all the finer feelings through harsh and even inhuman methods of training? No, my friend, at bottom the human race is pretty savage and all that prevents it reverting to type is education and the laws of behaviour. The shelling of HMS *Ladybird* in the Yangtse on the orders of Colonel Hashimoto, who received a hero's welcome on his return to Japan from thousands of his followers of the youth's organizations, the attack on the USS *Panay*, in which they weren't content till they'd gunned men swimming for their lives—these incidents indicate pretty well, I think, what control the government or the better types have over the hot-heads. Mark my words, Nanking is only the beginning!"

III

Germany and Italy were now Japan's partners in an Anti-Comintern agreement. Italian and German flags were strung out with those of Japan between the lamp-posts on the main streets, and so to add a little colour I fixed a long bamboo pole to our roof from which proudly flew the Union Jack. The students seemed greatly intrigued and called our home the British Consulate.

Two or three times a month a plain-clothes policeman sought an interview when he'd ask me absurd questions on the Sudetenland, Britain's attitude towards the Polish problem, whether President Roosevelt was a Jew, and assiduously wrote down my answers in his note-book.

One day, an hour after I'd returned from a week-end visit to Tokyo he arrived to ask me how long I'd been friendly with the Soviet consul at Hakodate?

"I've never met him," I replied.

"Oh, you must tell the truth," he answered, with a sly grin.

"But I have never even seen the man, did not even know that Russia had a consul in Hakodate."

"Now are you really sure what you say is true?"

"Of course."

He lit a cigarette, and asked if I denied having travelled with Mr. Boloslavsky, or whatever his name was, in the same train from Tokyo?

"Why, of course I do."

"Then you are lying because he was with you in the same sleeping compartment."

"Now please stop this nonsense. I do not know who was in the train with me. Damn it, because I travel in a train am I a friend of all the passengers?"

He looked rather dejected and said, "Yes, I believe you, but the Soviet consul was on that train and we thought that perhaps you knew him."

"Well, and supposing I did? Is there a law against my knowing a Soviet consul or for that matter an ambassador?"

He admitted that of course there was no such law but said the authorities were concerned about Soviet espionage.

There was an epidemic of spy mania. Plastered on the walls of railway stations were posters depicting a sinister looking foreigner rigged out in a Sherlock Holmes hunter and trapper outfit, even to the deerstalker hat, and smoking a large curly pipe and in large characters was the warning, Spy! Beware of spies! Once I'd had a crowd of school kids behind me chanting "Spy! Spy!—Spy! Spy! Spy!"

World war was still unthinkable, but the farms were gradually being bled of manpower and students and teachers would voluntarily go out to the country to assist the aged and the women-folk in gathering the harvest and other chores.

A regular visitor each morning was Joan's boy friend, a fine Airedale who lived at a haberdasher's and had developed a taste for bread and marmalade.

Joan's tastes now included doughnuts and ice-cream and if she got out she'd make straight for the restaurant and cake shop, nip upstairs, and to the amazement of customers perch herself on a chair and wait to be served.

Each evening I'd take her for a walk, during which we visited the beer-hall where to the delight of patrons she'd bark up to six at the command in English or Japanese, or on the required number of fingers being held out to her, to be rewarded with beer, ham, or a slice of cheese.

When our friends the Redmans went on home leave we agreed to look after their enormous Great Dane, a lazy individual named Rex, white with black markings and the gentlest animal I've known.

He was a sensation from the moment I took him from the train. It took him about five minutes to make water, a policeman inquired if he were not dangerous, and Rex jumped up to put two feet on my shoulders and demonstrate that he was at full stretch some six inches taller than I.

Peggy took an instant dislike to him, but never approached too near except to get behind him and take a swift nip at two very tender appendages. But there came a day when she was not quite quick enough and Rex picked her up gently by the scruff of the neck and flung her about ten feet across the garden. Henceforth she treated him with respect and affection.

In Hirakawa-Cho, in Tokyo, Rex was a celebrity, especially with the school children.

Once a new pupil at the nearby primary school remarked to a friend: "Oh, look at that big dog!" "Don't be silly," replied the other, "that's not a dog, that's Rex!"

On one occasion Rex was sitting sunning himself outside a restaurant when it came on to rain. At that moment a taxi drew up, disgorged a passenger, and before the driver realized what had happened Rex was inside his car.

The man was terrified and ran into the restaurant to inquire what he could do.

A waitress told him that the best thing would be to drive him up the hill to the residence of Redman San where if he opened the door Rex would be sure to get out.

The driver, still rather apprehensive about his strange fare, did as he was told, and to his relief the dog got out exactly as the waitress had predicted. The driver then opened the gate for the dog and rang the bell.

"Is this your dog?" he inquired of the maid.

"Oh, yes it's Rex."

"Well, I just brought him from the restaurant in my taxi."

"Oh, please wait while I call madame," said the girl, "for she'll wish to thank you."

"Thank you so much," said Madeleine Redman, "and how much do we owe you?" The man scratched his head, then replied with a grin. "Well, for a human being it would be fifty sen. It's the first time I've had such a passenger so would you mind paying half fare?"

The only time Rex was restive was when in love. Then if you did not watch out he'd be over the gate like a hunter taking a fence and he'd sit outside the home of the object of his affections, usually a little bitch about the size of a toy pomeranian, howling like a baby till an SOS would arrive for someone to come and take him away.

He took a great liking to my colleague, the Austrian priest, and especially his bald pate which he'd contrive to get a lick at by jumping up from behind. And when a truck ran over our little Peggy and she lay in her wooden coffin with leash, collar and her tartan coat, that dear old dog's moans of grief were heartrending.

Chapter Seventeen

I

In answering questions concerning Hitler and Mussolini I warned my students that Japan could trust them as much as one might a rattlesnake or a confirmed swindler and reminded them that, "Those the gods would destroy they first make mad."

One evening my good friend and colleague Tanaka came to warn me that a certain teacher had objected to the remarks I had made about Japan's friends, and had even recommended to the Principal that I be removed. This critic was a stupid old tyrant, a dyed-in-the-wood nationalistic fanatic, who was generally disliked. "You need not worry," said Tanaka. "The Principal won't listen to him, but you'd better be careful. If he went to the Gendarmerie they might take action against you."

The rather foolish old man lived next door and his radio had blasted us day and night when the mood took him with German and Japanese patriotic marches, as well as Hitler's screeching tantrums. My powerful radiogram countered with Sousa marches by the massed bands of the Guards, Sophie Tucker and Gracie Fields, with the windows open. This put a stop to the nuisance and as other neighbours had been just as annoyed as ourselves it was a popular victory.

Hardly an evening passed without visits from students, the Nugents had become very close friends, Father Holzer was a regular visitor, Eiko, the daughter of the fine art dealer, and Yukiko, the charming daughter of a local lawyer. The latter had lost her mother when very young, her father had not remarried, and she had brought up her young brothers and sisters. Yukiko had very firm ideas about marriage. Go-betweens were constantly approaching her father with offers but although in her mid-twenties she was determined that when and if she married it would be to a man of her own choice.

"I am not going to be a slave to a mother-in-law, taken into her household to be a servant and be an old woman by the time I am forty worn out with child-bearing. If I marry it will be to a man of courage and common sense. I've seen so many of my friends reduced to household drudges, and when they'd produced a son their husbands had no use for them, except as a servant."

Yukiko was a great admirer of Baroness Ishimoto, the advocate of birth-control then in trouble with the authorities who preached the need for more and more people to die for the glory of the empire.

In the summer of 1939 with a surge of Anglophobia sweeping

across the nation, Britain being charged with prolonging the war in China through assistance to the arch-criminal General Chiang Kai-shek, we went down to Nagahama. On arrival a delegation from the Nagahama Geisha Association was being sent off to demonstrate before the British Embassy in Tokyo and hand over a written demand to Sir Robert Craigie that Britain cease its criminal acts. To our amusement there were several friends and relatives among the see-ers off, dressed in the white aprons and sashes of the Women's Patriotic Association but we disturbed the affair as so many seemed much more interested in greeting us than their duty.

Father-in-law was a good deal better and pottered about raising potted plants and looking after his chickens. During his illness gifts had arrived from many of his friends, one a large stack of lumber which had been left outside the house by a grateful Korean he'd once assisted. But next day a policeman came around to inform him that it had been stolen from a local lumber yard.

The absence of young men was now very noticeable; three of Kaneko's cousins were in the Army, my bath-house friend Ishii, the policeman, had been called up, and dear old Ogawa was dead.

Mishima, the restaurant keeper, was quite despondent and glad to be able to air his views freely to me.

"The country is going mad," he said. "I should have stayed in Canada. There is nothing but misery ahead, for these Army people may do anything. None can stop them, none dare try, and the worse things become in China the more desperate they'll get."

Mother-in-law was deeply concerned over the possibilities of war with Great Britain and what would happen to her daughter.

"Well, if we cannot get away in time," said Kaneko, "then I shall probably be interned."

"But you are Japanese," said the old lady.

"I am not any longer. You ought to know that. I am British and I would be treated as an enemy."

Aunt from Formosa then suggested that we be divorced immediately and when the danger was over we could marry again. Kimi passed no opinion. She'd got rid of the Fox through taking up with a Shinto sect known as Tenrikyo of which it was said in those parts that they'd take everything they could from you except a persimmon tree on which to hang yourself. Father-in-law passed no opinion as he could not understand what was going on. The only really cheerful person was jolly Hidesaburo, the supreme optimist, who would arrive every day with vegetables, with sake or other gifts and became a great friend of Joan's and would to her delight spend hours throwing stones into the lake for her to retrieve.

Towards the end of August, just as we were preparing to return home, a veritable bombshell burst to disrupt the Japanese-German love-feast in the news of the Non-Aggression Pact signed between the prime movers in the German, Italian, Japanese anti-Comintern Pact and the Soviet Union!

The local policeman brought me the news and had apparently been sent round to find out my opinion. He did not seem to appreciate my roar of laughter and my observation that if you chose to deal with rattlesnakes you were likely to get bitten.

II

En route home I stopped off at Kobe.

Near the waterfront was the establishment of J. L. Thomson & Co., chemists, booksellers, publishers, and manufacturers of mineral waters, presided over by one of the most colourful and interesting characters ever to step foot on the shores of Nippon.

H. J. Griffiths, affectionately known as Caramel San through his partiality for this type of confectionery and his habit of distributing it to children, but "Griffy" to most, was a native of Bristol and arrived in Japan just after the turn of the century. In 1939 he was perhaps in his mid-sixties, a medium-sized, bald, cherub-like man whose eyes positively beamed and darted about inquiringly from behind large steel-rimmed spectacles. Even in the heat of August he wore his white, hard, cheese-cutter collar, and under his jacket a thick, grey flannel shirt.

The shop was anything but attractive, and cheek by jowl with toilet preparations you were as likely as not to find diaries for 1910, the *Gardener's Chronicle* for 1916, Mr. Maugham's latest novel, or the *New Yorker*.

On that August morning I came upon Griffy dealing with a group of American ladies off the President liner which was alongside the pier.

"Well, you can have that rubbish if you want it, madame," he was saying, "But it's a downright swindle. I can make you up a bottle for a tenth of the price and I'll make fifty per cent profit on it too."

"My dear, good lady, I wouldn't use that stuff on my teeth. Why not take some of my special preparation, a quarter of the price and it'll give you molars like cultured pearls."

"You all believe the advertisements like the gospel," he remarked as his customers left the shop.

We went upstairs where Griffy had his priceless collection of books on Japan and the Far East which had taken him a lifetime to assemble; precious works coveted by collectors all over the world who often visited Kobe for the purpose of trying to persuade him to part with his treasures. He did sell books if he had duplicates and the price would depend on his mood or in what esteem he held you. He had obtained several out of print works for me and had been most reasonable in his charges. He also supplied me with soda-water and ginger beer of his own making, and had latterly been sending me his special gin; but although he would join you in a pub crawl he never drank alcohol and never smoked. Once during an evening on the town he drank seventeen bottles of fizzy soft drinks, and we ate sixteen dozen oysters between us, on the shell, stewed and fried.

Griffy was a great exponent of Japanese classical dancing, a performer on the samisen and the bamboo flute, and an excellent singer of Japanese songs. He was also a pilgrim to shrines and temples and would set out clad in white kimono, *tabi*—the Japanese socks with the socket for the big toe—straw sandals, a wide rush hat on his head and grasping a stout staff. It took him years to do the famous eighty-eight temples of the Goddess of Mercy as he could only spare from Saturday noon to Monday morning and at each of these he had the special red stamp of the temple chopped on his kimono. He was also a first-class player of Japanese chess and perhaps more knowledgeable on things Japanese than any other foreigner or most natives.

Griffy took a pessimistic view of the international situation, and was certain that Japan would become embroiled with Hitler against us.

"Take my advice," he said, "and get away as soon as you can. I am an old man, I have seen this country rise from nothing to a great power and I can afford to wait and watch it reduced to scratch. Things will never get better here until they've been worse. It's a damned shame for the people at large. But until the Army is deflated of its opinion of its invincibility and the people know what war on their own doorstep means they'll never really understand."

That evening our party was large and there was an atmosphere of relief from the tension and frustration all had undergone in watching a policy of appeasement ridiculed and treated with contempt by those who knew only the methods of the rubber truncheon and the law of the jungle. For within a few hours Britain would in honour bound be at war with nazi Germany.

Chapter Eighteen

I

BONZO, a lovable old bulldog, lay sunning himself and watching the world go by from the steps of the British Embassy. As I patted him and said good morning he responded by cocking a baleful eye at me and then breaking wind, as if to express his personal opinion of my mission, a habit which a certain diplomatist's lady appeared to blame on Bonzo's master, as well his practice of enticing her well-bred hounds against the wire which separated them from the lesser creatures and nipping out tufts of their silky hair.

"Too old," I was told, "Be some time before they'll want chaps of your age. You can do a better job here . . ."

Pat, master of the bulldog, a very junior member of the staff and a top grade judoist, was scornful concerning what he described as the childlike faith in the Maginot Line, and incredulous that people were falling for stories of Hitler's plywood tanks and the papier-mâché boots of his soldiers.

"Too old at thirty! Just you wait me bhoy, they'll be glad of 'em at seventy afore they're through with this Hitler character," he observed.

"If you did not want to go and lend a hand I'd be disappointed in you," said the Viscount, "but stay here for a while. You can do a lot of good, for the Germans will be flooding the country with all manner of lies."

Herself was adamant that if I was to go, then she'd go, too, and find herself something to do for the Allied war effort.

In October Vere Redman returned from England to become head of the department of the Central Office of Information at the British Embassy, and Rex went home to Tokyo.

Possession of a short-wave radio was prohibited to all but embassies and legations. The Japanese radio, a semi-government organization, was markedly pro-Hitler-Mussolini, in spite of what had been termed the rebuff, even insult, provided by Hitler's deal with the Russians, so we endured atmospherics and interferences to listen to "Perfect Grind" Orcott in Shanghai, whose sponsored programme provided all the news and a sparkling commentary. Later, this fine American was in danger of his life from assassins hired by the Japanese; but he never relaxed and his talks inspired so many all over East Asia.

There was a nauseating imitativeness of nazi practices; folk were being urged to show their patriotism by wearing an ugly greenish-khaki form of national uniform. Newspapers parroted all manner of poppycock concerning Jews, Freemasons, and disseminated lies about Christian organizations; jazz and permanent waves came in for a great deal of condemnation as being representative of the unmoral and uncultured democracies, and signs in romanized Japanese were gradually removed from public places. In some cases the latter did not matter very much because for some time these had been employing the so-called Nippon system of romanization. The fanatic crackpots had apparently regarded it as nothing less than a national disgrace that the Hepburn system which had served for half a century was established by an American, and so for *Fuji* you now had *Huzi, Chichibu* became *Titibu, Chitose, Titose, Ichi* rendered *Iti*. Great consternation had been brought about when it was learned that the liner *Chichibu Maru,* named after a famous mountain and shrine, was now referred to on the West Coast of the United States as the *"Floating Titty"*. One of the directors of the company which owned the vessel had asked my opinion about this, and for an explanation of *tit* and *titty*. I quoted the little jingle about the "man from the city who knew a girl named Kitty whom he hit upon the titty with a hard-boiled egg". To save further embarrassment they changed the vessel's name to *Kamakura Maru.* Many well-known scholars had come out openly against this petty change-over from the well-tried and practical Hepburn system, but reason was fast giving way to chauvinistic madness.

At school the majority of my colleagues and students were sympathetic towards Hitler's victims, ridiculed any suggestion that Japan might throw in her lot with him, but were unable to understand why Britain and France were not on the offensive and content to wait behind the Maginot Line.

Mr. Neville Chamberlain's remark at the start of the nazi thrust into Norway that, "this time Hitler has missed the bus," buoyed our hopes and found me digging into gazetteers and drawing maps on the blackboard to satisfy the interest of my students in Narvik, Aalness and other places in the news. It turned out a fiasco, but it showed that the Nelson spirit was still dominant in the Royal Navy, and brought home the fact that you could not combat savage· beasts with well-meaning lapdogs and time-savers. And a lion of a man, whose predictions of the dire peril Europe faced from nazi Germany had been ignored, now roared his commands from the helm of state, began to unravel the mess which his predecessors had created, revived confidence, encouraged those labouring under the heel of the oppressor, and treated the threats of the "nazi guttersnipe" with the contempt and challenge they deserved.

II

After the fall of France I sent in my resignation to the school authorities. It seemed to me there was little excuse for my remaining in Japan; the people were so regimentated, so used to meekly obeying even the most outrageous demands of authority, parliamentary government was now but a mockery, expressions of anti-war sentiments branded those uttering them as Communists and traitors, and the notorious Military Secrets Act, Thought Police and Gendarmerie had just about humbled the nation into accepting anything the military and its extremist supporters might decide.

Dr. Sano, the Principal, insisted that I finish my contract, and told herself that in any case he was afraid that Hitler would have invaded Britain and the war be over before I could arrive home.

A brief visit from Graham Martyr, a retired teacher who'd started life as an apprentice in sail, served in the Royal Ulster Rifles in the Great War, had then taken Holy Orders, which he put down to a bad attack of shell-shock, was a great shot in the arm. At a lecture on his thirty-five years or so in and out of Japan he packed the school auditorium, reminded his listeners of what our island race had done with a character named Napoleon, predicted a sticky end for Hitler and his crew, and among many highly amusing anecdotes delighted the audience in telling them how many years before when teacher at the Etajima Naval Academy he'd been asked to teach two young Imperial Princes how to shake hands, one of whom is the present Emperor of Japan.

Dr. Anzai paid us a visit and seemed very pessimistic, but when I told him that I simply had to leave said that he'd do what he could to help, and in parting observed, "Well, I pray that Britain can hold out because if not the entire world will suffer the evils of fascism."

That evening while I was out for a stroll with Joan and our new wire-haired terrier, Peggy II, the Principal visited Kaneko. He told her that he could understand that the war situation was disturbing me and suggested we go down to Nagahama for a holiday. "Your family doctor will no doubt recognize that your husband is in a highly nervous state and if he writes a certificate to the effect that a change of air and scene would be best for his health, I am sure I can get the Education Ministry to release him from his contract and perhaps arrange for your passages to be paid to England or wherever you may wish to go."

"God bless dear old Anzai!" I cried, when she told me, "and let's start packing!"

III

Cigarettes, liquor, butter, meat and most imported goods were now difficult to obtain, but thanks to the generosity of Pat and an American friend we arrived in Nagahama well-stocked, and particularly welcome were three bottles of John Haig!

There was no difficulty about the medical certificate but it seemed to me to imply that all I'd ever be good for would be to grace a mental home.

"Good heavens! He has laid it on thick," I said.

"Well, better do it properly," replied herself, "if you want to get results."

No doubt about it, the Japanese *can* be the most kind and understanding people on earth.

Father-in-law looked disgustingly healthy and as handsome as ever, but he behaved like a child, still took his sugared water which passed for sake, and when he insisted on a tot of the John Haig and we passed off cold black tea watered down and sugared, observed that it was worse than his medicine, and that these foreigners did indeed have peculiar tastes.

Sitting in the cool home of Sato San, who'd been so kind on my first visit and had given us the Old Man and his mate of Takasago which was among our most treasured possessions, with the sun filtering through the leaves and branches of his maple tree to fleck the rocks and stones of their exquisite garden, I wondered if I should ever return and knew that I would miss terribly all these friendships and the surroundings I had come to love so well. Sato was telling me about his training as a youth in a Zen temple when Hidesaburo arrived with a telegram. This was from Redman, made no sense, but was quite obviously intended to get me to Tokyo.

As I said my goodbye, prophesying that I'd be back in a day or so, mother-in-law was in tears, said that she knew I'd not be back for a long, long time and that she'd regularly visit her favourite Shinto deity to pray for my safe return.

In the train I picked up a newspaper from which I learned that many British businessmen, newspaper correspondents, teachers and others had been arrested, that the Reuter's correspondent had committed suicide by jumping out of the window of Gendarmerie Headquarters where he was being interrogated, and that the authorities were in process of uncovering a very dangerous nest of British spies!

A bespectacled, furtive looking man sat opposite, and as I folded the paper started conversation with the usual questions. Where was I going, my nationality, my occupation. He got out at the next stop. An hour later, when the train pulled in to a large town, two obvious 'tecs came strutting into the carriage, stopped in front of me, one pointed to the rack and inquired, "Is that your bag?" and when I nodded grabbed it and said, "Please follow us."

God almighty! I thought, so now, I'm a member of this ridiculous nest of spies. Watched with much interest by passengers and serious-faced station officials I was led out of the station across a square and into a police-station and asked to produce my train ticket.

"Oh, you are going to Tokyo, yet you told a passenger that you were from Yamagata Higher School," observed the 'tec. I began to explain, but he took my ticket and told me to wait. I sat alone for about two hours wondering what on earth I might have said or written which could provide them with a scanty reason for throwing me in jail. Then, to my surprise, a woman entered with a cup of tea and sweet cakes, followed by the two 'tecs and couple of policemen all smiles and oozing apologies, who said they'd checked with Yamagata, established my identity, were very, very sorry, and had arranged for the special express to stop and pick me up which would get me to Tokyo even earlier than the slow train from which they'd taken me.

It was the first time I'd had a train flagged down for my benefit, or been seen off by half a dozen bowing policemen and detectives and as I entered the dining car all eyes were upon this obviously very important person. I sat down just as the boy was taking orders from three foreigners, one of whom had a large nazi badge in his buttonhole who ordered a brandy and ginger ale. As the boy passed me on his way to execute their order I asked him for a bottle of beer. He served me with this immediately while a waitress prepared the drinks for the Germans. When the boy took them their drinks he was greeted with a loud outburst from the swastika-decorated person who shouted in English, "Fool! You are insolent! You took our order and served that man first. I shall report you at Tokyo."

The wretched waiter did not understand what it was all about, passengers were surprised at the hullabaloo, but as he passed I begged him not to judge all foreigners by the behaviour of the nazi bore. "How dare you talk about me," shouted the nazi, standing up and wagging his finger.

"Can't you Germans ever behave?" I replied.

At this he started to rip off a string of oaths which I could not understand but guessed he was calling me every kind of an English swine.

When the trio left the car a Japanese gentleman approached me and said: "The Germans are terribly arrogant aren't they!"

"Well, perhaps they'll learn manners by the time this war is ended," I replied.

IV

"Oh, we just thought you ought to get up here," said Redman when I arrived at the Embassy. "I think you were down on their list for arrest, but perhaps retaliation on some innocent Japanese in London will calm things down. However, you'd better stick around here for a while."

I stayed with Pat and obtained some idea of the workings of one of His Majesty's diplomatic establishments. Then to help out I volunteered to do cypher work. The Ambassador was a much harassed man with a thousand and one problems whom all admired and respected. But it seemed to me that many of the so-called diplomats would have been better suited as principals of girls' schools. Some seemed to think that every day was Christmas, and judged all Japanese by the very charming people who had been to England or received the benefits of an Oxford or Cambridge education. It was refreshing to talk to men like Redman or the naval or air attachés who spoke a straightforward language and did not pull punches. When a certain junior member of the staff through persistent efforts and much initiative nailed a British traitor who was selling secrets to Japanese intelligence it took the naval attaché to get action and the matter laid before the ambassador. Sir Robert moved fast. The propaganda machine was busy as ever condemning the espionage activities of the Salvation Army, the Methodists and Baptists, the Episcopalians and other religious organizations, but most of the British subjects arrested had now been released. Retaliation in London had helped and the case of Reuter's manager had shocked the Japanese. There was no proof of foul play, but one could guess what sort of treatment the *kempei* had meted out to force him to take his life through the window. It was to become a general practice and many unfortunate people were to smash to their deaths on the pavement outside the infamous Bridge House, headquarters of the Japanese gendarmerie at Shanghai.

I had almost decided to accept the air attaché's offer to send me off to the RAF when his naval counterpart informed me that I had been given a commission as sub-lieutenant in the Hong Kong Royal Naval Volunteer Reserve and would train in Hong Kong prior to being sent to UK.

The majority of the British women in Hong Kong had been sent off to Australia, so I enlisted Redman's support to arrange permission for Kaneko to follow me, settled to leave in *Empress of Asia*, and then returned to Yamagata.

The medical certificate had done the trick. The Principal told me that they'd pay me the equivalent of two first-class passages to England, said the whole school was proud of me, and that he knew there would always be a job for me on my return to Japan.

This was magnanimous, to say the least, but it was typical of the treatment I received in those days as a teacher.

For a few days prior to departure there was a succession of parties. One student had his sisters stand in the rain for two days collecting stitches for a *senninbari*—a belt to protect me from harm. I was deeply touched. Around my waist I'd be wearing a thousand wisps of hair from a thousand women, each of which had been given with a prayer for my safety by those whose sons and brothers and husbands I might someday have to fight. It was a terribly depressing thought.

The evening before departure the students gave me a farewell party at a restaurant; many speeches were made, many toasts drunk, including one for the victory of Britain over her enemies, for our Royal Family, and I responded accordingly in wishing their prosperity and happiness, and prayed Japan would not become involved. Much sake and beer were consumed, it was gay and wild, and then a sad affair when a student sang a song about bidding goodbye to a friend in the rain. But soon they were roaring out their favourite—the *Dekansho*:

"Dekansho! Dekansho!
Let's warm our wine
In a kettle
And drink, drink;
For there's not a god
Who doesn't love wine!"

The whole school seemed to be assembled at the railway station; the Nugents, Father Holzer, the policeman who'd pestered me so often, the butcher, the baker, Eiko and Yukiko and their brothers and sisters and parents, even old Bob, the Airedale, was on the platform sensing that he was losing his friends, and of course his favourite bread and marmalade.

"There has never been a finer send-off here in Yamagata," said Kikuo Tanaka. "And it is because we all love and respect you both. You have tried to understand us, you have always been sympathetic and understanding; but first and foremost you have always been a true Englishman."

I hung on to the rail by the carriage step until the sea of kind faces faded and all that remained was the red eye of a signal and the loom of light above the city, my eyes bathed in tears of gratitude and happiness, and the soul-consuming despair in the thought that someday, somewhere, those young men and I might in line of duty be engaged in mortal combat.

Chapter Nineteen

I

THE RMS *Empress of Asia*, surely one of the most graceful vessels ever to ply Pacific waters, was now painted a sombre grey, and I stood at her stern, the red ensign slatting overhead in the stiff breeze, watching Yokohama fade into the smoke and haze. Still fluttering from stanchions were the remnants of the coloured streamers which passengers held with those on shore until the wind or distance parted them; a piece of red paper which had connected me to Kaneko was still in my hand.

By sunset we were well out to sea, Fuji San's peak just discernible, a pinkish wraith above the clouds, and inshore among the dark skyline of low hills was Inamura, where, if fate were kind, we might still make our home.

There'd been a rush of farewells in Tokyo; the Viscount, Yoshi and Aiko, old friends of the Ginza coffee shop, Vere and Madeleine who'd promised to assist Kaneko to join me as soon as possible, at the pier was Eiko, from Yamagata, and even our old maid Tatsu, and in my pocket reposed a sheaf of telegrams from Yamagata and Hirosaki to wish me *bon voyage* and safe return!

At Nagasaki we embarked de Trafford, English lecturer at the Nagasaki Higher Commercial School who'd been arrested on suspicion of espionage. He was in high spirits and said the whole thing had been a put-up job to get him out of the area. Sydney Ringer, a businessman whose family had been in the Nagasaki area for over fifty years, and his charming wife, whose two sons were in the Indian Army, entertained us right royally in their suite all the way to Shanghai.

Shanghai was completely under the thumb of the Japanese Army and Navy who by their actions were proceeding to make things more difficult and intolerable for Chinese and foreigner alike. On the railings of the Bund gardens was still the sign, "Dogs and Chinese Prohibited by Order, Shanghai Municipal Council."

Hong Kong Harbour was devoid of any suggestion that the British Far Eastern Fleet existed, but no sooner was the *Empress* berthed than a smart picket boat plying the White Ensign came alongside, and Jack Grenham, now a lieutenant-commander RNVR, and an old friend, greeted me, and whisked me off to the Hong Kong "Wavy Navy".

II

On December 8th, 1941, I was serving as a sub-lieutenant in a motor torpedo boat flotilla. Herself had joined me earlier in the year and we had a small apartment at Kai Tak, opposite the Royal Air Force base. I had implored her to go to Australia where we had many friends, or to accept the offer of a job in Ceylon; but she refused to leave, although it was fairly obvious that war with Japan could only be a matter of time.

On my arrival at Hong Kong I had undergone two months' training in small craft handling, gunnery, minesweeping, signals, anti-submarine attack methods, navigation and a host of other subjects. I then served in minesweepers patrolling the waters of the Crown Colony, in which most of our time was spent in chasing junks off our mine-fields, and was then posted to motor torpedo boats.

My brother officers were a jolly and enthusiastic crowd from all walks of life and various parts of the Far East and, without exception, all waited impatiently to be drafted to the United Kingdom in order to do our share in the Atlantic or Mediterranean, instead of kicking our heels playing sailors at Hong Kong.

The 2nd Motor Torpedo Boat Flotilla comprised six Scott-Paine and two old Thornycroft type boats, the latter having been acquired from the Chinese Navy. Each was armed with two torpedo tubes, depth charges and machine guns, and manned by two officers and ratings all of whom were regulars.

In addition to the MTBs, the naval defences of Hong Kong consisted of two old destroyers, several tugs used as auxiliary patrol vessels and minesweepers, a river gunboat, two boom defence vessels, the Royal Navy depot ship HMS *Tamar,* and the naval volunteer reserve depot vessel, HMS *Cornflower.*

The land forces comprised a battalion each of the Middlesex Regiment, Royal Scots, the Indian Punjabis and Rajputs, plus the Royal Rifles of Canada and the Winnipeg Grenadiers which had arrived only recently, Royal and Indian Artillery, Engineers, Ordnance, and a small detachment of the Royal Air Force which possessed but a few obsolete aircraft used chiefly for towing targets for anti-aircraft firing practice. In addition there were the various units of the Hong Kong Volunteer Defence Corps.

I had returned from sea on the morning of December 7th. That evening we sat on the roof with the dogs, watching the harbour, talking of friends and relatives. It was a calm and silent night. There was hardly a breath of air. The sunset was a riot of red, orange, and yellow hues, and the cloud effects were weird and almost ominous as if presaging a disaster, much like the sort of sky one sees before a typhoon.

At seven o'clock the next morning, just as we were starting breakfast, the air raid sirens started wailing, anti-aircraft opened up and Joan dived under a chair. "Why do they have these silly practices to frighten my dog!" exclaimed Kaneko. "Get down in the cellar!" I shouted as I spotted three light bombers with the red ball markings coming in from the sun at about two hundred feet. The next moment they dropped light bombs as they met sporadic machine gun fire and two old Albacores and a Walrus were blazing on the airstrip. A few wooden buildings started blazing over on the civil side of the airfield and now anti-aircraft and small arms fire woke up as if it was just then realized that this was the real thing. Kaneko, the dogs, the landlord and his wife and the servants, were crouched down back of the pen in which turkeys were being fattened for Christmas. "I do not know when I shall be back," I told her, "but keep in touch with the RAF and do as they tell you," and hastened off to my base and MTB 08.

III

The defenders of Hong Kong put up a gallant but hopeless fight. The Japanese Army had been poised for the attack just a few miles away over the border. The enemy naval forces were but a few miles outside the harbour limits, and their air forces within minutes' flying time of the Colony. So that it was only a matter of days before we were compelled to withdraw from the mainland; and then the Japanese were soon across the harbour and commenced battering us on the island.

On the night of December 9th our flotilla had carried out an attack on Japanese light naval craft off Lantau Island and although we were unable to verify results and feared that most of our torpedoes stuck in the mud because of the shallow waters, yet Tokyo announced that their forces suffered slight damage but claimed to sinking vessels and aircraft which we did not possess!

Kaneko was evacuated with the dogs by the RAF and on December 12th reported to be somewhere on the Peak.

On December 15th, MTB 08 was blown up through a bomb fragment entering the fuel tanks. It was a miracle we suffered not a single casualty. At about the same time three of our boats were destroyed during an attempt to shoot up the Japanese forces on the Kowloon mainland.

Our tiny naval force was then concentrated at our emergency naval base at Aberdeen on the other side of the island with headquarters at an industrial school. Most were sailors without ships and issued with rifles and bayonets, revolvers, and a bag of Mills grenades apiece and I felt like a walking arsenal. Rumours were rife, and many believed that General Chiang Kai-shek's forces were advancing to our relief, that aircraft carriers were on the way, and that US marines were to be parachuted to our assistance. The news of the sinking of the battleship *Prince of Wales*, and the battle-cruiser *Repulse* by Japanese naval dive bombers in the South China Sea had shaken our morale as much as the dreadful news of Pearl Harbour.

Those two great ships were like sitting ducks for the intrepid Japanese bombers. They had been without adequate air support, trusting to their armour and their anti-aircraft defences.

The Japanese were now driving down the Malay Peninsula,

threatening Burma, had taken Wake Island, and were consolidating in the Philippines.

Hong Kong was in a state of siege and at Aberdeen the Japanese were fast closing in on us.

A signal was received from the Commodore: "The Navy will fight to the last man."

Congratulatory messages were received from Mr. Winston Churchill and other leaders, extolling our efforts and urging us to stand fast until help could arrive.

We were bombarded by a Japanese cruiser. One shell which failed to explode was found to have been made in England in 1912. Every thirty minutes there was a most unpleasant bombardment by Japanese mountain guns whose shells screamed into us with a nerve-racking whine and with deadly accuracy.

In between covering the hillside with a machine gun from the window of a toilet, I spent the rest of my time assisting the medical staff, for our sick bay was filled with the wounded and the dying. One afternoon a doctor, Lieut. Whitfield RNVR, went out with a truck which displayed a Red Cross flag to bring in about a dozen casualties who had run into an ambush. The Japanese held their fire.

On December 22nd, I was summoned by a senior officer who told me that herself was to be arrested as a Japanese spy! The house in which she was living had been badly shelled, the roof had been blown off, and someone had reported that signals had been seen flashed there to the Japanese batteries on the Kowloon side.

The "Battle Box" near the naval dockyard was under constant bombardment and one had to run for it between explosions. Few people were on the streets apart from the military, and the whole area was clouded in a pall of smoke. The battle H.Q. was deep in the ground and one entered after being screened by sentries at half a dozen points.

Most of the senior officers were men brought out of retirement, for younger men were needed in areas which were of more importance and, despite talk of the impregnability of the island, all must have known that without reinforcements and air support it could withstand siege for but a limited period. The staff appeared to have little to do. Some were playing cards, chess, or drinking tea. There was an atmosphere of utter hopelessness, but all were eager for news from the outside as most had not seen the daylight for days on end. Nobody seemed to attach importance to the absurd report that Kaneko was a spy. Some busybody, learning she was Japanese by birth, had probably convinced himself that she must be one. I got out of the Battle Box and made for the Peak which I reached after about an hour dodging shells, bullets and bombs.

The house was situated on the edge of the mountain and right in the line of fire of the Japanese batteries which were shelling a wireless station and observation post. It had belonged to Wagstaffe, a brother officer who had been killed a few days

previously, when his MTB was sunk. In civil life he had been an
interior decorator and designer. Samples of his exquisite designs
lay among the rubble.

Herself and the dogs were crouched under a pile of tables and
chairs. There she had what few belongings she had been able
to bring from Kai Tak and a store of tinned goods. She told me
that Canadian soldiers visited her each hour to make sure she
was all right and that she was to go down to stay at their headquarters that evening when the shelling would probably relax
and there would be little fear of air raids. She'd had a fierce battle
of words with a police inspector who had ordered her out and said
he would shoot the dogs. But some British soldiers who appeared
during the argument took her part, drove the inspector away and
then brought her milk and meat for the animals. She'd had no
sleep for days, but was courageous and overjoyed to see me, because
she had seen the destruction of two motor torpedo boats by
Japanese gunfire and had been beset with the fear that one of
them had been MTB 08.

The racket of shells bursting all around, bombs and small arms,
was intense. Joan had shaken off her fear of noise and she and
Peggy seemed to realize that Kaneko needed them now more than
ever.

"We cannot hope to hold out much longer," I told my dear,
loyal wife, "and if I am spared I shall try to escape. You must
stick with the Canadians at their headquarters, and when the
Japanese arrive demand internment as a British subject." She
smiled between her tears and patted her stomach. She had her
passport and other documents sewn into her girdle.

Above the gunfire was a loud knocking on the door. I opened it
to find a Canadian sergeant and several privates.

"Thanks a lot, sergeant, for looking after my wife," I said.

"Why it's a pleasure, sir," he replied, "and she's a grand little
woman. Don't worry, we'll look after her for as long as we can.
She'll be all right down at H.Q. There's a fine deep shelter, plenty
of stores and she's best there when we get out."

As I clasped her to me in farewell I feared that the curtain was
almost lowered on our years of great happiness, for there seemed
but a remote chance that we'd be together again in life.

It was now obvious that it could only be a matter of hours
before the Japanese had us surrounded. Bands of weary soldiers
and sailors, Indians, British, Canadians, Chinese and Portuguese
Hong Kong Volunteers, straggled into the base from the hillsides where they had been clumping about in their heavy nailed
boots to run into Japanese ambushes at almost every turn. For
they could not see the Japanese, who were so well camouflaged,
let alone hear them.

The volunteer nurses had just been ordered to leave the base
and get into the city, when Kaneko arrived exhausted with Joan,
having been escorted down the mountain by two Indian soldiers.
The Canadians had left and taken Peggy and she decided that

she'd be better giving our wounded the benefit of her nursing experience. But the senior naval officer would not hear of her staying and she joined the nurses and left for the city, leaving Joan with me.

Overhead the White Ensigns were flying proudly; shells from the mountain guns screamed into and around the building. Some soldiers were burying the dead, and as I looked into Joan's trusting and inquiring brown eyes I knew we had to say goodbye. A chief petty officer took her to the back of the building and put a ·45 bullet into her head. It was the only way. The Chinese would have eaten her. I dug her grave, my face streaming with tears, wrapped her in a small naval ensign, put her in a beer crate and heaped a mound of stones over her, and at that moment I hated the Japanese more I think than at any time during the war.

Shortly after Kaneko left the base an officer came in from the city and said that a Japanese party had that morning crossed the harbour under a flag of truce to offer terms of surrender, and with a sneer and looking hard at me, said that she had accompanied them as interpreter.

I was about to drive my fist into his face when a friend pushed me aside and said, "Why you lying bastard, she was in this base but an hour ago!"

There had been unsuccessful attempts by the Japanese to persuade the Governor to surrender unconditionally. But the siege went on and now the water mains had been bombed to pose a most serious threat, our communications with the city were being strangled, and bands of armed Chinese roamed the island looting and killing.

Chapter Twenty

I

Lieut.-Commander G. H. Gandy, r.n., commanding officer 2nd MTB Flotilla, ordered preparation of the remaining boats for a long voyage and provisions were to be made for scuttling them if necessary and for long marches across country and mountain climbing. This meant a trip into the city with a petty-officer.

Burned-out cars and trucks strewed the roads, the streets of West Point, usually bustling with life, were deserted and shops all barred. We had to make a department store open up at gun-point. The manager and staff were terrified of looters. After filling a couple of sacks with torches, batteries, and other stores, I gave a receipt and then bought a few necessities which I hoped to pass on to Kaneko if I could find her quickly.

She was in a large office building in the Queen's Road which was packed with refugees, sharing a tiny room with a Mrs. Cheng, an attractive Chinese lady with three children. They had no water, so the petty-officer went down to the hotel and returned with a case of soda water. The whole building stank of foul lavatories; wretched men, some of whom ought to have been in uniform, women and children, were parked with bags and packs on the stairways.

Mrs. Cheng's clothes were not far short of gorgeous, jade pendants hung from her ears, rings glistened on her fingers. I told her that she'd better hide her jewellery, wear less conspicuous clothes, and no make-up. There were characters roaming the streets who'd cut off her fingers for her rings, the Japanese were now only a mile or so away, and there was no telling what might happen to attractive women judging by what had happened at Nanking.

Mrs. Cheng told me that her husband, who'd been a purchasing agent for General Chiang Kai-shek, had escaped to Chungking. I said that she should destroy any evidences of her relationship, take an assumed name and stick close to Kaneko when the Japanese arrived.

She replied that she had good connections to get her away to Macao whence she could make her way to Chungking and would take Kaneko with her.

So once again we said goodbye, the future still in the balance, and I went back to Aberdeen. Whilst awaiting a lift we watched the police dispose of a gang of looters in an alleyway by the side of a bookshop.

"Christ! How can we fight the Japanese and looters and Fifth Columnists at the same time?" exclaimed a police inspector.

II

It was Christmas Day—"Peace on Earth, Goodwill to all Men," and all around were the dead and dying, the Japanese closing in from three sides, the screech of those mountain guns, constant rattle of machine-gun and rifle fire, the plomp, plomp of bombs, and the drone of aircraft. Houses, and junks in the harbour, now sported Japanese flags, all nice and new, which demonstrated what the Chinese thought about Hong Kong's impregnability.

We often heard Japanese voices on the hillsides but never saw our enemies and so blasted away at shrubs, bushes and trees, or anything which provided camouflage. God knows how many times the building had been hit by those mountain guns yet the shells had only slight effect on the concrete.

The place was simply crammed with men from all manner of units, all bleary-eyed and at a complete loss as to what they could do.

Above the racket of siege some Cockney wag was bawling—

> "Then the voice of the workhouse master
> Rang out through the halls,
> 'What will you 'ave for Christmas boys?'
> And the poor sods shouted 'Balls'!"

A gunner was reading aloud from a newspaper of but a few days previous: "Chinese divisions under the direct overall command of General Chiang Kai-shek are now believed to be approaching to relieve the Colony."

"Now what do you think about that, sir?" he inquired.

"I'd say you can forget it and the chap who thought up that one should be shipped across to the mainland to find the Chinese Army and tell it to get a move on."

"Well what about the Yank marines and the reinforcements from Singapore?" inquired another.

"I don't know, but they'd better hurry else I doubt we'll ever see them," I replied. "What we've got to do is to hold on as long as we can so that the Japs will be tied up here and unable to send those attacking us to the south."

From first light the cooks had been preparing the Christmas dinner which was served to the men in shifts with the officers waiting on them. Weary soldiers still staggered in from the hillsides with stories of being cut off from their units, or were the survivors of ambushes. Some of the medical staff hadn't slept for days. During the afternoon shells screamed in from seawards, one or two scoring direct hits and causing considerable damage and casualties. Then mortars started lobbing stuff over. HMS *Aberdeen* was like a tin can floating in a pond and being pelted with stones by a host of boys; a few more bulls-eyes and it would all be over.

III

At 4 p.m. came the signal that the Governor, Sir Mark Young, had surrendered. Lack of water, looting, the welfare of the civilian population rendered further resistance quite hopeless and ridiculous.

It was a grim and tragic moment. The Royal Navy knew not surrender, the word is not in the naval vocabulary. But it was entirely out of the hands of the Senior Service, which must have gone on fighting, if necessary, to the last man. Most of us sighed with relief, and surely there must be something sacred about human life and values. The Creator did not make man to have him destroy his fellows, and surely the days are past when pride must demand the useless sacrifice of human flesh and blood. For us amateurs who came from all walks of life it was not so bad, we could face the facts, and consoled ourselves that we had done our best and need have no shame. But for the older professional sailors the whole bottom had fallen out of their world.

We now prepared for escape. The Philippines was now ruled out, we had not the fuel to reach Singapore, and it was decided to make for Bias Bay, just outside of Hong Kong, where we knew that contact could be made with the Chinese, scuttle the boats, and then make for India across the mainland.

But within minutes of departure a signal was received naming me as liaison officer for the surrender of the base to the Japanese. It was with a heavy heart that I said my goodbyes to my shipmates, and so the remaining boats of the 2nd Motor Torpedo Boat Flotilla set out on their last voyage, to find their resting place beneath the waters of a Chinese bay. My comrades got through to India; some served in the Atlantic, the Mediterranean, the Pacific, many with great distinction, and some were to fall in action. It was an honour to have served with them.

IV

Sporadic firing could still be heard from the direction of the fort at Stanley. Some wondered if a mistake had not been made in the surrender signal. We were to hear later that Stanley Fort had not received clear instructions concerning the surrender and as a result many died who might have been spared.

Now bands of Chinese looters gathered outside the base. A murderous looking lot who threw rocks when out of our reach.

Orders were received to destroy all stocks of wines, spirits and beer. It was heartrending to watch hundreds of bottles of whisky, gin and other liquor, smashed in the concrete gutters, and to watch stone jars of Nelson's Blood being poured away, and one was soon almost intoxicated with the smell.

While this jettisoning of alcohol was going on I stayed at the main gate by the senior naval officer, a destroyer captain named Pears, to await the arrival of the victors. It was almost dark when they did appear; a corporal and a first-class private.

They seemed doubtful about the wisdom of approaching too close and so I went to meet them and spoke in Japanese. The corporal smiled as if greatly relieved and pointing to his bandaged neck said that he'd been wounded by one of our bullets, that his company commander would arrive shortly, and asked if there was anything they could do for us. I pointed to the crowd of ruffianly looters. He caught the ringleader and tied him to a tree.

About half an hour later a lieutenant arrived who said his name was Suzuki, whom I conducted to my senior officer who was then waiting in the base office. Suzuki saluted him and then gave a smart salute before the picture of our King. His chief concern was our arms and ammunition. But these had already been collected and put under guard after much had been rendered useless. We suggested that he provide his own men to replace our guards who were not permitted arms; but he replied that he could not spare his men until the next day and would hold me personally responsible until that time.

We removed them to a store and Suzuki sealed the doors and windows.

The three Japanese created a good impression on my comrades, many of whom had been sceptical about what to expect.

Few slept that night. There were stores enough to feed an army, cigarettes in abundance, and all spent the hours in filling their haversacks and kitbags with whatever seemed to be most useful to prisoners of war. I realized that the disposal of the liquor had been a very wise move.

Early next morning Suzuki was back with half a dozen soldiers and an officer of the Japanese Ordnance Corps. It was then found that one of the windows of the arms store was open and the seal broken. I was told that I was responsible and that I might pay for this with my life. But one of our men pointed out that the heavy iron window was without a fastening and that its weight had been too much for the seal and all was well.

Suzuki informed us that all officers and men were to proceed to Murray Barracks, and so they started out in trucks and on foot, each loaded with more than he could carry very far. I was told to remain at the base and select ten officers and men to stay with me. The day passed without incident. The Japanese who drifted in and out were courteous and well-disciplined.

That night we were alone, the gates having been fastened and sealed by Suzuki before he went back to his headquarters which he said was above us on a hill. Then a petty-officer produced a large jar of navy rum which he had hidden in a lift shaft. Later we were to bless him for his foresight.

I worried very much about Kaneko and Suzuki had promised to try and locate her. He was greatly moved when my senior officer before leaving for Murray Barracks had presented him with a naval dress sword which had been offered previously, but refused. I doubt if it would have cut a wedding cake, but it was a beautiful souvenir and he said he'd sooner Suzuki had it than anyone.

Word had been received that several of our friends were patients in the Queen Mary Hospital, including Charles Boxer, who had received a bullet through his lung, and that they were short of food and certain medical supplies. Francis Carey and a naval mechanic had been tinkering about with a small car which had lost a wheel and did not look as if it would ever be of use again. But they got it going, having taken parts from another wrecked vehicle, and so I decided to take a chance and load it with comforts for those at the Queen Mary.

The hospital was only about three miles down the road and we went from top to bottom distributing what we had brought and found many friends whom we had presumed dead.

Charles Boxer, a scholar and an authority on Portuguese history, literature and language, was his usual cheery self. At his bedside was the charming and unpredictable Emily Hahn, the well-known American authoress, biographer of *Raffles of Singapore* and the *Soong Sisters*, now Mrs. Boxer, who had shocked Hong Kong with her habit of smoking strong cigars and her fondness for her two gibbons which she walked out on silver chains.

Soon after our return to Aberdeen Suzuki arrived and to my pleasure and surprise said that Francis should drive us into Hong Kong to look for Kaneko.

Civilians swarmed about us for news of husbands, fathers, sons, sweethearts; the horrors they had seen, their thoughts and fears written vividly in their eyes. At that moment their homes were being torn to pieces by the scavenging mobs of looters, men, women and childrer, who tore out the plaster from walls and ceilings to remove the wooden laths, took the locks off doors, extracted nails, tore out floors and window frames, and were to be seen laden with wash and toilet basins and every article which could be removed. The condition of those houses appeared as if millions of giant ants had been at work.

At Marina House the screams of children, the stench, and the condition of the aged were appalling. Mrs. Cheng had taken my advice and I could hardly recognize her. She was dressed in a suit of that black, oilskin material much favoured by Chinese boat-women, had removed her make-up and jewellery, her hair was frowsy and her face grimy. She said that Kaneko was still there but had gone out with a Captain Tanaka of the Communications Unit and a British officer. An old couple approached and asked Suzuki when he thought they might be able to return to their home out in the New Territories? They said they'd spent many summers in Japan where everyone had been so kind. There was a young mother with a child in her arms whose husband had been killed. Blind hatred blazed in her eyes and when a Japanese made to fondle her child I thought she would spit in his face. A well-known socialite was immaculate, powdered and perfumed, and demanded that Suzuki arrange for her to go to her home. Daughter of a marquis, niece of a general, her husband's grandfather was said to have had the honour of having a glass of brandy poured over his head at the dinner table by a drunken prince of England. To her the surrender was insufferable. She told me that in her opinion the Governor was a traitor, that the Colony should have been defended to the last man—even woman and child. She did not conceal her disgust at having to rub shoulders with the wives of bank clerks, Eurasian girls, wives of policemen and sanitary inspectors, with shopwalkers and even whores. The Chinese ladies she could tolerate, especially those who'd been received at Government House. But she was apparently untiring in her efforts to create order out of chaos in the building and, as Kaneko was to tell me, had tons of courage and seemed to overawe even the most arrogant Japanese.

We went into the lounge of the Hong Kong Hotel. Francis and I did not feel exactly comfortable; for we were in uniform and drinking beer with a Japanese officer and although we had come to respect him, he was still an enemy. By the looks we received from some I felt that we were already branded as arch collaborators of the Japanese.

As we were leaving the hotel we ran into Captain Cliff Weber of the Middlesex Regiment, with a Japanese sergeant. He told me that through some sort of misunderstanding, or sheer stupidity on the part of one of our liaison officers, the Japanese staff was being most difficult and would not allow stores to be brought in for the 6,000 officers and men then in Murray Barracks, and that they were almost out of food. He said that he could get hold of a number of trucks, and all he wanted was a permit for them to come to Aberdeen. I obtained this from Suzuki who agreed to allow us to send the food from our base.

The shops were thronged with Japanese buying or looting cloth and jewellery and anything which had for so long been in short supply in Japan. They seemed to have enormous quantities of Hong Kong money and I saw one fellow with a small suitcase filled with notes.

Hawkers were selling every conceivable kind of loot, and some had established wayside bars where they even dispensed champagne out of Chinese tea cups.

Soon after we returned to Aberdeen, Cliff Weber arrived with his trucks. They'd experienced difficulties and so Suzuki chalked a notice on each to the effect that it was under the supervision of his unit. Over fifty truckloads of food were loaded and, thanks to Suzuki, each man was able to leave Murray Barracks for POW camp with his own load of supplies. Then Kaneko arrived with the Captain Tanaka who was looking after the civilians at Marina House. She was well, but tired and worn out, and had just been in the midst of the shambles at Wongneichong to interpret in connection with broken telephone cables and where the sight and smell of the dead had sickened and horrified her. Another officer then joined us from Suzuki's regiment and said that we were to go with him to Government House where our general and other senior officers were staying and Kaneko was told to accompany us.

Government House was surrounded with Japanese sentries. There was no electricity and our general with twenty or so other senior army and naval officers were together in a lounge which was bathed in the soft light of candles. It was a heartrending meeting, for me one of the most tragic and impressive moments of my life. We were joined by a Japanese colonel and Kaneko interpreted.

The General asked if it was the practice of the Imperial Army to rape nurses and shoot and bayonet the wounded in their beds. This had happened at North Point and at Stanley. The Japanese replied that, if this were true, the culprits would be found and shot in accordance with military law. Some such sentence was actually carried out a few days later.

But the Japanese claimed that the shooting of the wounded at Stanley was justified because firing had come from the school which was being used as a hospital and armed men found inside, and that they could not know who were wounded men or who were shamming and waiting to shoot any Japanese who approached.

It was in the school that the wife of a friend was bayoneted to death whilst crouching under her wounded husband's bed. It was a ghastly business. There seemed to be a fixed idea in the minds of some that the Japanese were killing all our men found in the hills who had not reported after the surrender, and the General was particularly anxious about a large number known to have been at the magazines at Shouson Hill, near Aberdeen, and accused the Japanese of having shot them all.

The Japanese colonel said he knew nothing about them, but Suzuki hastened to explain that there was indeed a number of men in the magazines who refused to come out, who threatened to blow up the whole area, and said his men had been fired on whenever they approached.

A senior naval officer asked me if I could get the Japanese to agree to promise these men safe conduct and not punish them if I could get them to come out of the magazines. This was readily forthcoming and I was instructed to convey the General's orders to them to surrender immediately. I was warned that I might have difficulty as the officer in charge was a particularly stubborn Australian of the Royal Engineers who might choose to blow up the thousands of tons of munitions and explosives rather than surrender.

The General thanked Suzuki for his assistance in obtaining food for the troops in Murray Barracks, Kaneko was given all manner of messages for the wives of officers, and she promised to try and find the Scottish terrier of the General's aide-de-camp, and, after leaving her at Marina House, we returned to Aberdeen with two trucks for our attempt to get the Australian and his comrades out of the magazines.

It was almost 2 a.m. when we set out with Suzuki and he agreed that the less Japanese we took with us the more chance we stood of success.

The route was through man-made cuts in the mountains. and we drove into an open space, on both sides of which were barred doors leading into the magazines. Francis and I both shouted that we had come from the General and wished to speak with the senior officer. I heard someone say: "Tell them to bugger off!"

There seemed to be an argument going on inside and then Manning, a naval officer, appeared, astounded to see us, and was soon joined by several others, and then a well-built, imposing officer made his way forward. This was the reputedly tough Australian. He looked it. I repeated the order from the General and told him that safe conduct had been guaranteed and that I would stake my own life on their being escorted safely to Murray Barracks.

Suzuki now came forward. "Who's he?" I was asked. I told them how we had been treated by Suzuki's unit, and the Australian said, "Well, I still think it would be better to blow up the whole bloody dump, and believe me that is what was going to happen as soon as we ran out of grub, about the day after tomorrow. All right chaps. This is it. Open up!"

There were about twenty officers and men. We passed round the rum. Suzuki seemed to be greatly relieved and confessed that his unit had pondered for days over the problem of how to remove the inmates without bringing down half the mountain in the event of an explosion.

They had made themselves very comfortable, but had been on short rations, except for chocolate of which they had an abundance, but were almost out of water. Soon, twenty or thirty Japanese officers and men arrived who treated the Australian and his pals like heroes, and when we got down to Aberdeen a Japanese officer arrived with beer and whisky in plenty. The magazine heroes certainly did themselves well and we all shared in the liquid refreshment provided by the Imperial Japanese Army from our captured stores.

The next morning we took them into Murray Barracks, each weighed down with more than he could reasonably carry. Whether the idea was popular or not with his comrades, I am sure that had we not gone out to them, the Australian would have provided Hong Kong with the nearest thing to an atomic blast; for he had prepared everything for the big event.

He told Suzuki that if he survived the war he'd return the whisky and beer at his favourite pub on George Street, Sydney.

Chapter Twenty-one

I

LATE in the afternoon after our meeting with the chaps in the magazines, Lieutenant Suzuki approached and said: "My colonel has asked me to express his appreciation of the way you and your comrades have behaved. He wishes to see you this evening at our headquarters."

A naval mechanic drove me up to a house situated above the magazines at Shouson Hill. It was bitterly cold. A sentry was wearing a very handsome lady's mink coat which was probably worth about £1,000. The driver was taken in charge by an NCO and I was led into a typical English home. There were prints of English scenes around the walls, children's toys were scattered here and there as if discarded for the moment whilst the children were attracted by a more fascinating diversion. Little had been disturbed.

In the soft candlelight about a dozen officers stood around a large table which was laid out for what promised to be a banquet. I saluted and all came to attention and bowed. A tall, handsome man came forward, smiled and said: "My officers and I will be honoured if you will consent to dine with us tonight. We are enemies. You have been defeated, but you fought well and have no reason to be ashamed. So for a little while cannot we forget we are adversaries, but just men. It is the fortune of war."

We sat down to a delicious meal of chicken *sukiyaki* washed down with plenty of sake and beer. During that dinner not a word was spoken which might have embarrassed me in any way. We talked a lot about food. We discussed our favourite brands of sake, a major sang *"Tanko Bushi"*—"The Coalminer's Song"— with great gusto and I guessed rightly that he was from Kyushu, and a captain and I discovered that we had both patronized an *O'denya* on the Ginza in Tokyo named "I-Pei," where a middle-aged but extremely handsome dispenser of *O'den*, a particular and rather tasteless type of Tokyo food, had presided.

With dinner over all insisted on shaking hands, and the Colonel said: "Tomorrow we shall be gone. Please look after your health."

"I cannot wish you good fortune in fighting," I replied, "but I pray that you will all return safe to your families and that we shall meet again in happier circumstances, and I thank you not only for myself but for my comrades."

My comrades were indeed sorry to learn that Suzuki was to leave us and pressed upon him all manner of small personal mementoes such as badges and charms and cigarette cases. He was deeply touched and said that as long as we were enemies he could not possibly accept such gifts.

When we said our good-byes he saluted—and then held out his hand, and that handshake, firm and long, said a great deal, for it was that of any enemy through duty, but a friend through human understanding. We were not to meet again until 1956.

That night we were again alone, but I knew that we should not be allowed to stay much longer at Aberdeen and so advised my comrades to pack everything useful and edible they could carry so as to be ready to leave at a moment's notice. We shared the remaining rum which we put in our water-bottles. One of my most prized possessions was a heavy brass crest from a motor torpedo boat, triangular in shape with waves and a flying fish under the naval crown. I was to hold on to it until October or November of 1943.

Just after an enormous breakfast of fried sausages, bacon, tinned fruits, biscuits, jam, treacle, coffee and tea, a large bus arrived from which emerged—the *"kempeitai"*.

We were told to get into the bus and to leave our belongings behind. A *"kempei"* sergeant told me that we might return for our kit later. However, we managed to hang on to our water-bottles and small haversacks and said good-bye to our kitbags into which we had crammed cigarettes and food and plenty of new clothes.

After a short drive we entered the Repulse Bay Hotel. The place was filled with soldiers, most of them *"kempei"*, and Chinese whores. We were greeted with jeers, and led upstairs where a corporal, much the worse for liquor, was urinating in the corridor, and put in a room furnished with two large double beds, which had its own private bathroom and toilet. One bed was loaded with all manner of parcels; rolls of cloth, wireless sets, civilian suits, ladies' underwear, boots and shoes, and children's toys.

The door swung open to admit a short stocky man dressed in a bright silk dressing-gown with enormous dragons embroidered on the back. He threw himself on the bed, smiled, and told me to write down our names, ranks and service units. In the meantime a soldier entered and started massaging his neck.

I finished the list and sat there awaiting his pleasure.

"Do you have any cameras?" he asked. The answer was, of course, in the negative.

"Well then, where are all the cameras which I hear were at Aberdeen?"

We did not know. There might be some there.

"They were taken by those thieving artillery people, weren't they?"

I said I thought that the naval cameras had been taken away by the Japanese ordnance when they removed the arms and ammunition.

"Well then, what is left in that place?"

"Stores of clothing, tinned foods, plenty of cigarettes, paint, ships' stores of all kinds."

The telephone rang. He took it and listened for a while, grunting as he noted points from the speaker.

He then turned to me and said, "There are no cigarettes there."

"Well, there were cases containing several hundreds of thousands when we left this morning," I replied.

He seemed interested and so I said: "If we are not being returned to Aberdeen, could we go back there and collect our kit?"

"No, you must stay here until we decide where you are to be sent," he replied gruffly.

"Well, couldn't one of us go and collect our belongings?"

He thought for a moment and then said: "If I send one of you and allow him to collect your things, do you think he could find the cigarettes?"

"Why of course," I replied, "But I do not think one man could handle all our gear."

He agreed that two could go in the bus and Francis Carey and I accompanied by two soldiers were back there within an hour since leaving the place.

Our things had been pilfered and our cigarettes and certain small valuables taken. They had not bothered about clothing or foodstuffs; there was so much else to be had for the taking.

We were told to be quick and just stuffed those bags with everything which came to hand.

In one hour most of the cigarettes had been removed. But we managed to find about 20,000 which we handed to the soldiers and mustered another four or five thousand for ourselves, as well as a few tins of naval pipe tobacco, and Francis found a box-type Brownie camera which he decided to take back to Repulse Bay for the gentleman who seemed so interested in photography.

I took one last look around the place, and at the pile of stones where rested our beloved Joan. In that moment I heard once again the screech of the shells, the crumble of masonry, the shouts of men, and saw again the heroic figure of the naval doctor, Whitfield, and the naval ensigns flying proudly on every staff and pole.

And now flying overhead was the red ball of the sun.

II

We returned to the Repulse Bay Hotel to find that our friends had been removed to another room. We did not see the fellow in the embroidered dressing-gown. Francis gave the Brownie camera to a guard. We were left alone except for visits by curious NCOs, most of whom wished to know the whereabouts of cigarettes, whisky, cameras and other valuables which they seemed convinced we had hidden. One relieved some of my friends of their watches and when I protested was told that I should remember we were prisoners and that they could kill us if they wished. This was an entirely new breed of Japanese. I gathered that most had just arrived from Japan and had not heard a shot fired in anger. We were now among the followers-on, like a crowd of vultures come to lord it over the local populace after the real hard and dirty work had been carried out by the fighting men who were now gone to other battlefields.

We had little sleep, for all night long there was a pandemonium of singing, shouting, screaming of women, and visits by the soldiery.

On the following morning we were taken in a bus to Happy Valley, where the Hong Kong Race Course is situated, and handed over to the *"kempeitai"* which had its headquarters in a Catholic convent school and there put into a bare room with a stone floor and its barred door then locked. Some of the guards were Sikhs from the Hong Kong Police. One old sergeant, who was wearing medal ribbons from the First World War, whispered to me that he was ashamed at serving the Japanese but had a wife and children in the Colony and feared for their safety. We decided to be very careful of the Indians. Some, I am sure, were victims of circumstance and were quite all right, but it was best not to take chances. I had always sympathized with the Indian desire for independence and had the greatest admiration for Gandhi and Nehru and other patriots. But I could not but despise those who had taken the oath to serve in the armed forces and had subsequently turned traitor. Yet thousands of Indian officers and men were to suffer starvation rather than submit to Japanese demands to co-operate with the Indian Independence Army.

Hundreds of Chinese were brought into the court-yard, many of whom were beaten with rifle butts, given the water treatment, which consisted of having water poured into their nostrils until they choked, and other revolting tortures.

The soldier guards were not *"kempei"* but men from a Tochigi regiment who went out of their way to do us all manner of small kindnesses and who openly showed us their loathing of the *"kempei"*. One had been a country school teacher who knew of me through the translations which Kaneko and I had made of the books of the Japanese writer Ashihei Hino. One evening, he said: "Please talk to your comrades about Japan—please do not let them think we are all like these *'kempei'*, who are beasts." I was reminded of a passage in one of Hino's books in which he tells of seeing the execution of several brave Chinese, and remarks: "I turned my head away, deeply grateful that I, too, had not become an unfeeling beast."

One day when I was in the toilet someone whispered to me from the next cubicle. It was a British soldier named Frelford of the Middlesex Regiment. He said that he was being well-treated but had been told not to speak to us. The next day a Japanese officer came to question us about the stores at Aberdeen and I took the opportunity to ask him about Frelford, who was now to be seen walking about the courtyard. He said that the man had been left in their charge by a Japanese unit which had gone south. They had been requested to give him every consideration as he had saved the life of a Japanese soldier by tending his wounds. I pointed out that such special treatment would only put the man in a very embarrassing position and I was sure he would like to join us. Shortly after this Frelford was telling us his story.

He had been fighting in the Stanley area and was cut off from his unit, most of which had been killed, when he stumbled on a Japanese soldier behind a rock. The man was unconscious and bleeding from wounds in the head and chest. He gave him water and bound his wounds, but just as he opened his eyes, four or five Japanese appeared and were going to shoot Frelford when the wounded man spoke up.

Frelford was taken before a Japanese officer who inquired: "Why did you assist an enemy?"

"A wounded man, whether he be friend or foe, is just the same. Any human being would act as I did," replied Frelford.

From that moment the Japanese made him their special charge.

Frelford was a decent fellow and a good soldier and had a Union Jack wrapped round his waist which he said he was keeping for our day of victory. Although not a Roman Catholic he spent a great deal of time searching in the rubbish heaps for holy pictures and books which had been thrown out by the *"kempei"*, and also cleaned and decorated a shrine and a statue of Christ which stood in the courtyard.

He was of great help to us because he was allowed out with a pass during daylight and was able to do our shopping.

One day an American negro was thrown in with us. He was as black as the ace of spades and some of the Japanese in fun used to try to rub him white. We nicknamed him "Speed", because of his stories of the facility with which he broke down the resistance of any female to whom he took a fancy. The stories of his amours would have brought blushes to the cheeks of the most hardened roué. All day long he'd talk and sing, and grumble about the hardness of the floor, and extol the virtues of his Chinese woman. And then he seemed to fade away. He complained of stomach pains, he'd groan in his sleep, and seemed convinced that he was not long for this world.

Speed was a happy-go-lucky ne'er-do-well. Born in Alabama, he'd been a sailor, boxer, musician, and had roamed around the world with his trumpet.

It was an anxious and boring existence. Day after day an endless stream of Chinese went out to execution on the reclamation down by the harbour where they were made to dig their own graves before being decapitated by *"kempei"* officers and NCOs, without any sort of proper trial.

Shades of General Nogi, Admiral Togo, and Takamori Saigo! What had come over the Japanese military? The Russo-Japanese War and World War I had seen them humane and civilized towards their prisoners. Whatever these Chinese may have done could not have warranted such an undignified and bestial death.

Even a bullock, in any civilized land, is despatched with a humane killer. The sight of *"kempei"* returning from such blood baths boasting of the efficiency of their swordsmanship was ghastly and sickening.

On the twenty-third day after our arrival from Repulse Bay Hotel we were taken by truck to the prisoner of war camp which had been established temporarily at North Point, facing the harbour. But Frelford was not allowed to accompany us.

III

At North Point Camp were British, Canadians, Indians, and men of the local volunteer defence forces, composed of British, Portuguese, Eurasians, French, Americans and various other nationalities. We received a great welcome from our friends, many of whom we believed had been killed in action.

One of my friends had been one of some forty volunteers and regulars who had been surrounded and captured by the Japanese just outside the Repulse Bay Hotel. They were disarmed, given a few minutes to smoke a cigarette, and then bayoneted and pushed over a cliff. My friend fell backwards before the bayonet pierced him. The next thing he remembered he was surrounded by Japanese who carried him back up the cliff, and he fully expected that this time there would not be any mistake over his execution. But to his surprise he found some twenty of his comrades still alive. The Japanese had stopped the murder and he was told that the bayonetings were reprisals for Japanese who had been shot by our snipers after the Governor had announced our surrender.

Things were pretty easy at that time. Quite a number of my friends had already escaped. Some used to crawl out at night through the sewer pipes and go exploring for food, and others even slipped out to spend a few hours with Chinese girl friends. The camp was wired off from the road and all day there were crowds of women and children outside looking for fathers, husbands, sweethearts and relatives. Most were Chinese, Eurasians, Portuguese, or other neutrals.

There were faces, lined with tears, of those who had lost their breadwinners, and those who knew not what was to become of them with their men behind the wire.

I had been there only about 24 hours when I was summoned to my hut to find a *"kempei"* awaiting who told me to pack my kit, and within twenty minutes I was back once again at the convent school.

Frelford was overjoyed to see me. He had been carrying on with a sort of deaf and dumb language and said he had been terribly lonely. He was free to roam the city during the day but said that he could sense the scorn of people who believed him some sort of collaborator with the Japanese.

I lived alone in the room with the stone floor, Frelford was with about twenty Chinese who appeared to be important political prisoners, for all had beds and proper bedclothes, could send out for food, had wine and spirits, and played mahjongg all night. One morning they had gone. All met death on the reclamation by the harbour.

I found a book on Buddhism on a rubbish heap in the courtyard and read avidly a wonderful translation by Max Muller of the "Dhammapada" which I found of much comfort. It served to humble me and make me realize my own insignificance and the trivial nature of my own personal worries and sorrows.

IV

One afternoon a *"kempei"* sergeant whom I had not seen before took me by car to Queen's Building in the city and, as we reached the top of the first flight of stairs, a door flew open and Kaneko hurled herself into my arms. But she was dragged away and I was hurried upstairs to a small room and left alone for half an hour. Then a short, stocky man, with a Hitler moustache, came in and started questioning me.

"When did the British Government order you to translate the books of Ashihei Hino?" he inquired.

"As I remember it was suggested by a newspaperman on the staff of the Asahi or Mainichi," I replied.

"How much did the British Government pay you to spy during your years in Japan?"

"I am sure I would be the last person they'd employ for such a purpose."

"Why did you choose to teach at Hirosaki Higher School which is situated near an army divisional headquarters?"

"I had no control over the whereabouts of my school."

"Aren't you friendly with the notorious Redman who is now being punished for his crimes as a spy?"

"Vere Redman is a good friend of mine, but I am sure he has never been a spy and always tried to be a friend of Japan."

"When did your wife commence broadcasting anti-Japanese and anti-war propaganda from Stonecutter's Island?"

"To the best of my knowledge my wife has broadcast only once in her life which was from the BBC at the time of the Coronation of King George VI. Stonecutter's Island was a military wireless station, not a broadcasting station."

"Well, your country has lost Hong Kong, we are already in Singapore (this was not then true), we have taken the Philippines, we shall take Burma and India, and meet the Germans at the Suez Canal. What are you people going to do?"

"We may lose battles but we shall not lose the war, and so we shall win back these territories," I replied.

He knocked me down with a hard blow in the face and then stamped out of the room.

A few minutes later a soldier appeared with a tray on which were a bottle of beer, some steak and fried potatoes and fruit, and told me to eat and drink. As the soldier poured the beer I recognized him as the son of a shopkeeper over at Kowloon from whom we used to buy mosquito sticks and other Japanese products. He whispered that Kaneko was all right and being treated well.

Two *"kempei"* sergeants came into the room with a wizened old man dressed in some sort of uniform who carried a sword almost as big as himself. He introduced himself as an interpreter and said that he had been a teacher of English at a middle school in Yokohama. The questioning commenced all over again, and now and then one of the sergeants would leave the room. I realized that all I said was being checked with my wife and prayed she would be alive to the situation. There was nothing to hide except that she had designed some pamphlets: "Soldiers of Japan! Do not dance to the tap of Hitler's drum. War can bring you only ruin. We are not your enemies. Your enemies are those militarists who seek only their own selfish ends. A peaceful Japan can be a prosperous Japan. Go back to the factories and the rice-fields where now your womenfolk slave away without the benefit of your loving care."

Unfortunately, the Japanese found the filing cabinets at headquarters intact and Kaneko was shown her original manuscript, and asked if she wrote it. She readily admitted she had done so and said she was, of course, against all forms of war and did not wish to see the land of her birth involved in a conflict which could only bring disaster. She reminded them that she believed it was General Nogi, or Admiral Togo, who once wrote to the effect that "a man who loved war was nothing but a beast".

The little ex-teacher interpreter was quite hopeless, and admitted that he had not spoken English for years. I had to assist him because he got in an awful mess and the *"kempei"* seemed to make him very nervous. All they seemed to care about was establishing evidence that I had been a spy during my years in Japan.

When the interview appeared to be at an end I begged the old interpreter to try to arrange for me to see my wife. He spoke to the sergeants, and although they did not seem optimistic about obtaining permission, were not unsympathetic. Then the door opened to admit a well-built lieutenant-colonel who asked me if I had been well treated. I replied that I had no complaints except that I wished to be sent to a prisoner of war camp.

"But there is no need for you to suffer," he said. "You must make the best of things. You can be quite happy and comfortable. We have now started an English language newspaper and are broadcasting in English. Why not assist us?"

"What would be your reply were you in my position?" I inquired.

He smiled. "I expected such an answer. Your wife told me you would never accept. And now you may see her alone; but you are not to speak of your interrogation here."

Kaneko was in a small room with an old Chinese gentleman and his wife, well but terribly worried, and told me that the *"kempei"* had on several occasions told her that I had been beheaded. She had asked to be interned with other British women, but the *"kempei"* said that they could not recognize her as being British, despite the fact that she had a British passport. I told her in whispers to try to get outside and run to the Swiss or Swedish consulates, both of which were then protecting British interests.

I had never felt so proud of her. She was brave and loyal and a credit to Japanese womanhood and her adopted land. I was not to see her again until the spring of 1946!

I had expected to be taken to the officers' prisoner of war camp at Kowloon, but was returned to Happy Valley.

A few days later I was told to pack my kit, and that afternoon an officer drove me over the hills to Stanley Camp, where all the civilians had been interned.

Chapter Twenty-two

I

IN THE middle of January the civilians had been ordered to assemble at Murray Barracks, whence they had been marched to West Point and quartered in a number of the most disreputable Chinese brothels and hotels. The entire proceeding had obviously been designed to humiliate them as far as possible before the Chinese populace. But it misfired; for the Chinese showed only sympathy for those whom the Japanese labelled "exploiters and barbarians", and people have described the march to West Point as more like a funeral procession. The Chinese knew what they could expect from their so-called liberators of the Co-Prosperity Sphere; for they were now having to bow or salute anyone wearing a Japanese uniform, or suffer a beating.

There were about two thousand people in the camp which was situated around the Stanley civil prison, overlooking the sea.

Men, women and children roamed the hills and roads inside the wire, under the guard of former members of the Indian branch of the Hong Kong Police. The camp office was situated in the house formerly occupied by the prison governor and was in charge of a young Japanese merchant named Nakazawa, and Yamashita, who had been a barber in the Hong Kong Hotel.

I was assigned living quarters on the second floor of St. Stephen's College and shared a room with a tough old character who was a building overseer, the most foul-mouthed man I have ever encountered, and Desmond, a young Australian marine engineer. The windows had been blown out during the fighting, the roof leaked.

I went all over the camp to inquire of Kaneko from people who had only recently been brought in, including General "Two Gun" Cohen, once a bodyguard for Dr. Sun Yat-sen, who had been taken out for questioning. Poor Cohen had been given a bad time by the "kempei". Our former landlord and his wife were there with their two adopted orphan Chinese children who showered me with kindness and shared with me the little luxuries they had managed to hoard.

The food was atrocious. Broken, weevilly rice, which had been condemned, stinking fish, and all manner of peculiar greenstuffs. I still had some canned food, which came in very handy, especially as I was not in a position to receive parcels from outside, as was the case with many of the internees, and I had no money to buy on the blackmarket or from the canteen which was then selling foodstuffs at exorbitant prices.

Outside the wire were large storehouses of food put down by the government in preparation for a siege and many brave sorties were made through the wire by the stalwart inmates of Stanley. And when the Japanese did empty them we provided the labour and had plenty of friends standing by to carry away whatever we could lay our hands on.

Stanley Camp was a great leveller of the classes and social grades. People who had been living with their heads in the clouds, conscious of their social position, found that all that mattered was whether you had bedding, tobacco, black tea and other appurtenances which made life worth living. The fact that you were Mrs. No. 1 Sanitary Inspector, or Mrs. No. 1 Public Works Department did not amount to a row of beans. But in the main they were all good, kind and decent people, who bore their lot with great good humour and fortitude.

A school had been established and there was a library and a hospital. Camp affairs were conducted by a committee elected by the inmates, which was presided over by senior members of the Hong Kong Government.

Several of the inmates were serving sentences in the prison. From time to time they were released to the camp and judging by their condition it was a regular hell hole.

One day a Japanese soldier came to see me who said he had been sent to locate me by one of my old friends and that on the following day he would drive into the camp in a truck. I was to wait near a certain tree where he would throw out a package.

I was at the appointed place well ahead of time with my two room-mates waiting near by. The package which hurtled out of the truck was a large sack which after nightfall we carried to our room. There were cigarettes, pipe tobacco, shirts, soap, tinned food, oatmeal and a bottle of whisky! We really celebrated that night and I was able to repay the kindness I had received from my old landlord, from Olive Grenham and others.

I never discovered the identity of my benefactor. He may have been a former student, or friend from Japan who through his position could not approach me personally.

Olive shared a room with a very interesting Australian woman journalist who had been caught at Hong Kong while on a newspaper reporting trip to the Far East. Dorothy was attractive, and a hard case. She had been married several times, had been an actress in Hollywood, placed little trust in men, had a wonderful sense of humour, a great fund of stories, and was a gay and solid companion.

We used to sit and talk for hours in the old cemetery, one of the most beautiful parts of the camp which overlooked the sea. Here were graves of British soldiers and their families dating back to the early years of the last century, and the headstones testified to the terrible toll which cholera and typhoid took in those days.

One afternoon, after a heavy fall of rain, Desmond spotted a boot sticking out of the soil on the other side of the wire.

The building overseer looked down at his shabby footwear. "That bloke won't need his boots any more," he said, "and I could certainly do with them."

That evening he climbed under the wire and came back wearing a pair of Canadian army issue.

The next day we obtained permission from the Japanese to dig up the body and give it a proper burial.

The cemetery was popular with the camp lovers, for there were plenty of trees, rocks and headstones, to shelter them from prying eyes. One would imagine that love-making was the last thing to bother about in such circumstances. But there were a number of full-blooded young men, and many healthy and lonesome women. Unfortunately there were many tragic love affairs, broken marriages, and the infidelity of some whose husbands were across the water in the prisoner of war camps in Kowloon.

The representative of the Japanese Foreign Office, under whose jurisdiction the camp was officially functioning, was a very fine gentleman named Takeo Oda, now Ambassador at Djakarta, who earned the respect of all. Mr. Oda admitted that Kaneko should be interned as a British subject, but he did not appear too optimistic and I could sense that he was up against the narrow and stubborn military mind. But he promised to do his best to have me transferred to a POW camp.

Shortly after my first interview with him I was summoned to the camp office to be informed that a parcel had arrived for me. Anderson, the dour Scots quartermaster, said: "You must have been leading a double life, Bushy."

The parcel was from a Miss Mary Wong of Wanchai and contained some of my own clothing, in addition to tins of food, cigarettes, and a bottle of sherry! Later, I was to learn that Kaneko was at that time incarcerated at the Central Police Station and had enlisted the help of Miss Wong to send the parcel to me. Mary Wong procured Chinese clothes for her and planned her escape to Macao; but she was brought back when only about fifty yards from the gates of the Central Police Station!

II

Singapore and Corregidor had fallen, MacArthur had left the Philippines for Australia, the Japanese Navy had lunged out into the Indian Ocean, and Colombo had been bombed. But the Battle of Britain had been won, and very soon the Allies could expect the benefit of the full weight of American productive power.

Rumours circulated, the majority worthless, and products of the "latrine radio" or "bamboo wireless".

One was always hungry, and tobacco had become very scarce. We made cigarettes from collected butt-ends mixed with blanket fluff, and from dried tea-leaves, and experimented with all manner of dried grasses, coffee-grounds and various leaves.

At Stanley were a number of missionaries and nuns who were

the most unselfish and fine people, taught the children, tended the sick, and brought great spiritual comfort to those sensitive folk to whom the confined and unnatural life proved such a strain.

At about three o'clock one morning we were ordered out of bed and made to assemble for a check-up. It transpired that two Englishmen and an American woman journalist had escaped.

For some days there was a great deal of unpleasantness in the form of inspections, and difficulties about food, and the whole camp was paraded in the open for hours on end. But none complained and all were glad they had got away. The general opinion was that it could not have been done without co-operation from outside and that anyone could get across to Free China at a price!

After this the guards were tightened up and we had to be in billets by 7 p.m.

Most of the guards did a lucrative business in Chinese tobacco; a red, foul-smelling stuff which was, however, better than nothing, although those who smoked it were never welcome indoors. They also delivered messages to town and brought replies for a fee of $5.00 a time.

A most unpleasant Japanese major used to visit the camp who gave sweets to the children but would brutally strike any adult who did not bow or otherwise salute him. He knocked an elderly, near-sighted man unconscious, because the poor old fellow did not rise to his feet and bow when he approached.

Gymson, the former colonial secretary, who had been elected representative of the internees, and his interpreter Nellie Hardie, born in Kobe of a Japanese mother and a foreign father, had no easy task in dealing with the Japanese civil authorities who, although willing to do all they could, were nearly always up against the narrow-minded, unreasonable military.

"Uncle John" was the name given to the Rev. Watanabe, a Lutheran priest, who did all in his power to help the internees, as did "Uncle" George Sekiguchi—an interpreter.

There was a kindly sergeant-major who used to go out of his way to do us little kindnesses. I found that he came from Numazu and was acquainted with a friend of mine named Uno, the landlord of Abe Millar, who lived at Togo-mura, and used to have the monopoly on lunch box sales, at Numazu station.

The tragedy of the *Lisbon Maru* which had been torpedoed off the China coast by an American submarine in the late summer of 1942, plunged the whole camp in gloom, for this vessel had been carrying a large number of British prisoners of war from Hong Kong to Japan, and the newspapers reported a heavy loss of life. Many of the women internees lost their husbands and most of us friends.

On board the *Lisbon Maru* were the Middlesex Regiment, Royal Scots, Royal Navy and RAF. She was struck by a torpedo at about six o'clock one morning in fairly rough weather when the prisoners were battened down in the holds, but she was still able to proceed at a reduced speed. The second struck about an hour and a half later and she started to sink. Survivors have described the conditions of stark horror which prevailed below decks, where the cries of the wounded and the dying mingled with the noise of escaping steam and the shouts of those trying to escape from the sinking coffin. But when one hold had been forced open those gaining the decks were able to release those still battened down, and all took to the water, many of whom died by Japanese machine-gun fire and from the depth-charges which destroyers were dropping over the entire area.

Several hundred survivors were taken to Moji by destroyers and patrol vessels where many died later as a result of exposure, including my old friend, Commander Horsewell, R.N.

III

During the summer months the Japanese permitted us to use the bay for swimming. This was a great blessing, although it was ridiculous to have our own guards posted to ensure that people did not swim farther out than about ten yards from the shore. Where we could have swum to perhaps only the Japanese knew!

Twice each week an auctioneer used to function and offer every conceivable and inconceivable object for sale or barter. Old clothes, shoes, articles of furniture, half-used lipsticks, second-hand boxes of face powder, used underwear, books, smoking pipes, perambulators, blankets, pots and pans, and I saw a set of false teeth offered for sale!

Conditions soon told on many of the older people and I put in several spells of grave-digging in the cemetery, which had now been cleared up and put in beautiful shape by a band of tireless workers. It seemed to me a disgrace that the graves of those early colonists had been neglected for so long by a local government which certainly never lacked funds.

Hong Kong is a beautiful colony of the British Crown and a great credit to those who developed it from a barren island which even the Chinese could not conceive as being of use.

But in spite of the great wealth of its trading concerns and the enormous volume of trade which had poured through its fine harbour to swell the coffers of its treasuries and banks, Hong Kong, at that time, still lacked a good public library, a town hall worthy of its position, and did not even provide a building for its art treasures. It was more interested in its race course, its golf links and its clubs.

I boiled ricve, dug graves, studied the stars, learnt how to lay bricks, wrote quantities of bad poetry, listened to concerts, tried to teach certain interested people the elements of the intricate Japanese language, talked law with Frank Loseby, a solicitor, talked animals with Rosa, his charming wife, who operated an animals' home and veterinary surgery, sang at concerts, assisted in producing a play; and when a year had passed since the surrender

I received word that Kaneko had been shipped to Japan and was living in Osaka.

One morning, in April, 1943, I was told to pack my kit. At the camp office a host of friends saw me off escorted by a Japanese major. I was sorry in many ways to leave the many good friends I had made at Stanley, but was eager to join my comrades, and looked forward to hearing how they had fared and being able to relay the tidings from Stanley to husbands, fathers, brothers, sweethearts and friends.

Chapter Twenty-three

I

HONG KONG was so very quiet. The streets which once teemed with life were now almost deserted.

We stopped at Blake Pier where I saw several Chinese boatmen who recognized me. One had served in the Navy as a mess boy and gave me a cheerful wink and the V sign.

The Japanese prison camp headquarters was situated just outside the Argylle Street officers' prisoner of war camp and as we went inside I spotted two or three old friends standing by the wire and had time to give them a wave of the hand.

Leaving me in charge of a sergeant the Major then left the room to return in a few moments with a very grim look, ordered me to stand to attention and in a very loud voice, delivered an oration:

"You have caused a great deal of trouble to the authorities by taking up the matter of your transfer from Stanley, which has been referred to Tokyo. You should have appreciated being in Stanley; you are ungrateful. You must apologize for all the trouble you have caused and be grateful to the Japanese Army for acceding to your request."

He then smiled, held out his cigarette case, and asked if I were hungry. I was given a plate of curry and rice and expected that any moment I would be taken to join my friends, and soon be exchanging experiences.

But the Major beckoned me to gather my kit and we drove into Nathan Road and soon entered Shamsuipo, a camp for all ranks, which had been a barracks of the regular Hong Kong garrison.

In the camp office I was handed over to a Lieutenant Wada, and given a document to sign which was in effect my promise not to attempt to escape on pain of being shot or bayoneted to death. I signed this because I knew that all prisoners had been ordered to do so by our own authorities, after a long and unpleasant period during which many were severely punished and victimized for their proper contention that a prisoner of war by any civilized standards has, as his principal duty to his country, to try and escape from captivity by any means.

Wada, the camp commandant, told me that he had been aboard the ill-fated *Lisbon Maru*.

I was then taken to another office where I made the acquaintance of a British officer who was the administrative official appointed by the Japanese, an effeminate looking individual, well-shaved, powdered and perfumed, and well-uniformed, with a slender waist which seemed to indicate that he used corsets. He did not seem to be at all pleased that I spoke a little Japanese. His nickname was "Queenie". My kit was inspected and he warned me concerning my behaviour in the camp and said that there were far too many trouble-makers.

And then I was behind the wire and in a small stone room surrounded by dozens of old friends, again the hero of the hour, a chap from other parts who might have bits and pieces of news to add spice to their humdrum lives.

Captain Campbell, R.N., the senior naval officer, was a grand person who had left retirement, in which he had been happily rearing pigs and playing golf, to serve his country. But he was not physically fit and lived in a section of the camp known as the "Old Men's Home".

It was heartwarming to be able to meet the husbands, fathers, sweethearts and friends, of those I had known at Stanley, all so eager for news of their beloved ones. But in some cases it was embarrassing to be compelled to lie for the sake of helping someone retain his illusions.

II

Some kind soul produced a camp bed and I spent a couple of hours trying to eradicate the bed bugs which simply swarmed out of every crevice. A sailor was appointed as batman who collected my food and made himself generally useful.

I had my first meal with a major-paymaster, Captain Green, an R.C. chaplain, and Cliff Weber, captain, Middlesex Regiment, who had procured the trucks with which we had been able to victual the men in Murray Barracks from Aberdeen, and was introduced to the famous water heater and electric hot-plate.

Water was heated and special food cooked with guards posted at the doors to watch out for the infamous interpreter known as "Slap Happy", a Canadian *nisei* who later was to pay for his crimes by being hanged. He claimed Canadian citizenship, but this did not save him, for he participated in the murder of a Portuguese.

The heater was simply a cigarette tin with an electric lead. You merely plunged this into water and turned the switch, and you had hot water in three minutes. If you were in a hurry you just tossed in a pinch of salt and had hot water instantaneously. The hot-plate was made of barbed wire. The bars glowed a bright red and one always wondered when the whole camp electric circuit would fuse. But none cared. The camp engineers could soon fix it up, and one just had to lay off cooking for a while.

Some had water-heaters made from 7-lb jam tins which with a pinch of salt would heat a large bath in five minutes. These things really drove the Japanese frantic. I had many, and as fast as they were confiscated we made others.

For my first meal we had fried duck eggs as a special treat. Hong Kong is famous for its walkie-walkie ducks. There were thousands out in the New Territories at Taipo, and the eggs were sold in the camp canteen. Father Green did the cooking and the wire heated, glowed, and plinged and planged until I thought that any minute there would be an explosion.

I was also introduced to "Green Horror". A soup of greens of most doubtful origin which tasted hateful.

Afterwards we walked four or five abreast on the parade-ground. There the camp characters were pointed out to me. There was one chap who used to walk up and down for hours telling himself stories and laughing long and loud at his own jokes.

There was another with a long beard known as Jesus Christ.

Major Ashton-Rose, the senior medical officer, a fine figure of a man was doing a splendid job. There was a great deal of sickness, especially beri-beri, one form of which was known as "electric feet". The sufferers from this unpleasant disease were to be seen with their feet in buckets of water for this was the only way they could obtain relief and, for most of them, sleep was impossible, and the lack of it was testified by their sunken eyes and ghastly pallor. Ashton-Rose was getting along very well indeed with the Japanese authorities and in his own way had managed to amass supplies of most valuable medicines and equipment which were to save a great many lives.

The colonel in charge of Hong Kong POW camps was a fat individual known as the "Pig".

"I do not care, indeed I hope you all die," was the retort of this former dean of a famous university in response to protests over the shocking conditions in the camp hospital. The "Pig" lived in a splendid house near the officers' camp with his Chinese mistress, but every Saturday she contrived to send parcels from his store to her old friends in the Argylle Street and Shamsuipo camps.

At the end of the parade ground was a hall which was used as a church on Sundays and as a concert and assembly hall during the week. The camp orchestra was engaged in practice and from what one could hear it contained some excellent musicians and I looked forward to hearing some good music.

I felt happier that night than at any time since the surrender. Kaneko was in Japan, where I was sure she would be well cared for by her family, and the Swiss, who were looking after British interests; and I was among servicemen, and many, many friends.

III

There was speculation about the next draft for Japan. I heard in detail concerning those who had been in the ill-fated *Lisbon Maru*, but none knew about survivors. Just prior to my arrival at Shamsuipo, a draft which contained many friends had left for Japan aboard the fine NYK luxury liner *Kamakura Maru*, the former *Titibu Maru*.

It would indeed be a strange trick of fate were I to return to Japan as a prisoner!

The next morning I took my place on the parade ground for

"*tenko*"* at the head of the combined naval and merchant service units. Lined up were the Royal Navy, the Royal Rifles of Canada, under their fine colonel, John Price, the Winnipeg Grenadiers, the Royal Air Force, the Middlesex Regiment, the Royal Scots, the Royal Engineers, the Royal Army Service Corps, and the Hong Kong Volunteer Defence Corps.

After our breakfast of "Green Horror" and mouldy rice, or if a supply had come perhaps a duck's egg, the gardeners went off to their gardens, the fatigue details to cleaning up the camp, and others to all manner of activities. There were always dozens of fellows trying to de-bug their beds.

Philip Samuel, the son of Lord Samuel, a member of the Hong Kong Volunteer Defence Corps, was conducting a reading circle for the patients in the dysentery ward of the camp hospital and I readily agreed to join him in this work and started to search for suitable material.

There was a continous witch hunt in progress for radio receiving sets. Slap Happy would appear at all hours of the day and night, usually accompanied by two British prisoners. I did not know the location of these radio sets until years later and learned that I used regularly to sit on one in the hut of Captain "Chippy" Woods of the Royal Army Service Corps, who had it concealed under a chair.

There were some excellent artisans and inventors, wood-carvers, artists, engineers, painters, scientists, electricians and, given the material, they could make almost anything. There was a 'cello made by a Canadian out of an iron petrol drum. This had a sweet and full tone and was used in the camp orchestra and I understand that it now reposes in a museum in Canada. Some of the men made rugs out of pieces of old stockings, old shirts, and all kinds of odds and ends. One handsome, embroidered piece, made by men of the Middlesex Regiment, was a roll of honour containing the names of those of their battalion who had fallen in the fighting at Hong Kong, woven out of woollen stockings and scraps in red, gold and blue, and which bore a fine large regimental crest. Later this was presented as a souvenir to the Reverend Junsho Hayashi, of Kyoju-in, Zenkoji, Nagano City, who was a captain in charge of POW camps in the Yokohama area where he was affectionately known to the prisoners as "Heidelberg Henry".

In 1951, during the Korean War, the Reverend Hayashi having learned that the Middlesex Regiment was serving in Korea, asked me to arrange the return of the roll of honour to the regiment and when Colonel Mann, of the 2nd Battalion, was on leave in Tokyo, I presented it to him on Hayashi's behalf. He was most grateful and it now reposes in the regimental headquarters at Mill Hill, near London.

* Roll call.

IV

Several officers and men, as well as civilians at Stanley like Fraser, the kindly Scotsman who'd been in charge of defence, were beheaded by the *"kempei"* for attempting or allegedly planning escapes. Flight-Lieutenant "Dolly" Grey RAF, was an old friend and the camp sports officer who'd been wireless officer on the record-breaking flight from Ismailia, in Egypt, to Australia in 1938, and had operated the wireless station at Sheko, on Hong Kong Island until the Japanese were but twenty-five yards away. Grey had also escorted Kaneko and the dogs from Kai Tak when the RAF evacuated their base.

One afternoon, when several of us including "Dolly" were talking, a Japanese told him to get ready to go out of camp for the purpose of buying sports equipment. It was the last we saw of him. He was beheaded. Apparently a mass escape was being planned and messages passed between Shamsuipo and Argylle Street by the ration truck. A tiny piece of paper containing a message dropped in the street from the truck was picked up by an Indian and handed over to the Japanese.

A Canadian sergeant named Arthur was a swarthy, sturdy fellow with a fine, wavy moustache and one's idea of a Hollywood Mexican bandit chief. He spoke Japanese, having studied at Waseda University for about a year, had a fine baritone voice and a fund of the most lurid jokes. Twice a week Arthur went to the Kai Tak airport as interpreter with a working party of prisoners who spent the day cutting the grass, and he suggested that I now take turn about with him as it was a good day's outing and one got double rations.

About fifty of us, and four or five Japanese guards, left camp at about 6 a.m., marched down to the pier nearby and boarded a ferry boat. Cooks brought along the food and a small field kitchen. Earlier the working parties had been on excavations for enlarging the airport. This had been back-breaking and terrible for men in poor physical condition. My friend, John Abbott, a barrister in civil life, had refused to perform this labour, not only on account of being an officer, but because it was contributing to the Japanese war effort and strictly against the Geneva Convention covering treatment of prisoners of war. John was sent for by the "Pig", given a cigarette and a cup of tea, and then asked to voice his complaint.

"Why do you refuse the orders of the Japanese Army?" he was asked.

"Because, in the first place I am an officer and cannot be made to do manual labour, and in the second place that work is contributing to the Japanese war effort."

The Colonel took off his sword and hit John a smack over the head, which knocked him to the ground. He then left the room without another word and his aide-de-camp gave the surprised John another cup of tea.

But the work at Kai Tak was now a farce. When we marched to the airport from the Kai Tak pier, along the road were the wives and sweethearts of many, with small parcels of food, cigarettes and other comforts, who knew their men were on the detail through the Japanese guards who told me they did not mind the men talking to their women or even receiving parcels from them, as long as officers or NCOs did not see.

We set up our field kitchen, and the men were issued scythes and spread out to cut the grass. But they did not do any cutting, as long as no unpleasant NCOs or officers were around.

A number of Chinese women were working on the construction of bays to protect aircraft against bombing attacks. They were the usual working type and wore jackets and trousers made of that material which looks like oilskin. Many of our men seemed on most friendly terms with these ladies and would go off and spend a few minutes with them in the bomb bays out of sight of prying eyes.

A sergeant commenting on the amorous activities said to me: "God knows how they do it on this food, sir."

"Yes, sergeant," I replied. "The charms of that assortment of unwashed women would not, I think, move me even though someone filled me with a charge of dynamite, or though I might be dead drunk!"

There was not much movement in the harbour. A Japanese hospital ship was alongside one wharf and we had noticed armed men embarking. Masts and spars of sunken ships jutted up through the blue waters and just off the airport was a sunken Soviet vessel. This had been one of the first ship victims which had been used as a screen by the Japanese in their first attempts to cross the harbour and had received the concentrated fire of British guns from the naval dockyard.

The masts and superstructure of HMS *Tamar*, a relic of the old days of steam and sail, were still visible. She was scuttled during the siege. An interesting reminder of other days, she had been used as a depot ship, but in the early days of the century had been employed as a naval prison.

We returned to our camp that evening refreshed in body and mind. A good day had been experienced by all, including our guards, who had been kind and considerate in every way.

v

The camp hospital buildings were in a shocking condition and better fitted for pigs than human beings and the lime-washed walls produced the effect of a cattle pen.

Practically all the patients were sufferers from beri-beri and particularly that form which had been christened "electric feet". A strange peculiarity of this complaint was that it was experienced only at Shamsuipo Camp and not at the other camps in the area, and was most perplexing to the medical authorities.

Dysentery was the other terrible scourge, and the sufferers were segregated in a special ward which I visited to read to the patients as one of Philip Samuel's team.

There were usually about fifty inmates, all of whom were in a serious condition. The stench was horrible; light, because of the black-out, came from low-power bulbs shielded with cigarette tins, and you had to sit directly below one which provided just a circle on your book.

The spirit of those sufferers was wonderful, they joked about their condition, they even had bets on who would die first. None complained unreasonably, and all were conscious of the fact that everything humanly possible was being done by Ashton-Rose and his orderlies to get them well.

I read them thrillers, stories by Poe, Maugham, Edgar Wallace and Wodehouse and it was most rewarding when they laughed out loud, although this may have aggravated the condition of their weakened bowels. The greatest success I had was with a story, hardly appropriate in such circumstances, which I read from *Esquire* magazine, entitled—"The Morticians, Embalmers, and Funeral Decorators Convention at Niagara Falls." This really had them rolling with laughter and I was implored to read it time and again.

On April 29th—the birthday of the Emperor of Japan—the Japanese issued us with parcels sent by the British Red Cross Society as if these were a special bounty from their Sovereign. These were magnificent, and contained jam, sugar, meat puddings, tea, cocoa, milk and other delicacies.

We also received a shipment of a cereal from India which made a very fine porridge and also did a great deal of good to those suffering from beri-beri.

Apart from the *tenko* parades and inspections by visiting officials from Tokyo, the Japanese did not interfere with us very much.

We played volley-ball and soft-ball, had three-day cricket matches and other sports.

Slap Happy was just a moron and I suspected that he was an informer to the *"kempei"*. But we soon had him under an obligation for one night he came to my room and asked if I would do him a favour. It appeared that he had contracted a venereal disease which was giving him a great deal of pain and, scared to go to a Japanese army doctor, he desired me to take him to Major Ashton-Rose. The doctor diagnosed his complaint as being very serious indeed and started his treatment that night. It looked extremely painful. After this, Slap Happy was quite subdued and gave little trouble.

After that I received many requests to escort Japanese soldier sufferers from "ladies' disease" to our genial medical officer, and it was from these grateful patients that the doctor obtained many valuable drugs from town. And so, the street walkers of Kowloon rendered a great service to the prisoners of war in Shamsuipo and it was jokingly said by many that these roving young women had inflicted more casualties on the Japanese Army than the entire British defence force.

Each evening we'd line up for our daily shower bath which was situated outside the camp canteen. It was an extraordinary sight with lines of men of every shape, size and colour, and most of them naked, although modest types wore Japanese *fundoshi*—loin cloths—which were issued us each month, together with a small towel, tooth powder and a toothbrush.

Cockney humour was always absolutely irrepressible even in the most difficult and ridiculous circumstances. I was standing in line for my shower one evening and immediately in front of me was a huge fellow extremely well proportioned in his productive organs. A Cockney voice from behind me chuckled: "You can see he never had no toys to play with when he was a baby!"

VI

One day in May, 1943, I was ordered to the camp office, outside of which were lined up a very odd assortment. British, Americans, Dutch, Chinese, Eurasian, Portuguese, Russian, Turkish, Czechoslovakian, Hungarian, Spanish, Jamaican, Cuban, West African negroes, short and tall, fat and thin, ebony, brown, yellow and white.

We boarded a truck and were soon spinning down Nathan Road waving to the girls—for there were always numbers of girl friends of prisoners at the entrance to the camp—and pulled up at prison headquarters at Argylle Street.

In a large room there were four or five Japanese wearing long white coats and masks. "My God," said a soldier, "They are going to bloody well castrate us!"

"What did that man say?" said one of the Japanese.

"Oh, he thinks you might be going to remove some rather important accessories of his body," I replied. He did not quite understand and so I repeated it in Japanese.

Those Japanese exploded with laughter, one beckoned him to come forward and, to his surprise, nicked his ear with a sharp knife, the blood from which he put in a test-tube. We all had this treatment, were then weighed and measured all over, our teeth were inspected, even our privates, and all the time one of the Japanese would be making notes on filing cards.

The Japanese have a passion for useless statistics and unnecessary paper work, and filling in forms. Millions must be wasted each year in their institutions through this, and I always grieve to think of all the trees which have to be felled for such a useless purpose. I wonder if the information they obtained that day was of any practical use? But we did not mind in the least; for it was a day's outing and quite a picnic to brighten our humdrum lives.

The main topic with everyone at this time was the next draft for Japan. Most were anxious for a move and I was continually asked my opinion concerning the treatment they might expect. Hong Kong was hot for the greater part of the year. It was not a good climate for men on short rations and, as it was no longer practicable to escape, I felt sure that removal to Japan would be best for all of us. The very senior officers had by this time been sent to Formosa and the Governor, Sir Mark Young, to Shanghai.

VII

There was to be a super musical show. The Japanese authorities had frowned upon our beauty chorus of handsome young men dressed as girls. But their attitude had changed and every co-operation was given in assisting to provide the producers with women's clothing.

New songs were written to new music, there were parodies on hymns, ditties by Cole Porter, Noël Coward, and Rodgers and Hammerstein, scenery was painted, and rehearsals went on all day long. Our beauty chorus and our female star, a certain Hong Kong Portuguese lad named Sonny Castro, were terrific, and would have packed the house at normal admission prices.

I was the master of ceremonies and, for the opening night, we were to have the attendance of the senior Japanese military officer and his staff. For their benefit our band rehearsed a medley of Japanese tunes—*Kojo no Tsuki, Sakura Sakura*, and others. I suggested to Sonny Castro, the leading lady, that when they finished their high kicking number he threw a bouquet at the senior Japanese officer.

"Suppose he takes offence," he said. "They'll probably chop my head off!"

"Go on, Sonny," said one of his friends. "The old bugger will probably put you in his harem with all his geisha girls."

I assured Sonny that all would be well and that the gesture would be appreciated by the audience. So we made a bouquet of artificial flowers which felt a little heavy, and I hoped that Sonny would not throw it too hard and with too good aim.

The house was packed and the Japanese came in full force, and I introduced things with a short speech in Japanese, during which I nearly fell off the stage.

Our girls were a tremendous hit; they could dance and sing well, looked quite fascinating. As they finished their final number I tossed the bouquet to Sonny and he timidly flung it into the audience. It struck a Japanese smack on the nose. The house roared its approval, and the Japanese seemed delighted.

From start to finish it was a first-class show which few professional companies could have bettered. The orchestra might have been that of the London Palladium, striking out a zimmy-to-zam beat which set the senses glowing and toes tapping, and at any moment one expected that Flanagan and Allen might be on stage. It was all good, robust, lavatory humour—just what the lads needed, and all joined in singing "Roll me over", "Take me back to dear old Blighty", "Long, Long Trail", "Swannee", "Sidewalks of New York", and other favourites. It would have packed houses any-where—if it could have passed censorship—and was such a great success that the producers immediately made plans for a next show.

None enjoyed it more than a frequent visitor from Argylle Street named Matsuda, a delightful man whom we affectionately called *Cardiff Joe* because he spoke English with a Welsh accent. Joe had been an officer in British merchant ships and was for many years manager at Cardiff for the Yamashita Steamship Com-pany. He'd left Britain in the autumn of 1940 during the blitz, and provided us with much first-hand news of how our folk were standing up to Hermann Goering's much-vaunted Luftwaffe, for whom he had a healthy hate.

Chapter Twenty-four

I

ONE day "Cardiff Joe" said: "Well, I understand that you are to come with me on the draft to Japan!"

Five hundred men were selected, plus a Canadian chaplain, a doctor, Captain Howard Bush, Canadian Army Service Corps, one company officer each from the Royal Rifles of Canada and the Winnipeg Grenadiers, and myself.

All manner of rumours were in circulation concerning our transport. Some said that a large passenger liner was already at the pier. They all anticipated another *Kamakura Maru* and by the attitude of some, you would have fancied they were off on a luxury cruise round the world.

Those on draft were segregated. One of my new room-mates was a captain in the Winnipeg Grenadiers, a six-footer, who in civilian life was an undertaker and embalmer. He told us the most hair-raising stories of his trade. Of how he once flew from Canada to Mexico to embalm the wife of a millionaire who'd been dead for some days and had not been put in a refrigerator. He'd had to pump her full of paraffin wax, paint her face, and fit her out in a wedding costume, and then fly back to Canada with her. According to him people often spent more money on their wives when they were dead than when alive, even to the extent of putting them in their coffins with new and valuable jewellery and costly new clothes.

A few days later all officers but myself were withdrawn from the draft, leaving us without benefit of a doctor.

There were now about four hundred and twenty Canadians, fifty assorted British; army service corps, engineers, ordnance, artillery; a few Royal Air Force, some British military policemen and the Dutch submarine crew, a total of five hundred and one.

Colonel John Price, of the Royal Rifles, and the commanding officer of the Winnipeg Grenadiers hated parting from the men and desired very much to accompany us. I promised I would do my level best for their welfare, but I did not like the idea of going off with so many unfit to travel.

Just after dawn on August 25th, 1943, we assembled on the parade ground for our march to the pier at Kowloon docks, the men dressed as best they were able, some with their buttons shining and uniforms pressed. But there were many who could hardly walk, were without boots, and stumbled about in home-made wooden clogs.

We formed up in units, myself at the head of the column, and at 7 o'clock marched through the gate out on to the main road. Two trucks brought up the rear with our kit and these were soon filled with those unable to walk.

A Royal Air Force warrant officer marched beside me and I told him to get the men whistling and in step and show the people that we were by no means downhearted. They started whistling "Roll out the Barrel", and were soon marching as though on a parade ground. The route was lined with Japanese soldiers, Indian police, and a *"kempei"* car kept ahead of us. As soon as we reached Nathan Road people swarmed out of the neighbouring streets and thronged the side-walks, despite the efforts of the police to keep them away. Men were shouting at their girls, answering queries of women who wanted news of their loved ones, and the *"kempei"* and guards soon gave up trying to do anything about it, and before long there was a regular column marching with us till we passed through the gates of the Kowloon wharves and on to the pier where a fine large vessel was waiting. She looked beautiful, a modern motor vessel of the OSK line. "Cardiff Joe" was now marching beside me and as we drew abreast of the gangway I slowed my pace, expecting that he would soon give us the word to halt. But we marched on and there, dwarfed by the OSK ship, was a dirty vessel lying at the end of the pier with a white feather of steam at her funnel.

Manryu Maru was a cargo ship of about 1,000 tons, recently salvaged from the bottom of Hong Kong harbour, and built as a river steamer for the run between Hong Kong and Canton! With her shallow draught, I shuddered to think what she was going to be like in a heavy sea.

All down the ranks one could hear a steady moan as the men caught sight of this miserable craft. She lay well below the wharf so that you could jump down on her decks and no time was lost in getting us aboard with half the men going down the fore-hatch and the others aft. She was half-filled with coal and the only air and light provided came down the wooden gangways on top of which were rough wooden covers. When all the men were below there was just about room, provided they did not lie full length anywhere.

"Cardiff Joe" escorted me to a cabin on the main deck and told me that I should use this and, if I liked, share it with Arthur and as many of the senior non-commissioned officers as I pleased. I realized this was his accommodation and asked him what he was going to do?

"Now don't worry about me, I'll sleep on the saloon settee," he replied.

The sun was now high and from out of the holds poured a steady stream of curses.

Then the "Pig" came on board with his staff, including the handsome major who had brought me over from Stanley, and a captain named Ito, who was to be in charge of us on the voyage. The guards were Koreans or Formosans.

The "Pig" told me that we would be well-treated in Japan *if we were sincere* and gave us the sickly hypocritical admonition to look after our health. The Major expressed his concern over the physical condition of the men and said that many of them should not have been selected.

"I hope we get them all to Japan alive," I replied.

As my deputy I appointed an elderly chief warrant officer of the ordnance corps, who was next to myself in seniority. The RAF warrant officer was placed in charge of the after-hold and a Canadian sergeant-major in charge of the fore-hold. Arthur and an RAF corporal medical orderly named Edmunds were to share the cabin with me and we decided that it should also be our surgery and first-aid post.

"Joe" told me that Ito had given orders for the holds to be battened down and all to be below whilst the ship was leaving harbour, and that we should remain in the room.

"It is going to be hell down those holds," he said, "but I'll get windsails rigged as soon as we get clear." He grinned at me. "Sorry we've got such a bloody coffin to travel in, but the skipper seems a good fellow and you can rely on me to do my best. I'll get those holds open and have you out on deck as soon as I can."

We sat in the darkened room discussing matters.

"I feel sea-sick already," said Arthur. "I always feel sick even when I look at the bloody sea."

"Fat lot of bloody good you're going to be," snorted Edmunds. "With half the buggers sick and lots of tough boys to make trouble we are going to have a muckin' fine cruise."

"Well, it doesn't matter much," said Arthur. "For we'll probably catch a Yankee torpedo like the *Lisbon*."

"Never torpedo this scow," I replied, "a tin-fish would pass right under her bottom."

We could hear the engines turning over and wires being hauled along the iron decks.

"All aboard the 'Skylark'—next stop Southend Pier!" cracked Edmunds.

"The next bloody pier's going to be Nagasaki or Moji," snorted Arthur, "and the sooner the better I'm thinking."

II

We had stripped to our *fundoshi* when "Joe" let us out to gulp the good sea breeze and were now clear of Lyemoon Pass and heading out to sea between the islands which I knew so well through my patrols in MTB 08 and other vessels of the Hong Kong Navy, and last in line of a convoy of some seven vessels escorted by a single destroyer. The latrines were at the stern of the vessel and we organized a line of men from each hold so that they might relieve themselves and get a breath of air. A soldier came on deck and threw his hat over the side. "I never thought I'd have to do it in my hat," he said, with a grin.

Edmunds and the Canadian medical orderly were soon in demand and in no time we had some fifty men prostrate on deck. Some were seriously ill, especially three or four who had just been released from hospital to catch the draft. "Joe" saw Captain Ito to request that all be allowed to stay on deck. He would not agree, but said that twenty of the most seriously sick could remain.

The galley was on the after-deck opposite the latrines. Practically every man wanted to be a cook so that he'd be out of the stinking holds for the major part of the day; but we had to use those with experience in the camp. Sacks of weevilly, broken rice had been put aboard, as well as a very small quantity of meat and quite a lot of fish. The latter was stored in a lazarette on the poop and was already smelling foul.

For our first meal we had a gluey mess of rice with whatever we had managed to buy from the canteen. I was just starting to eat when Arthur grabbed my mess tin and his own and Edmunds' and disappeared on deck. We stared at each other. Arthur was a queer customer and we guessed that he was on to some racket or other.

He returned in a few minutes and handed us our tins packed full of quite good rice, winked, stuck his fork into his tin and brought out a large piece of fried steak. It was the most delicious piece of meat I'd had in nearly two years.

"Chink cook used to work in Blue Funnel boats out of Liverpool," he explained. "Says he'll do us all right."

I felt a bit guilty considering that the rest of the men had no such luxuries.

We had been joined by the RAF warrant officer. "Don't worry about them, sir," he said. "They are already negotiating with the Chinese crew."

I finished my food and went down the after hold. The atmosphere was foul and overpowering. There was not enough space to walk anywhere, even though large numbers of men were in the chain leading to the latrines.

I went back on deck. There appeared to be three Japanese deck officers, two wireless operators, and two engineers, Captain Ito, a sergeant-major named Sato, a corporal, about twenty guards, and Cardiff Joe. The rest were Chinese.

We were now well astern of the convoy, and the destroyer was no longer in sight. Out to port could be seen the rocky outline of the China coast. "You know, sir," said the Canadian sergeant, "we could pinch this bloody ship and run her into China."

"Yes, we could if it were not for all those poor buggers," said Edmunds, pointing to the men lying exhausted on the hatches, "and if that bloody destroyer was not around."

The crew were now engaged in fitting windsails for the holds and Joe was on the bridge engaged in conversation with the captain of the vessel. They were joined by Captain Ito and seemed to be engaged in some sort of argument in which the ships captain and Joe seemed at issue with the army man.

Joe came down on deck smiling. "The skipper's a good fellow;

The author (front, second left), Lieutenant Kilbee, crew of MTB 08 with special passengers, Hong Kong, October 1941

Group of POWs at Omori Camp, Tokyo, 1943. (Back row, left to right) Tom Quillan, RN; John Abbott, Middlesex Regiment; Gordon Braden, Australian Army; Harry Parker, RN; the author; Peter Frankcom, AEC; "Mac", Australian Army; "Hank", USAAF; Eric Marsden, Royal Signals; "Clarkie", US Navy. (Front row) "General", Royal Artillery; a US officer; "Sedgy" Hinson, US Army; "Mr. Brown"; Brian Penlington, Royal Engineers; a US officer; Bert Rees, Royal Engineers

Admiral Sir Bruce Fraser, Commander-in-Chief British Pacific Fleet talking with RN personnel (including author, wearing black peaked hat) aboard the US hospital ship after their liberation from Prison Camp No. 2, August 1945

The author with the late Prince Chichibu, Gotemba, 1946

The entrance to the home of the author at Inamura

he's going to rig hoses outside the latrines so that the men can have salt showers when they come on deck."

"That's going to help a lot, Joe, and please thank the skipper for me," I said. "Give me a seafaring man every time!"

Towards evening the *Manryu Maru* started a steady roll. But there was a fine cool breeze which was drunk in hungrily by the parched and sweaty men. Arthur lay outside the cabin complaining that his stomach was turning inside out.

"I'll get a nice piece of fat pork from that Chink cook, fasten it to a piece of string, and you can swallow it and then pull it in and out," said Edmunds. "Finest cure of all for seasickness."

"Fine," replied Arthur, "and we can pass it round the ship and all have a go at it, and the last man can keep it in his belly, string and all."

"I'm convinced we could pinch this bloody ship," said Shepherd, "were it not for the sick."

"Well don't bloody well broadcast your opinion," cautioned White. "Joe's next door in the saloon. He can hear every word if he is listening."

"Well, we've got twenty-four sleeping on deck, there are at least sixty below who might be dead tomorrow in this heat, and you can reckon on another hundred who'd be useless in a scrap," whispered Edmunds. I beckoned them to come into the room.

"It would have to be tonight, or never," I said. "As I see it, twenty men could rush the bridge, fifty deal with the guards, for although they might get off a few rounds with their rifles we'd soon have them under control."

"One of my chaps says he could put the wireless out of action any time," said Shepherd. "Well, that would have to be done first."

"All right then, just suppose we pinch the bloody ship. Sir, you can navigate, but what about engineers?"

"There are the Dutchmen. They ran a submarine, so I bet they can run this old tub."

"Well come to that, the junior engineers seem to be Chinese and we can bloody well make them keep the wheels turning."

Edmunds returned from a visit to the holds. "Well, what time does your balloon go up?" he inquired with some sarcasm.

"Oh, you're a regular bloody parcel of wind and misery," said Shepherd.

"Now Sarge, do you think I want to spend my young life in a Japanese prison if there's a chance I can get out of it?" inquired the medical orderly.

I left them arguing and went down the lower hold. The foul, hot air struck me like the blast from an open furnace. Many had been sick and the stench was shocking. Few could lie down full length. Some were playing cards, one man was playing a mouth organ, the others just squatted and lolled about jesting, grumbling, cursing or just staring up at the deckhead.

"Gord bloody blimey, sir," said a military policeman. "This muckin' ship will do for all of us if we can't get up on deck." I assured him that we were doing everything possible to get more men on deck, but that preference would have to be given to the sick.

The ordnance warrant officer lay at the foot of the gangway in his own spew. I told the military policeman to get him up to our cabin. The poor devil was ghastly pale, his eyes bloodshot. I stumbled around talking to the men. But despite their sufferings they were by no means downhearted.

I staggered up on deck and went forward. The forehold was a little better. There was slightly more wind being circulated than down the after hatch, but it was still pretty foul. Here conditions were a little more orderly, thanks to the NCOs of the Royal Rifles of Canada. The Dutch were together in a group and seemed to have fixed themselves up better than most. They had more equipment; buckets, washing bowls, and one even had a carved Chinese chest which served as an excellent bench or table.

"Could you run the engines of this ship?" I inquired of the Dutch chief petty-officer. He looked at me incredulously.

"Yah. I could. But . . ."

I motioned him to whisper. "I only wondered." I replied. His eyes were wide open. He looked around at the others, at the mass of sweating men, some of whom were either asleep, or unconscious.

"I understand you, sir, but we could not do it with this crowd."

"All right, forget it," I replied.

"Yah, but I could run the engines."

When I returned to the room I found Joe with Edmunds and White. The ordnance warrant officer was lying out on the deck. "You'd better have a sick parade first thing in the morning," Joe said, "and I'll get Captain Ito to be present so that he can see for himself what a bunch of invalids we have on our hands."

"Yes, we'll do that, Joe, but can't you get him to allow more men up tonight. The deck will easily take another hundred or so."

"No, I have already tried. He's not a bad chap, but he's scared. I don't think he likes the guard very much. I, too, think they are a useless bunch of bastards."

We were talking in pitch darkness. Joe was sitting on the steam-pipe casing. I hoped that none, who might not see him there, would mention the idea of seizing the ship, which I had by now convinced myself was almost entirely out of the question. Just then I saw a dark shape astern. It was the escort destroyer and she crept up and passed barely fifty yards away. That settled it. After tonight we would be too far off the China coast. Arthur stirred and struck a match.

"Put that bloody match out," snapped Joe. "Do you want a torpedo just to make you a little more cheerful?"

"Sorry, Matsuda San," he replied.

"I remember the last time I came up to Japan. It was a French boat. There was a lovely piece of tail I was square-pushing. Boy what a girl!" mused Arthur.

"Regular bloody old Casanova, aren't you, Arthur?" jeered Edmunds.

All was now quiet, except for the steady thump, thump of the engines, which seemed to sing Na-ga-sa-ki, Na-ga-sa-ki, the swirl of the bow wave, and the occasional scrape of a shovel from the stokehole. Arthur had started to snore.

III

From dawn a steady stream of men poured out from the holds to the latrines and the showers. One of the Canadian sergeants approached me and said: "What about getting the Japanese to issue that fish, sir? It's really starting to stink something terrible." I spoke to Joe, who called the supply corporal. The latter was little more than a boy named Fukushima and because Joe was a civilian he proved difficult and said he would issue the fish when he thought fit and no sooner. "Nasty little bastard," said Joe, "I'd like to put my boot right up his arse!" I agreed that nothing would give me greater pleasure.

Sick parade was a sorry affair and I sat there as a steady stream of claimants for the right to sleep on deck filed past and were examined by Edmunds and his Canadian partner. Edmunds took me aside, and said: "There are too many of these buggers swinging the lead, sir. You just watch me and I'll give you the wink when a lead-swinger appears." Captain Ito watched proceedings and the outcome was that he agreed to allow fifty men to sleep and stay on deck and a constant stream to proceed to the latrines and showers.

The Chinese cook continued to help us out with our rations but there were no more lumps of fried meat. It was the old Shampsuipo "Green Horror" all over again. But we did have plenty of black tea which was always refreshing, even without sugar.

That evening Joe told me that we should be putting in at Keelung, in Formosa, for bunkers, and were due there the next afternoon. "I'll see what I can do for you when we get there," he said. "I think there's plenty of bananas and pomelo to be had and fruit would be the best medicine for these chaps." I told White to collect a small sum from each man who had any money or was willing to subscribe towards buying supplies. This RAF warrant officer was a splendid type who knew how to command respect and treated me with every consideration.

Sergeant-Major Shepherd became seriously ill, was bilious, ran a high temperature, and complained of severe pains in the stomach. Edmunds was very grave. "The poor old sergeant's very bad, sir," he said, "and I just don't know what's the matter with him. He might have appendicitis on top of beri-beri."

Shepherd was a veteran of World War I, a strict disciplinarian who'd stand no nonsense from anyone and a power of strength as, indeed, were most of the NCOs.

The next day we went very short of food. We'd eaten what small supply we had been able to buy from the canteen and late in the afternoon it was found that water from a leaking hose had ruined the remaining rice. When this was discovered the supply corporal, Fukushima, released the fish, but it was found to be crawling with maggots and dumped overboard.

Towards evening the skipper called me into the saloon and offered me a meal of salt fish, soup, rice and pickles. I could not accept this, but did take some sake, and sat talking with him and the chief engineer and Captain Ito and Joe. This captain was the usual, decent, seafaring type; the sea is a common leveller of persons, and those who live close to her are invariably broad-minded and kindly in their ways. He had been in most ports of the world and could talk with equal facility of San Francisco, Liverpool, Cardiff, Singapore or Tampico.

"What about a sing-song," suggested Joe. "Must be plenty of your boys who can give us a turn."

The sea was calm, bathed in the glow of sunset. There was not a thing in sight. The convoy must have been miles ahead and the destroyer had probably given up worrying about the *Manryu Maru*. And across the waters of the China Sea rang out the songs of England, Scotland, Ireland and Canada, the USA, and those of Wales.

Joe had a splendid voice; his years in Wales, the land of song, had inspired in him a love of those beautiful and stirring traditional Welsh melodies and he sang "Men of Harlech", "Land of My Fathers", and "All through the Night". There were a couple of mouth organs and an accordion to provide accompaniments, and Arthur sang some very amusing ditties as well as several in Japanese. But Edmunds stole the show with "There's Silver on the Sage Tonight" and "Home on the Range", and his soft tenor voice certainly brought tears to my eyes as I looked about me at those haggard men who listened to the man who, with the Canadian, was doing so much with so little for our sick. That sing-song certainly put new life into them and even brought poor Shepherd to his feet. "Well, wherever you are going, you have the makings of a fine concert party," said Joe.

"Better still if you stay with us," I replied.

"Somewhere around Kobe would suit me," he said. I knew that his wife and child lived in that city. "But not much hope of that. I shall probably be on my way back to Hong Kong within a few days of arrival."

A Canadian soldier, a thin, elderly man, well over fifty years of age, approached and asked if I could get him some old electric lamp bulbs.

"Yes, get him some old bulbs sir," urged one of his companions, "and he'll give you a show."

"What about a bottle?" suggested Joe.

"Well, all right," replied the soldier, whose friends called him Jock.

A Japanese engineer produced a bucket filled with old bulbs and Joe came out of the saloon with an assortment of bottles. And then Jock commenced to astound us all with an exhibition of chewing and swallowing light bulbs, bottles and razor blades; bending keys with his teeth, and all manner of gastronomic acrobatics. The Japanese were astounded and Captain Ito asked if there were no danger of him becoming ill? "I used to do this for a living," said Jock. "Used to make five hundred dollars a week, playing at night clubs in Canada and in the States."

"Well, why on earth did you join the Army at your age?" I inquired. Jock smiled and pulled out a soiled wallet from his pocket from which he extracted a photograph. It was a picture of a young soldier in the uniform of a Canadian Scottish regiment.

"That's why I joined up," said Jock. "That's my boy. He's nineteen. Couldn't have him doing his duty with me at home living on the fat of the land."

"But how on earth can you swallow all that glass and steel?"

"Oh, all sorts of doctors have examined me. They say I've got some kind of a queer inside. Everything goes down and then out. Doesn't even seem to touch the sides."

Captain Ito gave him a few packets of cigarettes, the ship's captain donated some tinned food, and various other gifts were showered on the little Scotch Canadian, which he shared with his friends.

The next morning we sighted the mountainous coast of Formosa and as we came up with the land the old ship seemed to become imbued with new life. Her engines seemed to strike a more vigorous beat. The poor old thing was probably terrified when out of sight of land. Shepherd had improved, but there were half a dozen serious cases which Edmunds said should be in hospital and I asked Joe if their transfer at Keelung to a hospital could be arranged. He seemed doubtful. At mid-day we all had rice bust, —rice without anything to go with it. There were no vegetables of any description, even to make "Green Horror". But we still had plenty of tea and whoever discovered how to use this wonderful leaf certainly had our blessings.

Entering Keelung harbour all were on deck. Just outside the breakwater a large Japanese whaling mother ship had been beached. Her back was broken, there were great holes in her sides, and her superstructure was shot to pieces. She certainly had been in a fight and the fact that her crew had been able to bring her in and beach her was a tribute to their seamanship. This evidence of American naval activity was a great shot in the arm.

We made fast to a buoy just astern of a large German cargo vessel. There were loud boos as we came abreast of her and glimpsed the hated swastika flag. The German officers and crew grinned and seemed highly amused at seeing their enemies in such a plight.

"Grin, you muckin' squareheads," shouted someone. "We'll make you bastards grin all right." A roar of insults were flung

across at the Germans. Joe was smiling, and the rest of the
Japanese seemed to find the situation somewhat amusing.

As soon as the vessel was made fast a launch came alongside.
"Christ! here come the mucking' *'kempei'*," exclaimed Arthur.

The *"kempei"* were not slow in sending for me. They knew all
about me, and Kaneko. Apparently she had passed through
Keelung on her way to Japan and her arrival there had been
reported in the Japanese newspapers. I gathered that we might
be in port for several days. Probably waiting to pick up a convoy.

Now the men were all on deck and seemed much happier. All
they wanted was a good feed.

I walked aft where a crowd of men were shouting insults across
to the Germans standing on the poop of the large German ship.
Two of our men stood outside the latrine with a large bucket. A
small boat with an outboard motor was just leaving the German
vessel carrying three men who looked like ship's officers and which
was making to pass under our stern.

"Stop those fellows playing the fool, sergeant," I ordered. "This
is no time for getting into trouble. And stop them shouting across
at the Jerries. We are trying to get some food and the Japs are not
going to be pleased if there is any trouble."

"You are right, sir," he replied. "But I'd love to empty that
bucket on those nazi bastards."

"Well, they'll be getting their whack in full measure, don't
worry, and they'll be wishing it had been a bucket of crap."

Just before sunset Arthur cried. "Look, here's Joe with the
grub!" Sure enough, Matsuda was standing up in a sampan surrounded by baskets and bales.

"All right, tell the cooks to move lively," he said as he climbed
the accommodation ladder. Joe, God bless him, had ninety-five
pounds of pork, several crates of bananas, two crates of pomeloes,
about five thousand cigarettes, two or three baskets of onions and
carrots as well as a sack of potatoes! I called the NCOs together
to decide how to divide the food.

"Well, it is my opinion," said White, "that we'd better have one
good feed for a start. Let's use fifty pounds of the pork with plenty
of the veg. That's not much to split among five hundred of us, and
it will do the sick a lot of good." All agreed. The result was a
delicious pork stew, the like of which I had never appreciated so
much. All had a fair share of the fruit, and that evening there were
songs and great rejoicing, with every man happily puffing on
tailor-made cigarettes instead of those made of butt-ends and rope
rolled in news- or toilet-paper. And one and all agreed that no
finer man lived than Cardiff Joe.

Chapter Twenty-five

I

THAT night we went to bed as satisfied as prisoners could ever hope to be.

The next morning Joe told me that all would be given a stool test for cholera. At about 11 o'clock a launch pulled alongside and up the accommodation ladder came half a dozen Japanese dressed in white coats, and two young women. I was called into the saloon and Joe explained that each man would have a chopstick inserted up his rectum around the end of which would be wrapped a piece of cotton wool. Whilst this was taking place the man would hold a test tube in his hand in which the chopstick would be placed when the operation had been successfully completed.

"You'd better get yours over now," he said, "and we can then organize the whole business."

I looked at the nurses. Joe laughed, and said: "You are not bashful, are you?" They went outside for my benefit and I submitted myself to the chopstick test with Arthur and other NCOs watching to see the drill. We then organized the men in lines on each side of the deck.

"On the word One," shouted White, "drop your trousers!"

"On the word Two, touch your toes!"

This naturally encouraged a great deal of ribald jests. None liked the idea of the young women being present but they seemed to be part of the team and made notes on cards as each man was attended to.

What humiliated us most of all was the fact that this operation was watched by the Jerries from the nazi ship, who seemed to enjoy it immensely.

"Yes, laugh you muckin' bastards," shouted someone, "we'll test you with rat-tailed files!"

That afternoon Jock entertained the port authorities and the *"kempei"* with some more glass eating, and received boxes of sugared bananas and cigarettes for his efforts.

"I'll soon have a stock of bananas and fags to last me till the end of the bloody war," he said.

The next morning we steamed out of Keelung in a convoy of ten vessels, which included a large oil tanker and the *Asahi Maru*, with a destroyer as escort and aircraft circling overhead. Joe confided that we were bound for Osaka.

"Well, that's fine, Joe. The Hankyu line will soon get you home to Ashiya," I replied.

Osaka! Somewhere in that great, smoky city was Kaneko.

II

It was now a much more orderly convoy and its speed seemed to
have been ordered to suit the slowest vessel, which was obviously
Manryu Maru.

Since arrival at Keelung the sick had shown remarkable improvement, although there were still many who were far from fit,
and some who would perhaps never recover from beri-beri and
other malnutrition complaints. The onions seemed to make a
great deal of difference.

Now that fifty men were allowed to sleep on deck things were
much easier in the holds where each man had his own space.
There had been incidents with bullies and trouble makers but
these had been very quickly settled by a group of NCOs who had
not hesitated to use their fists on the offenders. Arthur had been
particularly useful in this respect.

That night there was a strong breeze and the vessel started
to act very lively. But it was a godsend after the unbearable
hot days we had experienced in Keelung, and the salt spray
which swept the decks did not bother those sleeping there in the
least.

We entered the straits of Shimonoseki on the morning of August
31st. I had been awake since dawn, watching for the first glimpse
of the islands of Nippon.

There were the orderly, terraced hills of Kyushu, the smoking
chimneys of busy Yawata, and all the bustle of the coastwise shipping and fishing boats in and out of the straits.

I could not see an early end in sight to the stupid and costly
war although day by day the resources of Japan were being drained,
her armies stretched out far beyond their sources of supply, the
Allies whipping up production, and for the first time since the
invasion by the hordes of Kublai Khan, the people of Japan faced
the prospect of war being brought right to their own doorsteps.

It had turned out a glorious day and the prisoners poured out
of the holds to feast their eyes on the scenery.

"Well, what do you know! Millionaires pay good dollars for a
cruise like this!" cried a Canadian.

"Garn, but you don't catch the muckers on a trip like this.
They're all at home stacking up the dollars to buy their tarts mink
coats."

Steaming through the Inland Sea was really pleasant. It seemed
to revive even the very sick and depressed, and Shepherd had
vastly improved under the attention of the medical orderlies and
as a result of the liberal ration of onions. Arthur was no longer
grumbling about the sea, which he seemed to hate, and he sang
and joked, and even indulged in wrestling with one of the more
robust Canadians in Japanese *Sumo* style.

III

There were very strong tides in the Inland Sea, the weather had taken a turn for the worse and it was not until the afternoon of September 2nd that we steamed alongside a wharf at Chiko, Osaka.

There was very little activity in the harbour. On the wharf a number of Japanese officers and soldiers were awaiting us and instructions were shouted for us to get ready for immediate disembarkation.

As each man filed down the gangway, many had to be carried, there was a hurried medical inspection. A Japanese medical officer said, "Who selected these men? Most of them are not fit to work."

I was told to arrange for the Canadians and Dutch to parade on the wharf separately from the British, and that I should head the Canadian unit, and Chief Warrant Officer White the British When we were lined up Captain Ito stood on a railway truck and made a speech, said we had behaved ourselves well during the voyage, hoped that we should conduct ourselves properly in the future, and added the stupid warning about anyone trying to escape would be shot or bayoneted to death.

Then Joe stood up and addressed us in English. There was little he could say, but we had all come to love and respect him and if we had not been pestered to get moving I am sure we'd have sung "For He's a Jolly Good Fellow" and chaired him round the wharf. As I shook hands with this fine man, he winked and said, "Keep your pecker up, Bush, things are getting better." It was another three years before I found out the real meaning behind that wink.

Then, led by a stout Japanese army captain and numerous guards, we marched off the wharf and into the streets of Osaka.

Everything looked drab, the roads out of repair. Outside each house or shop some sort of patch had been dug to grow pumpkins which trailed their tentacles everywhere. Passers-by took little notice of us. Occasionally a schoolboy jeered, but I saw no hostility of any sort. The people looked shoddy, the women mostly in *mompei*, the men in the dreary-looking national uniform. None looked particularly happy, despite the fact that, according to Imperial Headquarters, the Japanese were experiencing victories on every front.

Here and there were pitiful apologies for air raid shelters. Looking about me at the flimsy wooden buildings I could imagine what was going to happen once the Americans started their bombings of the Japanese mainland. These thickly populated streets would soon be masses of flames, and no fire fighting equipment in existence could save them.

After marching for some fifteen minutes we came to a street car depot and piled into the waiting cars. Arthur was soon joking with the conductress who looked astounded and almost afraid at being spoken to in her own language by this swarthy moustachioed Canadian, who even used the Osaka dialect. It was now almost dark and the Japanese captain was shouting to the

drivers to get started before the black-out exercise which was
scheduled for that evening.

The men were all in high spirits. Riding in a street car in
Japan of all places was a novelty; but we had not gone far when
we were ordered out and divided into two columns. Arthur went
with one and I with the other. The streets were by now as black
as pitch and we could see ahead only by means of the glistening
tramway lines. We trudged along until we came to an intersec-
tion; here there was a conference among our guards about the way
to the railway station and we soon discovered that half our column
was missing. It was impossible to search for them and the air was
rent with the loud shouts of the guards. By now many of the sick
men could hardly walk and had to be carried by those who were
more or less physically fit. The guards were kind and encouraging,
urging the men to stick it out, and promising that soon they would
get a fine meal. The men were all over the place; on the sidewalks
mixing with the Japanese passers-by, on one side of the road and
the other.

Trucks and bicycles were moving about without lights and to
avoid these we were in a terrible mix-up. The Osaka folk must
have been surprised at this phantom crowd moving about their
city and we must have appeared quite frightening to those who
bumped into us. Finally we came to the plaza of Osaka Station.
Street cars were stopped all over the place and after edging our
way between them I found myself with only five Canadians.

We made for a chink of light and walked through the doors of
Osaka Station unescorted to find fifty or sixty men already there
and the guards shouting and running about all over the place
trying to round up their charges.

There was plenty of light inside, the station was well blacked-
out with curtains and shaded lights, and filled with people.

We assembled outside of the toilets and opposite a store which
was selling postcards and pills and a lot of useless rubbish, and
sat down on our bags and packs while the guards rounded up the
stragglers. Arthur arrived bathed in perspiration. His column
had got on to the wrong road and had been brought back at the
double.

I was now able to take stock of our escorts. The captain, a tall,
sturdy fellow, named Nemoto, a young cadet doctor named Fuji,
and some dozen or so private soldiers together with a soldier
interpreter who confided that we were bound for Niigata!

A small trolley was pushed up by two men, from which they
unloaded *bento*—lunch-boxes—which were immediately distribu-
ted. Each had its wooden chopsticks and considerable amusement
was now provided by the attempts of the men to use these and the
crowds grew thicker and thicker until the guards started to move
them away. The *bento* was a fine wholesome meal, smoked fish
pickles, whale meat which had been fried, and white rice.

"Well, if we are going to eat like this," said a Canadian,
"Japan'll suit me."

In the toilet I found myself standing in the next urinal to an old man who spoke to me in English and asked where we came from, and when I replied said, "Why doesn't your country make peace with Hitler and Japan? We shall soon meet the Germans at the Suez Canal. It is a pity that we have to fight like this. All those men should be back in their homes. It is all because of Roosevelt and Churchill."

"Well, I think we'd all sooner be dead than be the slaves of Hitler or Tojo," I replied smiling.

He pressed a packet of "Golden Bat" cigarettes into my hand, and murmured, "Well, take care of yourself."

We were now told to form into two groups of Royal Rifles of Canada and Winnipeg Grenadiers.

The cadet doctor told me that we were to take different trains. One would leave at 8.30 and the other at 10 p.m. He said that we should meet again at our destination as he was to go with the first train with the Winnipeg Grenadiers, and I would follow with the Royal Rifles.

IV

In the train I sat at one end of a coach with the soldier interpreter and two Canadian sergeants. At the other end were Captain Nemoto and a Japanese sergeant. As usual, before we entrained, there was the inevitable speech about our being bayoneted or shot to death should we attempt to escape, which nearly always brought forth a raspberry from some wag.

The train was blacked out but I was able, much to his surprise, to tell the soldier interpreter the names of all the stations. At Maibara, surely one of the most depressing stations, I said: "Tell the stationmaster that *Mr. Six Feet Two* sends his best regards."

My heart really contracted as we pulled into Nagahama. Outside was Lake Biwa and Chikubu Island, and Mount Ibuki and all those places I knew and loved so well. And my parents-in-law and other relatives, and friends.

Torahime, Kinomoto, Tsuruga ... I dozed off, and awoke just as we were pulling into Kanazawa. The blinds had now been raised and I gazed out on a beautiful sunlit day.

All through that morning and early afternoon I was busy answering questions about Japan. Many were farmers in civil life and expressed great admiration for Japanese skill in agriculture.

On arrival at Niigata there was an enormous crowd outside the station with a band playing and the city decorated with Japanese, Italian and nazi flags.

"Well, what do you know about that? They've turned out a welcome committee," gasped a Canadian.

We got into trucks and drove out of town for several miles through streets lined with the curious populace until we came to a cluster of wooden buildings, some of which were not yet completed, at the foot of a hill.

Arthur and the Winnipeg Grenadiers had already started to settle in. It was a miserable-looking place, the huts were constructed of thin boards, and the men were to sleep on matting which lined wide, wooden shelves. The camp commandant was an elderly man who knew Father Holzer at Yamagata.

Arthur and I decided that we'd occupy a tiny two-mat room at the entrance to one of the huts and I had just thrown down my kit when the young doctor, Fuji, told me that I was to leave immediately with him and the rest of the guards for Tokyo. This was a blow. Here we were at the end of the journey, and now I was to leave those fine Canadians.

I went round and said good-bye to all, told them to rely on Arthur, and hoped that we'd all soon meet once again for a grand and happy reunion. Over one hundred of them died during their first winter through sickness, and a tragic avalanche which almost buried the camp. They now rest in the British Commonwealth Cemetery at Hodogaya, near Yokohama.

In the train to Tokyo I had no less than fifteen guards.

It was interesting to listen to the speculations concerning my identity.

"He is an American captain."

"No, he is an American airman, shot down over the Japan Sea."

"He's an American spy who was dropped by parachute."

None ventured the thought that I might be other than an officer of the United States Forces.

The young doctor and I chatted about all manner of things. He came from near Chichibu, in Saitama Prefecture, where his father was a dentist.

It was a slow train and a succession of travellers took part in a sort of guessing game about my rank, nationality, and the diabolical crimes I had committed. One thing that probably perplexed them was the wavy stripe of the Royal Naval Volunteer Reserve.

Tokyo Ueno Station was drab and dreary, *mompei* and uniforms everywhere, and not a gaily dressed girl to be seen. We sat outside the station awaiting a truck and I asked a soldier if I might go to the toilet. He said he did not know where it was situated and I replied that I would show him.

"Interesting," he remarked, "for a British prisoner from Hong Kong to have to direct me to the toilet at Ueno Station."

A crowd of people gathered and one man spat at me and was promptly punched by Doctor Fuji. Another shouted: "Why don't you bring your aeroplanes? We are ready for you. But you can't, can you?"

"You poor ignorant lout," I thought, "They will come soon enough, and when they do, heaven help this great city of yours."

When the truck arrived, I said jokingly to Doctor Fuji: "What about taking me through the Ginza, or down past the Imperial Hotel?"

We passed through the Ginza, turned at Owaricho, up to

Hibiya Park and then turned right and straight down to Shinagawa.

It was now a vastly different Tokyo, a tired and shoddy city —a great metropolis which appeared to have lost its energy and seemed just like a tired old man who neglects to shave, wets the bed and just waits for something which he cannot prevent, much as he boasts he can.

Shinagawa, Oimachi, the restaurants of Omori, and then we stopped in a side turning and there before me was the "Bamboo Bridge" which I was to come to know and hate so well.

Chapter Twenty-six

I

ON SEPTEMBER 4th, 1943, Omori Camp was tolerable.

My kit was inspected by a young soldier-interpreter named Suguhara, and I was then conducted to Barracks No. 2, where in a small four-mat room were five officer prisoners, just finishing their mid-day meal.

"Poop" Badger was a captain in the Middlesex Regiment—the "Die Hards"—affectionately known as the "Hermaphrodites." Harry Parker, a commissioned writer, Royal Navy; Bob Thompson, a flight-lieutenant, Royal Australian Air Force, "Mac," a captain in the Australian Army, Peter Frankcom, a major in the Army Educational Corps, and "Quillie" Quilliam, commissioned gunner of HMS *Thracian* which had been bombed while in dry dock at Aberdeen, Hong Kong.

The room was soon filled with prisoners of all ranks. Americans, Dutch, and British, and to my pleasure and surprise, our old coxwain of MTB o8, Petty-Officer Mitchell.

Omori, H.Q. POW Camp for the Tokyo area, was at that period populated mainly by one of the first drafts to be sent from Hong Kong. They had actually worked on the reclamation of the land from Tokyo Bay, and had only recently been moved from Shinagawa Camp which had been converted to a POW Hospital.

While we were all talking nineteen to the dozen a soldier brought in a plate of stew—it actually contained a few pieces of pork—and said it was with the compliments of First-Class Private Suguhara.

"Well, I think I'm going to like this," I said.

"Oh, it's not too bad, but it was better at Shinagawa. Sometimes used to get a bottle of 'Suntory'."

A pot of tea was produced. Poop told Harry to see if there were any Japanese around and then lifted one of the floor boards and took out a large cardboard box from which he extracted some fine white sugar which he dumped into my tea.

At Omori were men from Hong Kong, the Philippines, Wake Island, from Singapore and Java, from Dutch and American naval vessels which had been sunk in the Battle of the Java Sea, and American airmen of Chenault's Flying Tigers.

"What's the news, what's the news?" this was the standard cry from all I met. But all I had was the names of those who had come with me to Japan and news of the first American air raids on Hong Kong.

There were some 500 prisoners in the camp at this stage, housed in five barracks each identical in design. At the entrance of each were two four-mat rooms for officers, behind which main barracks contained two shelves covered with matting on which the prisoners slept and ate and had their being when they were not working; for all other ranks went out each day on working parties. One gang went to Shiodome railway yard, near Shimbashi Station—this was the elite gang, and the men would give anything to work there, for at Shiodome they had all the best pickings of all manner of edible goods. Another worked at the Mitsubishi warehouse where they loaded sugar. A good job was the Shinagawa railway yard. But an unfortunate gang went to Sumidagawa, where they loaded wood on to trucks, and yet another worked at a coal yard.

The conversation, after it was found that I had little of importance in the way of news, then centred on advice to me on camp routine and the Japanese personnel.

"Colonel Suzuki seems a decent chap. Trouble is we can only talk to him through the interpreters, and the civilian guy is a bit of a snake."

"Suguhara? Oh he's a nice little fellow."

"Be careful of the 'Little Beast'—he's mad and ought to be in a loony bin."

"If you hear a lot of diabolical screaming going on at any time, don't worry, it's only the 'Little Beast'."

"Nemoto? Don't know."

"Fuji's all right."

"The 'Geisha's' a fine little chap—a lieutenant. He used to get us the 'Suntory'."

"The senior doctor is a swine; at Shinagawa he ripped open the guts of our little dog—just to see what was inside. We sewed up the little fellow with twine."

"Captain Muragishi—'Gentleman Jim'—is one of the best."

"'Heidelberg Henry' Lieutenant Hayashi—is a cracker-jack, used to be a priest."

"Remember when he met us at Yokohama? Christ! When we saw his Hitler moustache and his high-crowned German style cap, we thought he looked a bastard, a real 'Heidelberg Henry'."

"But coming up in the trucks when it started to rain, to our surprise 'Henry' stopped to put a sick bloke in his seat in the cab, and came in the back with us? Yes, you're going to like 'Henry', he's a great guy. Wish I could get to one of his camps, at the brick works or the peanut oil factory."

"Hell! they even fry their millet and yellow rice and barley at the peanut oil factory. Lucky bastards!" said an American.

At five o'clock the first working gang came in, and with them Cadet Hunting, RNVR, who had served with me in patrol vessels at Hong Kong.

"Poop" was the administrative officer with whom I was to share the room at one side of the entrance to Barracks No 2. A solicitor in civil life, he was a mild-mannered methodical man, with the lawyer's rather dry cynicism. He had been confined in Stanley

Prison at Hong Kong because of his refusal to sign the parole form.

In the room opposite were Peter, who had been captured at Singapore, and "Bob"—a slow-speaking, dry-humoured Australian from Perth, West Australia, who had been the first to spot the Japanese fleet off New Guinea just after the attack on Pearl Harbour.

The officers' rooms were standard—two mats raised from the floor, on which we slept, and two mats of boards with a small table. We ate together with Harry, Peter and Bob.

Just before the evening meal we had a visit from Colonel Suzuki, tall for a Japanese and a fine looking man.

We stood up and saluted as he entered and he beckoned us to sit down, and came in and talked pleasantly for some minutes. I was impressed, decided that things were going to be all right, and hoped the Canadians with Arthur at Niigata were faring as well.

II

Our batman, a British naval rating, brought our food. One wooden bucket with a stew of vegetables, which might contain a few pieces of potato or even a minute piece of meat, and another, containing a mixture of millet, yellow rice and barley.

We ate from Japanese army rice bowls and soup dishes, all of which were marked with a blue Japanese army star.

"Now you'll have to think up some good plans," said Peter. "We'll expect one from you to-morrow."

He drew five squares on a piece of paper, each of which he numbered. The mixture of yellow rice, barley and millet, and the soup were then ladled out by Harry into separate bowls and placed in order on the table. Then Peter read his plan.

"Now the war is over and on your first night out of captivity you can have the choice of the following:

You can spend the evening with:
   Marlene Dietrich,
   'Two Tits' Turner,
   The Headmistress of a Home for Delinquent Girls,
   The 'Little Beast's' Girl Friend, or
   The Fat Lady in a Circus."

"I'll take the Turner," said Bob.

"Number three," said Peter, and Harry handed him his bowl and Bob explored for any hidden delicacy.

"The Fat Lady," said "Poop".

"Number two."

"Headmistress."

"Number one."

"Well, all right, I'm stuck with the 'Little Beast's Girl Friend'."

"The prospect disgusts me. I can imagine what she must be like to go out with that little bastard."

"Cheers! I've got a bit of potato!"

The author and Kaneko at Tokyo, 1960

Looking down the crater of Mount Fuji from a BOAC jet airliner

The author illustrating a talk on bells over Radio Japan (NHK) in 1958 with a practical demonstration

"Honourable Nose-Paper and his Japanese bride": a dramatized version in Japanese of the first chapter of *The Road to Inamura* telecast on Channel 6, Tokyo, on April 1, 1961. Meiko Nakamura appeared as Kaneko, and William Ross played the part of the author

"Well, how's Lana, Bob?"

"Cripes, she's lousy. Why it's all bloody water with a lump of woody turnip?"

"Well don't be so bloody greedy next time. And what are you grumbling about."

"Well, who's going out with her on a lump of bloody turnip?"

There was no measuring, no inquests, and never a single argument over food.

We ate the millet, barley and yellow rice sprinkled with sugar.

During the meal an American came in and inquired whether we wanted any sugar? I bought a bowl, filled up to the blue star for three yen.

"Price will be going up," said the Yank, "the guards are getting a bit tough."

Tenko was at 7 o'clock, and before this Captain Goad, the American army doctor, held his sick parade in the surgery in the office building.

There was a great deal of beri-beri and men were often injured at work.

We lined up in columns of huts on the parade ground in front of the cookhouse. Numbering in Japanese was quite fantastic with the queer Cockney, Brooklyn, Deep South, Scottish, Welsh, Lancashire and Yorkshire accents. The hut commander reported in Japanese such details as—

"Two men in the Shinagawa hospital, one man in the lavatory, two sick in quarters."

Most of this was quite unintelligible, but the Japanese already had the information in writing, so they did not care.

It was on this first *tenko* that I met Captain Muragishi and the "Little Beast".

"Gentleman Jim" was an athletic looking man with a keen eye and open countenance. "Little Beast" certainly looked mental.

After *tenko* we had an hour to spare before lights out at 8 o'clock and I met Captain "Sedgy" Hinson, a rosy-cheeked impish young American from Tylertown, Mississippi; Weimer, an American army signals officer, from San Antonio, Texas; Captain Bert Rees, from South Africa; Brian Pendleton, captain, Royal Engineers, and others.

When "Gentleman Jim" came to our room I learned that he had formerly rowed for the University of Commerce, and that Vere Redman had been his teacher.

The men in our barracks were mostly gunners from a Welsh yeomanry artillery regiment, Middlesex and Royal Scots, with the odd Navy, Air Force and Engineer types.

Like all Welshmen, the gunners never missed a chance to sing. And that evening they sang in such manner that brought out the whole camp to listen. They made a superb choir, and sang "Men of Harlech", "Lords of the Air", "All Through the Night", and "God Bless America".

Well, I thought, this is as good a place as any to sweat out this

cursed war. If only there were a letter from Kaneko, just to let me
know she is well and being cared for!

III

Morning *tenko* was at 5.30 a.m. There was no warning, just a lot
of shouting by the night guards and you jumped into your clothes
and made for the parade ground as fast as you could go. Then,
with *tenko* over, along came our first meal of the day—watery soup
flavoured slightly with soy sauce or bean paste, in which were
seaweed, chunks of *gobo*—burdock, *daikon*—turnip,—turnip
leaves and a faint hint of bones, which were boiled and boiled
over and over again.

Sometimes you might find a piece of *konnyaku*—devil's tongue,
but it was very tough, grey, jelly-like stuff, which I could not
recognize from that I had been used to eating in former days.

My comrades did not much appreciate *gobo,* which they called
"walking stick", or the seaweed; and still less the *konnyaku,* which
they labelled "Elephant's semen".

The men who went out to work received double the rations of
those who stayed in camp, but these were scanty, so that the white
sugar, of which at that time there seemed to be plenty if you had
the money to buy it, proved a wonderful addition to the diet.

The sugar racket was well-organized. The men who worked it
at the Mitsubishi warehouse had specially made socks, like long
sausages, some of them about four feet long, which they hung
from the neck right down their bodies and legs. Others made a
hole in a sack when carrying it, and allowed the sugar to run
down their necks into their clothes, and would return to camp
just packed with the stuff. The civilian guards were all mixed up in
the racket and for them the men filled specially made receptacles in
the floors of the trucks. The "Big Boss" was a hefty Scot, a corporal
who was reputed never to have less than two thousand yen round
his waist at any time. He controlled the market price, did little
work on the job, but spent most of his time down in a boat with a
girl friend he had picked up among the women working on the
wharf. But no sick man went short of sugar through being without
the means to buy it. Later I was to be one of the select few invited
to Jock's birthday party when to my amazement I was given a
piece of iced cake, sweet tea and a mouthful of wine!

Jock dealt not only in sugar but with commodities brought in by
other gangs outside the select Shiodome crowd, for they did their
own marketing. It was from this gang that one might be lucky
enough to buy a pound of cheese, tinned fish, or even strawberries!
The Japanese people could not, of course, buy such luxuries and
most was for export to South Asia.

At one period there was quite a lot of wine on sale and even
strawberry jam. The wine had been part of a consignment for the
German Ambassador at Bangkok. Seeing the destination of those
cases which were accompanied by several pieces of furniture and

other household goods for His Excellency, the representative of Mr. Adolf Hitler, was like a red rag to a bull when the boys cast their eyes upon it and each case was just dropped hard and the leaking wine went to fill their water bottles and, according to my informant, there was nothing left for the nazi representative in Thailand.

In our mess we were never so fortunate as to be able to buy the wine. This went to the bosses among the working men. But sometimes we obtained a water-bottle full of industrial alcohol, and used just a tea-spoonful in a cup of tea.

"Want to buy some fish, sir," whispered a grimy looking American to us one evening as we sat down to our evening meal.

"Sure," said Harry, "how much?"

"Two yen apiece, I've got four."

"Okay, let's have them quick before the 'Little Beast' comes around."

The soldier slipped down his trousers and extracted the fish which were secreted round his crotch.

"Poop" decided that the Japanese would smell them from the camp office, decided he'd have no part of it, and went off to visit friends in the next hut. The rest of us made short work of those herrings, or whatever they were.

IV

Every day after breakfast the officers repaired to a hut which was used as a POW post office for sorting letters delivered by the Red Cross for prisoners of war all over the Far East. Each officer had a small filing cabinet knocked up by the camp carpenter, which contained cards for all prisoners of whom we had knowledge, written on pieces of cardboard from packets of "Golden Bat" cigarettes. So, as a stack of letters came in we'd check to find out if we could locate the addressees.

I took over the letters P–T. I had already been able to provide the names of the men who had come up from Hong Kong with me, and it was only through new prisoners that we could keep our files more or less up to date.

The idea of this post office, which was doing a great job, was that of Colonel Suzuki, and the officers were only too glad to volunteer for such work. As we worked there would be all kinds of running conversation.

"You Yanks are still wet behind the ears, you've hardly got your diapers off," would taunt Harry.

"Aw, shit, we've got Joe Louis, and Benny Goodman, and all the gold in the world—and boy we got Texas!"

"Texas! Jesus! attached to the United States for rationing," would cry "Sedgy".

"What do you go on this, chaps. Come and have a smell of this letter."

"Good God!" says Peter, "It's positively immoral. Keep it away from "Sedgy". He's got enough bad habits."

"And you can say what you like but we'll never have honesty until we get a Republican government."

"Horse's arse! Why, they'll make Huey Long and Al Capone look like a couple of candy snitchers!"

"When we get those Yanks out of politics and bring the federal capital down to Texas, why then boy, we'll really have something!"

"Aw, listen to Texas, why down there the barmaids eat their young and drink their bath water!"

"Aw for Christ's sake can it," says Ray, a Flying Tiger, "there's only one god-damned place in this world and I'm telling you that's Brooklyn."

"Up the Bums, up the Bums!"

"East side, west side, all around the town!"

"Shut up, you silly buggers, here comes the 'Little Beast'."

The post office would assume an air of great industry and we'd shout to the other end of the hut to warn of "Little Beast's" approach to the men sick in quarters, who worked there making ear flaps for Japanese soldiers out of rabbit skins.

"Too much noise! You no work. You no work, I punish," screams "Little Beast", his crazy little eyes flashing.

"Hinson, you *benjo soji*—latrine emptying—tonight, after work."

There were also really earnest and heated discussions, many of which were interesting and helped to keep one's brain ticking over.

"The republics have failed. Show me a really successful one?"

"Well, what about the United States and France?"

"The United States. Well, with all our wealth and resources, our so-called rugged individualism, our technical know-how, we are still politically immature and there's hardly any dignity in our politics. As to France, she's crooked all through."

"Switzerland is the only example of a successful republic."

"Well, the United States may be politically immature but she's god-damned useful to practically every country which is on the bum for Uncle Sam's dollars."

"Yes, we know, poor bloody Britain's debts from the last dust up, in which we lost half a million men while you guys sat on the fence for nearly three years to see which way the cat would jump. Why you'd not be in this thing now if the Japanese hadn't been so bloody crazy as to bomb Pearl Harbour. Your Congress would still be debating the point."

"Hell, Harry, why my brother was fighting with the RAF in early '40. Went over the border to Canada to join up."

"Sorry, chum, but you Yanks do love to sling the bull-shit; give away the British Empire, curse us for not fighting Hitler at the time of Munich and then make a virtue of fighting in a war which you still would not be in had not old Tojo forced your hand."

"Well, anyway, we may have some crooked politicians but that's a darned sight better than having a lot of royal bums and their relatives to support, and the dukes and lords and all that crap."

"Bullshit!" says Texas, "Hell, the average American loves a king or a duke. And Jesus Christ, no American, except perhaps some of the New York stage Irish, can deny his admiration for the British Royal Family."

"Well, here's one country that's going to get a republic when Uncle Sam gets through whether they like it or not. The Son of Heaven can go play with his seashells—Japan is going to have a president in the good old American style."

"Yes, and that would be about as bad a blunder as Tojo's bombing of Pearl Harbour," I'd remark. "The Emperor system is the only one for Japan, a constitutional monarchy on British lines. The Japanese Emperors have never been tyrants. When they have held the reins of power this country has had peace and prosperity."

"Oh, they've got peace and prosperity now, haven't they?"

Many of my comrades were serious-minded fellows who gave much thought to the future and to existing political and economic problems. Many were genuinely interested in Japanese history and politics and in the events which had brought Japan from feudalism to the level of a first-class power in such a short period. Others, and who could blame them, had no interest in Japan other than a hatred which, even after the end of hostilities, would never heal, and regarded me as something of a crank.

v

One day news came from our batman that there was a British officer in the guardhouse. Within an hour we had a new member of our mess in the person of Captain David "Tough" James, M.C. —eldest of the James brothers, whose father, one of the early foreign pilots on the Inland Sea, had founded a sort of family dynasty in the foreign community of the port city of Kobe.

Of medium height, David was a lean, tough chap, with white hair and a small white moustache. He'd lost a lung in World War I, at the Battle of the Somme with the Northumberland Fusiliers, suffered with hernia, and although over age on the outbreak of war, had finally got himself posted to an intelligence unit in Singapore.

He'd spent most of his life in Japan, and although he had not been in the country for some years, his spoken Japanese was better than mine. I'd never met him but knew his brother Ernest who had done so much to develop Shioya, and the Shioya Country Club at Kobe. He had a lot to tell us of Changi Camp, at Singapore, where he had been liaison officer between the prisoners and the Japanese. He went in with Bob and Peter, and so now we had a mess of six.

A new barracks had been in course of construction and on the evening it was finished, we were told to stay in our huts, and the next morning found that we had some sixty or seventy Italians with us—officers and men of an Italian ship which they had scuttled at Shanghai.

That day our rations showed a marked decrease. For no extra rations had been provided for these newcomers. They were not very popular, but our good natured men did all they could to help them, although we were told by the Japanese that there was to be no fraternization.

A few days later they were visited by the Swedish consul who brought them a consignment of wine.

The inroads on our rations were serious business and despite protests to the interpreters, they did not seem to be able to do anything about it.

This decrease seriously affected the working men and beri-beri had assumed rather alarming proportions. It was then that Doctor Fuji put forward his plan of making *miso*—bean paste—beer, which he believed would prevent and even cure beri-beri. He had a hard fight with the supply people but eventually they gave way and agreed to grant him the supplies for making this brew for the men engaged in heavy labour.

It was made in the cook-house under his supervision from bean paste, sugar and fermented barley. It did not taste bad, but what was most important it soon had the desired effect. This was only one of the very excellent deeds of this young cadet doctor, but even so, he was tried as a war criminal. Today he is married and has his own practice in Tokyo. Many of my comrades did not, I am sure, realize all he did, or tried to do, in order to uphold the medical code.

The camp gradually absorbed more and more officers and men. One day a group came in from Cabanatuan in the Philippines. Some had been on the Bataan "death march", others were from Corregidor. Among them was a Captain Bryce Martin, U.S. Army, from Houston, Texas, who became a very good friend of mine and an Air Force captain—"Hank" Hankin. They arrived during one of our periodical shortages of tobacco and most generously shared their supplies of the dark, strong Filippino tobacco.

Harry Parker, and Weimer, another Texan, were the canteen officers and the goods were displayed in their small room—meagre stocks of pocket-combs, mirrors, note books and general rubbish. They issued the "Golden Bat" cigarettes—at that time we received two pieces per day, and the issue took place about once a fortnight. But we had been well off for cigarettes, as we had come by some 4,000 *Homare*—Japanese army issue.

One evening, the civilian in charge of the Japanese canteen had come to me in great distress. Apparently he was short in his canteen funds and as an audit was to take place he was in mortal terror as to what would happen to him. He knew that we had little on which to spend our money—we received the same rates of pay as Japanese officers of equivalent rank—and asked me to arrange a loan for him among my comrades. In return, he promised to provide us with as many cigarettes as possible. I had little difficulty in getting him his money.

A British soldier, returned to camp from the civil prison where he'd been serving a sentence for stealing whilst out at work, took a poor view of Omori, said that in the prison he'd received fairly good food, the warden had been kind, and had spent his time making envelopes. He got himself back there by stealing clothes hanging out to dry at a house near his place of work.

A new arrival was none other than John Abbott, Middlesex Regiment, former Crown Solicitor at Hong Kong, a comrade at Shamsuipo. John became one of our favourite plan makers. One of his efforts was: "The war is over and you want a job. They are pretty hard to find but you are offered the following choice:

'Rickshaw puller for General MacArthur's pet geisha.'

'The monopoly on Winston Churchill's cigar butts—with the band on.'

'Sales manager for the *Gobo* and *Konnyaku* Sales Promotion Syndicate in Texas.'

'Foreman of the Omori *Benjo* Cleaners' Association.'

'Promoter of Japanese Culture, in Sydney, Australia.'

'Scratcher off of rude words in London underground lavatories.' "

"Tough" James did not care for the plans—said they were damned silly and held up the serving of the food. He was the skinniest of all and down to a shadow, but had a voracious appetite and would eat fish heads which few would touch and which the men would collect for him.

We heard the most horrifying tales of treatment at an interrogation camp situated at Ofuna, not far from Yokohama, and these were confirmed when a number of officers and men arrived from that hell-hole.

Commander Maher, USN, had been gunnery officer of USS *Houston*, sunk in the Java Sea, "Dave" Hurt, USN, had been in command of the submarine USS *Perch*, and Lieutenant "Clarkie" Clark an American naval airman. Ofuna specialized in interrogation of airmen or submariners, and they were not listed as prisoners of war with the International Red Cross until and if this was finished. Some had been in solitary confinement for months on end and forbidden to speak to each other for long periods. In the autumn of 1943 Omori seemed to them some sort of paradise.

Chapter Twenty-seven

I

THE camp had its weekly bath on Thursday. The officers went at four o'clock and the other ranks as they came in from work. The unfortunate last gang into camp would be confronted with water black with grime. One could not bathe in the proper manner and soap and wash off the dirt before entering the large bath because only a trickle of water came through the ridiculous one inch pipe across the Bamboo Bridge.

New arrivals at Omori had all manner of stories which they'd usually vow came from absolutely reliable sources. According to some the Allies were but a few miles from Berlin, the Russians were already in the war and had taken Manchuria, and hostilities could last only between two or three weeks or three months at the most.

One of our American friends had a bet with a comrade over a certain piece of "news", and vowed that he'd kiss the other fellow's backside in public if he lost the wager. Half a dozen newcomers proved that the so-called news was simply *benjo* radio and we had just forced the American to carry out his bum-kissing pledge when Puss in Boots, an officer named Ichimura, came rushing into the bath-house shouting *kiotsuke!*—attention!

All stood up, some in the bath, some outside, and just behind Puss came a stocky looking individual attired in tweed suit, a light-grey felt hat, and carrying a walking-stick, the handle of which appeared to be shaped in the form of a dog's or horse's head.

Keirei!—salute! shouted Puss. We all bowed, and General Prime Minister Hideki Tojo raised his hat, gave a slight bow, smiled, and then proceeded to ply the almost petrified Puss in Boots with questions.

General Tojo had really caught the camp with its trousers down on one of his snap inspections, and he visited all barracks followed by the awe-stricken Puss in Boots, and other members of the staff, some of whom were so affected by his presence they could not answer his questions for spluttering and stuttering, and almost kicked themselves flat in clicking their heels. In one hut the camp idiot, who many considered was probably the greatest actor of all time, was sitting in a corner gnawing a large bone which had already been boiled as clear as a piece of ivory. He had wild eyes, used to break into the most maniacal, blood-chilling laughter and screams, and winter or summer wore a greatcoat about five sizes too large for him. Puss in Boots tried to steer Tojo away from this character, but the General went up close to have a better look while, according to my informant, the object of his interest let out some extraordinary noises which sounded suspiciously like raspberries.

The Japanese Prime Minister appeared most touched and, after telling our idiot to "look after his health", proceeded to the cook-house. Here, to the surprise of the cooks they had just previously been issued with unheard-of quantities of bones, meat and rice, which caused Tojo to tell them through the interpreter that they were being better fed than the Japanese people.

None of my comrades realized the identity of our visitor and when I told them were quite incredulous.

"Well, I'm damned," said John. "When my grandchildren ask me what I did in the Great War I'll be able to tell them that I bowed bollicky naked to the great General Tojo."

"Looked to me more like a Brooklyn ward-heeler," said Ray Lucia.

"Who was that fatherly old bastard?" inquired an Australian.

"Jesus! " he exclaimed, "I can just see him kissin' all the babies."

"Yeah, and goosin' all the geisha," said a Texan.

"Well, I'd like to goose 'im with a ruddy great meat 'ook," remarked a Cockney.

Tojo's visit was a subject for much discussion and those at work at the time seemed most disappointed at not having had the chance to see one of our arch-enemies. Whether there was any connection or not a few days later the officers were told to clean up, we were conducted to the camp office reception room, sat down before cakes and tea and trays of cigarettes, and then questioned by a number of senior officers. They asked us about the British Constitution, gangsterism in Chicago, freemasonry, and to state our complaints, which of course we voiced in good measure. But everything seemed rather too nice and polite and we left with our pockets filled with cigarettes, even the butts from the ash trays, the cakes and boxes of matches, all somewhat puzzled.

Shortly after this, Omori became a perfect patch of purgatory with the arrival of a tall, sturdy corporal, who was to make each day twenty-four hours of misery.

This fellow, whom we were to dub "Mr. Brown", sauntered into our room, dumped a package of sweets on the table and announced that henceforth he would be in charge of camp discipline. We ate his sweets and smoked his cigarettes and all except Peter expressed the opinion that he seemed quite a good chap.

"Well, I don't like the look of him, not that I like the look of any Japanese except Gentleman Jim," said Peter. However, for a few days the corporal seemed most reasonable and co-operative and we went to him on all manner of problems, which he dealt with to our satisfaction, so that even Peter wondered if he had judged the fellow too hastily.

One Sunday morning Brown was about to enter a barracks

through a crowd of prisoners when "Clarkie", an American navy flier, shouted, "Gangway, there!" Whereupon the Corporal knocked him down with a vicious blow in the face and kicked him.

Commander Maher USN, came over to see Poop about this unwarranted conduct on the part of Brown and I went over to the camp office to try and sort matters out. There I found Brown threatening "Clarkie" with a drawn sword and screaming hysterically that he was going to cut off his head. Fortunately Gentleman Jim arrived, dismissed Clarke, and ordered Brown into the office.

"You were right, Peter," I remarked when I returned to the barrack. "This chap is certainly going to give us trouble."

That evening, just as we were about to sit down to our meal, Brown arrived and, with a countenance black with fury, ordered me to the camp office.

He pushed me into a small room where there was a coal stove burning and screamed: "You are impertinent, you are insincere," and then knocked me across the red hot stove, jumped on me, tore my tie from my throat, then started in with his heavy boots. Then the door was flung open and there stood Gentleman Jim.

"Go to your room," he said, as he took in my sorry condition.

I staggered into the room and flung myself on the *tatami*. This was the most shocking humiliation I had ever suffered. Peter and my friends had heard all that went on and had saved my food to which had been added a few little delicacies from the working men. But I could not eat for rage against the monster.

After *tenko*, which Gentleman Jim conducted, attended by Brown, this officer came to our room and told me how angry he was that such a thing had happened, and said in an undertone: "You know, the Corporal knows that you know how any Japanese should behave who has had such an education as he received at Keio University, and he resents it. Be careful of him, especially when I am not on duty."

Just after midnight Brown, accompanied by a sentry, dragged me from my bed and ordered me to kneel on the board floor.

"Now I will show you how to treat prisoners," he said to the soldier, and drew his sword. Poor old Poop had his head under his blankets but uncovered one eye to see what was going on. Brown turned upon him. "You sleep!" he shouted.

He then proceeded to shave my head as near as possible with swipes of his sword; and when I tried to ease the pain from my knees which were numbed by the bare boards, kicked me down. It was a nightmare which lasted until 3 a.m. and I fell asleep utterly exhausted.

At about five o'clock, just before *tenko*, Brown appeared and telling me to get up put his arms around my shoulders and propelled me towards the camp office. Inside he burst into tears, embraced me, told me I was a good man, said that he was sorry and that he would never ill-treat me or other prisoners again, made me drink a bottle of beer, and thrust several packets of cigarettes and some sweets upon me.

I almost choked in drinking the beer and returned to my room more bewildered than ever.

That night he went berserk again with a wooden fencing stick, and raged through each hut beating at the sleeping men and anyone in his path. The whole camp was awakened and the screams and oaths would have put a madhouse to shame.

And there seemed nothing we could do. The young interpreter, Suguhara, had already run foul of Brown and urged me to do nothing to enrage him in any way.

All this encouraged the Little Beast, and he and Brown became great friends. Little Beast then beat the Scots camp shoemaker about the face with a clog until the poor devil could not see or even open his mouth to eat. We got Gentleman Jim to have a look at the shoemaker and Little Beast was severely reprimanded.

On the following Sunday, Brown and Little Beast assembled all the officers on the parade ground and Little Beast screamed: "I can kill you, anytime. I only go to guardhouse for two, three days. You tell Japanese officers, I kill, I kill!"

After this, Brown harangued us for several minutes and said that he had been sent into the camp by a high authority and did not care about the camp officers.

I now started on my career as a cleaner out of *benjos*.

II

Until Brown showed his hand, the work around the camp, such as cleaning out the latrines, was performed by a squad of soldiers kept in camp especially for that purpose. But now this was to stop and the officers were forced to perform these tasks.

It takes two men to work a *benjo soji* detail and so when Brown ordered me to do this work he had to fall upon some other wretched fellow to assist on the other end of the pole from which was suspended the "honey bucket".

We prayed Brown be struck dead, stricken of a loathsome disease —anything, so long as he was out of sight and reach. Gone were the days of laughing and joking, the cards on Sunday afternoons in our room or in the canteen. Our conversation was now conducted in whispers for fear that our arch enemy might be lurking outside. He spoke a little English and had beaten a man he heard mention his name and this was the reason we called him Brown or "The Bird".

A new prisoner was Colonel "Bill" Pike, an American flier who had been forced to bale out of his P40 fighter over Hankow, when his fuel pipe choked. Bill, a hefty six-footer, was terribly burned. The first day he appeared at *tenko* Brown slapped his face because he moved his eyes when he was supposed to be at attention. I believe Bill would have hit him had we not been able to whisper to control himself.

Another new chum was George Williams, a Devonian, administrative officer on one of the Gilbert and Ellice Isles. When the war broke out George was in process of training his local defence force which consisted of a squad of natives and a large canoe in which a machine-gun was mounted. Early one morning George was aroused to find a Japanese heavy cruiser in the bay.

After leaving Omori, at Bunka Camp, Tokyo, George was ordered to perform some propaganda work which he refused. He was then ordered to kneel down and a Japanese unsheathed a large sword. Poor George closed his eyes and hoped it would be a swift death, when he was told to stand up, told he was a very brave man, and he was then sent off to dig ditches.

When David James entered the camp, in view of his age, and general physical condition, I asked Gentleman Jim for him to be excused morning *tenko*, which was readily granted. But Brown did not take kindly to this and started a campaign against him. However, "Tough" James was able to reason with him for a while and at that time Brown had not sunk so low as to hit a weak and elderly man.

When Little Beast and Brown were off duty and out of camp our life was tolerable.

Captain Hayashi—"Heidelberg Henry"—would visit us whenever he had business in the camp and this always meant a pleasant chat and cigarettes. He was a decent, humane man, as was to be expected from a Buddhist priest, and promised to try and get news of Kaneko for me.

All longed to be sent to one of the camps at Yokohama where Henry was in charge, and one day Brown announced that he wanted an officer to volunteer to go to the Yokohama Brickworks Camp. We all applied in writing.

"Why did you apply to go to Yokohama?" Brown screamed. "You are not satisfied with my treatment?"

For being impertinent, as he called it, in response to his request for a volunteer, I was ordered to wash four pieces of clothing of the soldier prisoners each day for one month and at the same time given one month of *benjo soji* after my day's work in the post office!

Captain Eric Marsden, Royal Signals, was the lucky one to be sent to Hayashi's camp. Eric was once called to task for writing a post-card to Winston Churchill. The Prime Minister happened to be an old friend of his family.

Brown started a *blitz* on our books and papers which had to be handed to him for inspection. He retained my autograph book which I had kept since Shamsuipo and in which were some excellent sketches of POW camp life, but allowed me to keep my encyclopædia which I had found on a rubbish heap at the "*kempeitai*" at Hong Kong, and my *Dhammapada*.

One day a tall, handsome Japanese, dressed impeccably in clothes which might have been cut in Savile Row—actually they had been—visited us. He turned out to be Yoshitomo Tokugawa, on of Marquis Yoshichika Tokugawa, and brother-in-law of Prince Chichibu, who was to work for the prisoner of war camps as representative of the Japanese Red Cross. We told him our complaints and he promised that he would do whatever he could to assist us; what he did carry out immediately was get released to us from the camp office a whole lot of books which had been sent by the American Red Cross and the Swedish consul but which we had not up till then been able to obtain, through insistence on the part of the camp authorities that these be censored. Now we had plenty to read if Brown were not around; for if he caught you reading you were accused of being lazy and were sure to get some extra *benjo soji* or a beating.

After Yoshitomo's first visit Brown gave me another bashing, accused me of telling tales, and said that I was not in future to speak to him.

I asked Yoshitomo's opinion of our idea of petitioning the Colonel with regard to Brown, although we had not seen Colonel Suzuki for a long time and whenever he did come to the camp there was always the possibility that Brown would be one of those accompanying him on inspection.

Tokugawa thought that it would be unwise to make any petition at this time as the army system was quite unpredictable, but promised to do his level best for us.

III

With winter approaching, Omori became more gloomy than ever. It was just an island of sand a few feet above sea level and when there were high tides with strong winds the waters of Tokyo Bay would swamp our huts and wash the filth from the *benjos* all over the place.

The sugar gang had now emptied the warehouse and was working on scrap iron.

Just prior to the end of the sugar a Japanese officer approached me one evening and asked if I would do him the favour of buying him a couple of pounds of the stuff.

"Sugar!" I exclaimed. "I have forgotten what it tastes like."

"Oh but everyone knows the men bring it in for sale. Please do me this favour. I want some for my children."

A few days later he came to me and said: "It's all right, I managed to buy that sugar I asked you to get for me."

"Oh, that is very good, but I really had no idea where to obtain it," I replied.

When Brown was in camp we put into operation a system of warnings, similar to those used in Britain during air raids—"Green—green, changing to Red"—etc., so that each hut would know of his movements and be prepared accordingly.

When he was around there would be a rush on the *benjos*. He would come storming down there screaming my name, tell me that I was always trying to avoid him, and there would be extra *benjo soji* or I'd be made to stand at attention in some part of the camp under his eye or that of some unpleasant friend of his, like Little Beast.

One day there were some fifteen, mostly officers, standing at attention around the camp, including the camp carpenter, Petty Officer Lewis, who was a great favourite with Colonel Suzuki, and who would occasionally shout: "You wait till I get you after this bloody war, you little bastard. I'll cut your bloody heart out and use your guts for garters!"

Little Beast or Brown often sent Lewis out with the scrap-iron gang, but then some job of carpentering would be required and they'd get into trouble for interfering with the camp work.

Inspections by visiting officials were the plague of our existence, especially as the officers would be called upon to clean up the place while the men were at work.

On one occasion the canteen was well stocked with goods which we had never seen before—although Harry was told they must not be sold; the cooks were issued with the most unheard-of rations, and then we stood on the parade ground and were inspected by a number of unpleasant-looking high ranking officers covered with medals and gold lace, who went into the kitchens where a veritable feast was being prepared, saw the wonderful display in the canteen, and no doubt commented that it seemed the prisoners were doing better than the Japanese people.

But when they left the canteen stock was removed and the feast we had been licking our lips over went to a banquet held in the camp office.

One day three men came into camp from the Sagamihara Military Hospital. Private Plimmer, Royal Scots, had both legs amputated, not because of wounds but because they had wasted away through malnutrition. He was only nineteen, a bonny little Scot from Edinburgh, who had retained his army jacket and his Glengarry cap with its tartan edging, and whose buttons shone like dollars on a negro's backside. He shuffled along on his stumps which were covered with pads of leather, a cheerful, courageous little man, who inspired all of us with his splendid indomitable character.

He went to assist the shoemaker to learn the shoe repair trade, which he felt would be useful to him in civilian life.

Shortly afterwards he befriended a stray dog which had come into the camp, and despite the attempts of Brown to take the animal from him, he kept it with him always.

Chapter Twenty-eight

I

TOGETHER day by day, possessing different points of view on many subjects, except our loathing of captivity, varied and sometimes exasperating habits, was not conducive towards perfect harmony; and yet strangely enough we seldom quarrelled.

You'd be almost frantic at watching the way a chap held his spoon, picked his nose, scratched his backside, employed certain words, repeated the same tales and jokes, wore his clothes, played with his moustache, pulled at his earlobes, or ate his food.

Food, liquor and women were the ever recurring subjects for conversation. We'd talk of the restaurants we knew, of the menus we'd order, and of the bars we intended to visit on release from captivity.

Peter had a list of hundreds of pubs and restaurants throughout the length and breadth of the British Isles, "Sedgy" would extol the virtues of good old Southern American style cooking, and we'd argue the merits of how to prepare a sole, roast beef, or cure a ham, exchange recipes for making beer, rum, and even whisky.

"Sedgy" was an expert on home brew as his grandpappy had been in jail for running a still during prohibition. But Harry, too, had done quite a lot in the brewing and distilling line. He had a recipe for home-made rum which I have tried and found excellent.

You take a pumpkin, cut off the top, scrape out most of the inside, then pack it full of brown sugar. You then replace the top and tie the thing in a sling which you hang up until it starts to get dry and wither on the outside. You then place a wooden tub underneath and prick the bottom with a needle so that it will drip into the tub. It takes about four weeks to drip through, and the liquid is a tasty and powerful concoction.

During winter we were issued with beans. These were very wholesome, but they gave everyone severe diarrhœa and these and the cattle cake the men pinched on the job made our mess almost unlivable with the veritable mist of broken wind.

"Well, let's not waste the stuff," said Harry. "Let's get blankets over our legs and provide our own central heating."

It was most effective, and Brian, our engineer, said that there was enough natural gas in the camp to power a factory or light a village. We'd not at that time heard of atomic energy, but someone said that if all that gas could be concentrated it would serve to make such a bomb as would force the Germans and Japanese to surrender!

II

More Americans arrived; some were shot down in raids on Karafuto, others from the Philippines. There was a young ensign from Honolulu named "Bucky" Henshaw, who played the guitar and who had been one of the first prisoners taken in the war at Wake Island.

An addition to our mess was McGrath, an artillery lieutenant who sported a very fine moustache, whom we called "General". He did not smoke but would take his cigarette ration and issue it to us when all were miserable through lack of tobacco. In civil life he had been a law student and arrived at Singapore with reinforcements just in time to be taken prisoner.

Another crowd came from Korea with Captain Jack Mc-Naughton, of the Loyal North Lancashire Regiment, with the regimental bandmaster and several musicians.

But the Texans were now in the vast majority among the Americans and from whom we Limeys learned that Texas bred the finest men, the prettiest women, enjoyed the finest food, grew the most beautiful roses, boasted the highest state of literacy, maintained the best hospitals, the most tuneful dance bands, the greatest singers, politicians, and in short was a paradise on earth. So the United Kingdom, Australia, South Africa, and the rest of the Commonwealth lined up with the other forty-seven states just to balance the arguments. The Texans were grand chaps and someday I'll hope to visit the Lone Star State to see all its wonders for myself.

The bandmaster of the Loyals organized a makeshift band with a trumpet, saxophone, trombone, drums, a bass, and a few mandolines, accordions and other instruments which had been sent in by the Swedish Consul.

Legless Private Plimmer played the drums, perched on a stool, and the trumpeter, who had learned his trumpeting in the Salvation Army was, according to our American experts, one of the finest they'd heard, who was certain, they said, of a place with Louis Armstrong or other great possessors of hot lips.

Jack McNaughton was in civilian life an actor, and son of the famous comedian Gus McNaughton. Just before Christmas of 1943 at the suggestion of Gentleman Jim we started to prepare for a camp Christmas show. At this time we had a period of respite from the attentions of Brown when he went off somewhere on some special duty.

One afternoon a squad was taken out of camp on a special fatigue. When they returned all had their pockets filled with "Lucky Strike" and "Chesterfield" cigarettes! They had been unloading American Red Cross parcels from railway trucks into a warehouse at Shinagawa. All were enraged at this theft of Red Cross supplies and we had the American sergeant in charge up to explain matters. He said that as the Japanese workmen and soldiers were freely helping themselves they felt they might at least get some sort of share before the whole lot was stolen. We could not help but agree.

And when Brown returned from his duty he went round camp smoking "Lucky Strikes", while we were down to the butt ends collected from the camp office.

On Christmas Eve Gentleman Jim was the officer of the day. Brown issued us three-quarters of a Red Cross parcel each, although there was enough in the store to give each man his full share. But what a parcel! Cigarettes, jam, coffee, corned beef, chewing gum, lemon essence, and all manner of good things. There was also a bulk issue of cocoa and sugar from the good people of the United States. Gentleman Jim had arranged for lights-out and permission to smoke to be extended to eleven p.m. and when Colonel Suzuki arrived, accompanied by his wife and sons, our show opened in the camp bath-house.

It was a tremendous success. There was an American gangster play with Ray Lucia as Al Capone; nigger minstrels, crooners—led by "Bucky" Henshaw, and all kinds of nonsense, and all joined Jack McNaughton in singing his:

> "Sweet Fanny Adams, bright and gay ...
> And all you could see ...
> On the old apple tree was Sweet F.A.!"

For a grand finale the curtain opened on an old couple sitting by the fireside on Christmas Day talking of their boys away at the wars. Then came a knock on the door, and the boys were back, and amid great rejoicing all sang the old heart-warming songs, which bowled everyone over so that there was not a dry eye among us.

When it was over we entertained our great friend and saviour, Gentleman Jim, to a cup of Red Cross cocoa in the post office.

III

During one of my periodical punishments I was working with young Hunting, my usual partner, in a pit which we had dug to receive the contents of the *benjos*, when Tokugawa sought me out.

As he handed me some "Airship" cigarettes, he said, "Yesterday I met His Imperial Highness Prince Chichibu at a ceremony. He remembers you well from Hirosaki days and when you were in England with your wife at the time of the Coronation of King George VI and asked me to tell you how sorry he is that you are a prisoner, and hopes that you will look after yourself and come through these terrible times."

Needless to say I was most deeply moved to receive this kind message. But His Highness, the late Prince Chichibu, had always been a very humane and sporting gentleman.

In his death, Japan suffered a grievous loss and I shall never forget the kind message he sent me in those grim days of early 1944.

Later, in 1946, I was able to offer him my thanks for his message at his home at Gotemba, and I was also to have the privilege, a sad one indeed, of paying my respects to the gracious prince before he was taken to his final resting place.

At about this time I heard that many of the Canadians at Niigata had died of pneumonia, and through an avalanche which had struck the camp, and "Bill" Stewart, major in the Royal Army Medical Corps, from the officers' camp at Zentsuji, stopped over at Omori for an hour or so, on his way to Niigata, where he was apparently needed most desperately.

IV

In early spring 1944, each day all went outside to prepare the sandy soil in order to grow turnips, peanuts, and carrots.

Outside the canteen, Harry started a small garden of red, white and blue flowers. He obtained the seeds from the man who used to come in from the Keihin Department Store to supply any rubbish which the Japanese people would not buy. Our great mainstay was black tea which always seemed available, probably because the Japanese did not like it without sugar. But it was hard to get hot water and to obtain it one had to have influence in the cookhouse. My old coxswain helped a great deal, but often we had to use the water in which the cereals had been boiled.

At this period we had a great deal of trouble with Little Beast. He told us that in future he would punish any man who whistled or sang, said we were insincere, and that we should be humble and serious in view of the fact that we were disgraced in having been taken prisoner, and that our countries were being defeated on all fronts.

He was always damning Mr. Winston Churchill. One evening he devised a new form of punishment for his victims. He had them standing outside their huts shouting: "Mr. Churchill is a very good man, he is very kind to women and children—I don't think!"

When any showed signs of weakening he received a punch in the face. They kept it up until none could speak for hoarseness.

And yet, an hour later Little Beast presented a sick man with his own dinner.

The behaviour of our hosts was quite unpredictable. A British soldier was caught stealing from the Japanese army canteen into which he had tunnelled while detailed in the guardhouse. He was ordered special hard labour in the camp and to wear a placard round his neck on which was written in Japanese and in English: "I am a Thief." The guards thought this a most diabolical form of punishment, saw that he did little hard labour, gave him cigarettes, and even their own rations.

Colonel Suzuki had left and in his stead came a ghastly man, the very worst type of Japanese officer, arrogant and cruel. I believe Suzuki had always tried to be fair and, as he was in command of some thirty camps in the area one could realize that his was no easy job.

Another new member of the staff was a captain we called "The Rat", a quite unbalanced person, who was to prove worse than Brown.

One day Tokugawa announced that he'd arranged for us to have a film show and said he'd got hold of a print of an old German film "Congress Dances", and we'd see it on April 29th, the Emperor's Birthday. However, the new colonel objected to our being shown this film, which most of us had seen and enjoyed years before. He said it was bad for our morals. And so after some sports events, in the evening we were shown a documentary of the Yawata Iron and Steel Works, well calculated not to arouse any sexual ideas among us. This was followed by a short but superb film, *Kojo no Tsuki*—"Moon on the Ruined Castle"—with singing by Tamaki Miura, which was appreciated by all.

v

One afternoon I was summoned to the camp office and introduced to a Japanese professor who wished to give us a lecture but emphasized that this was not being forced upon us. He was extremely pleasant, spoke excellent English and was obviously a widely travelled man. He then came around the camp and talked with the officers and men.

Before he left I told him about the treatment meted out by Brown and The Rat and said that for the honour of the Japanese people he should see that such men never had charge of prisoners of war. He appeared shocked and promised to take up the matter with higher authorities.

The next day we assembled in the bath-house for his lecture in which he expounded his theory that it had been ordained that the people of the Sun should rule mankind, and that the Japanese were the chosen race. He said that the gods, and particularly the Sun, were angered at the Western nations and the Chinese. He pointed out that the Japanese were the only nation which used the true Sun in their national flag; the Americans used stars, the Australians—stars, the Turks—the Moon and a star; and worst of all, the Chinese used a white sun on a field of blue, which was a direct insult. He was of the opinion that if Mr. Churchill and President Roosevelt would only study his theory and that of *Yang* and *Yin*—the Chinese male and female principles—they would eventually see reason and acknowledge that it was quite useless to fight.

"Well," said a bright young Texan, "if you will arrange for one British and one American to have safe conduct to a neutral country they can at least acquaint our respective governments of your wonderful theory. It surely can do no harm!"

"I shall put the suggestion before the authorities," replied the professor, and then proceeded to answer questions.

He was a charming personality, could speak on most subjects and, apart from his ridiculous theory, was a most scholarly and kind man, who spoke of people like Henry Stimson, Woodrow Wilson, Lord Balfour and Sir Arthur Henderson, as personal friends.

We did not see him again, but next day I had my worst beating from Brown who said that the professor had tried to assist us.

Then the Rat had us on the parade ground and said that henceforth we would have to go to work with the men. We protested that as officers we could not be forced to do such work. He replied that he would give us one day to make up our minds, but that he would force us to work in any event.

At a conference we decided that we'd work in the post office, gardening, or at anything not of assistance to the Japanese war effort.

The next day Bryce Martin told the Rat that as an army officer he could not consent to being forced to do any kind of work and the swine took him to the camp office and committed the most brutal assault ever to take place at Omori.

He knocked Bryce down, kicked him in the face, broke his nose, and altogether made a shocking and bloody mess of him. The young Texan could not move for about two weeks and then went out to work at Sumidagawa in the wood-yard. He was a brave man, for in the Rat he was not dealing with a human being, but a sadist of the worst type.

With the coming of the warm weather, Harry's red, white and blue flower garden began to look lovely and was a most pleasant sight amid those gloomy surroundings.

Brown started to show great interest in this garden, took photos of it and also had one taken of himself and some of his victims.

"When the war is over, would you welcome me if I came to England?" he asked "General" McGrath.

"Why of course, we'll even meet you at the ship with a brass band," replied the "General".

A few days later Brown stormed into Harry's room and shouted that gardens could no longer be permitted and made him dig it up and plant turnips.

He now gave orders that Japanese of any rank, even civilians, were to be saluted by all prisoners.

Heidelberg Henry had been in touch with the Swiss consul at Yokohama and had broken all kinds of regulations in doing so; but the result was a letter from Kaneko, from Rokko, near Kobe. She was apparently well, and under the protection of the Swiss. This was a great relief. I had worried the camp staff and especially the civilian interpreter about her, until I had been told: "You should not worry about your wife when your country is being defeated in war."

The camp guards changed every week or so, and were by and

large a very decent crowd of men. One who used to warn us of the approach of our persecutors knew my relatives at Nagahama and Ohta who used to serve in the grill of the Imperial Hotel, at Tokyo, is now proprietor of a travel magazine, "This Week In Tokyo."

The camp sergeant-major was another good type, and the cook-house sergeant Fukuda was a decent fellow who would help weak prisoners carry heavy loads, and behaved excellently.

As Petty-Officer Mitchell had joined MTB o8 while she was building, on his birthday I gave him the MTB crest which I'd brought from Hong Kong. At the end of 1945 when I visited him at his home in Pompey it was hung in the place of honour above the fire-place.

One evening at *tenko*, Brown made me step forward and knocked me down, poured the contents of a fire bucket over me and struck me with the empty bucket. I managed to dodge one of his kicks, and his boot sank right through the woodwork of the barrack. He was about to brain me with a heavy fire extinguisher when Doctor Fuji appeared, threw Brown with a *judo* throw and ordered him to the camp office.

The next day we were ordered to be on parade at four o'clock in the afternoon to give some army cadets practice in English conversation. It was a dreary sort of business and Legless Private Plimmer was told by the cadet he was conversing with, that the Japanese soldier was noble and gentle, and possessed the spirit of *bushido*.

"Och, aye, well ye should ha' seen the nobility of your soldiery last night when one of them nearly killed one of our officers!" commented the young Scot.

VI

We lost some of our good friends including Jack McNaughton, "Bucky" Henshaw and George Williams who were taken to Bunka School, Tokyo, but fortunately, our happy mess was not disturbed.

On the now frequent visits across the bridge to bring in stores one obtained a vivid impression of the gradual deterioration in Japanese living. They had experienced the false illusions of early victories but now the inevitable and merciless retribution had commenced. The people's clothes were shabby, they did not look as if they were able to enjoy their usual daily bath, so essential to Japanese. The general shoddiness was even reflected in the little children, who looked so undernourished.

Often there would be an old woman standing near the bridge with a small girl. One of my comrades offered the child a piece of chocolate which he had saved from a Red Cross parcel, but she screamed when he approached her. He was deeply hurt and probably felt that the child regarded him as some kind of monster.

One Sunday afternoon I was invited by one of the cooks to participate in a bone sucking session in the cookhouse. The bones had been boiled and boiled for weeks and heaven only knew the types of animal from which they originated. They were stacked in a barrel and the favoured few stood around gnawing and sucking them for a couple of hours. How many times they had been subjected to the frantic biting and gnawing of human jaws I do not know. There was really nothing more to be got out of them. The next day they were buried or burnt.

Squadron-Leader Burchell, Royal Canadian Air Force, had joined us to be disciplined by Brown. He was a fine, courageous officer, who had been the first to spot the Japanese fleet in the Indian Ocean as it approached Ceylon, and it was his warning which he was just able to radio before being shot down by Japanese fighters, which probably saved the island.

Apparently Burchell had struck a Japanese medical orderly who had ill-treated a sick prisoner. Brown did a lot of threatening, but left him pretty much alone.

I had now really struck rock-bottom and I did not much care what happened to me, was coughing blood and my pillow was covered with it each morning, which convinced me that I had contracted consumption. Doctor Goad disagreed, and said he believed I had a hæmorrhage through being kicked in the stomach by Brown.

Then in August 1944 I was told I was to be transferred to another camp.

After all we had been through together it was indeed hard to leave Harry, Poop, and Peter, David and Bob, the "General" and other friends.

"You'll be better off anywhere," said Peter. "That Brown will surely kill or cripple you if you stay here."

"See you on the boat going home," said Bryce Martin.

"You'll find me around Piccadilly, sir," said Klot, in civil life a taxi driver.

Chapter Twenty-nine

I

I was handed over to a civilian interpreter I had never seen before and limped over the Bamboo Bridge and along to Omori station.

The electric train was packed with people of all ages, and I was the object of much curiosity. One man offered me his seat when he saw that I had a bandaged foot.

I feared that I was being taken to Ofuna, but we changed at Yokohama to the Sakuragi-cho train.

Outside Sakuragi-cho station was a lone charcoal-burning taxi which we entered, and were soon climbing the hill leading to the Bluff, passed the foreign cemetery, and stopped before an ordinary private house.

The door was opened by a Japanese naval petty-officer and I was escorted upstairs and shown into what I was told would be my room. The interpreter, Shinozaki, and the petty-officer left and I threw off my pack and coat and flung myself upon the built-in bed, completely exhausted.

Someone shook me. I jumped up to find a smiling young Japanese sailor who pointed to a plate of food and a cup of tea which he had placed upon a small table, and expressed his alarm on seeing blood on my pillow.

I took stock of my surroundings. The bedroom contained a cupboard, a chair, and a small table. I was to be interrogated here, I thought, and then sent off to a Yokohama camp which I hoped would be with Heidelberg Henry.

The interpreter returned and said that he was making arrangements for me to see a doctor, but that in the meantime I should stay in bed and my food would be brought to me.

"There is another officer here," he said, "but for the time being you must not see him. If you promise me that you will not attempt to do so then your door will not be locked and you can go out to the bath-room as you please."

I fell into a deep sleep, to be awakened in a cold sweat by a nightmare in which Brown was screaming and beating people all around me. I looked out of the window where a young British or American officer in khaki trousers, shirt and sweater, was walking up and down the garden. Two Japanese sailors were seated on a bench laughing and smoking.

The next morning I had the joy of being able to walk in the brilliant sunshine down past the foreign cemetery and Christ Church along the Bluff road to the International Hospital, which had been taken over by the Japanese Navy, accompanied by a very jolly sailor.

A queue of sailors waited outside the medical inspection room, mostly very young and many pitiful specimens, some of whom looked as if they were riddled with TB, and I felt that the Japanese Navy had certainly come to a critical state of affairs if it was reduced to accepting such poor material.

A grey-haired doctor received me. "You were at Hirosaki Higher School, weren't you?" he inquired. "You taught my son."

He gave me a thorough examination and then a young nurse escorted me to another room where I was X-rayed. The doctor told the sailor that I was to rest as much as possible and should be brought back the following day.

On the way back I had a good look at the harbour. No more gleaming white Empress liners, black-funnelled French ships or beautiful NYK Pacific vessels. All ships alongside the wharves and at the buoys wore the dull grey of war.

The sailor told me to rest and we sat on a patch of grass in the sunshine and he lit a cigarette and, as he did so, said: "Perhaps you should not smoke?"

I took a *Homare,* and he laughed. It was glorious sitting there with everything so very quiet. The sailor was a robust country boy who seemed delighted and mystified concerning my ability to speak a little Japanese.

The doctor had given me an envelope which contained about twenty packets of powders and the sailor took these from me and said that he would see that I took them as directed.

In the cupboard in my room I found a large stack of magazines, mostly "Atlantic Monthly", "Saturday Evening Post", and "Harpers". On some was the name "Dennistoun". Here was a feast of reading and I blessed Mr., Mrs., or Miss Dennistoun, who were connected with the Standard Oil Co.

Whenever I looked out of the window the young officer was walking round and round the small garden. Once he looked up, his eyes met mine, and he gave me the V sign and smiled.

When I went to the toilet I found "Lieut. John Gibson, Australian Infantry, Melbourne," pencilled on the wall. I rubbed out his name and pencilled in my own.

At the hospital next day, I was greatly relieved to hear that the X-ray had revealed no trace of any lung infection. The doctor confirmed that I had an internal hæmorrhage and beri-beri, and said that I should have to rest for several weeks.

Inside the cupboard door was pencilled the name "Best," I had heard of him and believed he, too, was an Australian. Then at the foot of the stairway was the name "Lempriere" written on the wall; another Australian whose family is well-known in the wool business.

Shinozaki, the interpreter, came to see me from time to time and was a delightful and decent man, a staunch Catholic with whom I had many interesting arguments on religion. Prior to the war he had worked for Butterfield and Swire, a British shipping company. Then to my great surprise, there arrived none other than my old friend Ken Sato of the Osaka Mainichi newspaper, a friend of many years' standing, accompanied by an interpreter named Nozawa.

"I know you've had a bad time," said Ken, "and we are ashamed at the treatment you and other prisoners have received. It has not been with the approval of the higher naval authorities. Now you will be left alone."

Ken said that his family was living near Takarazuka, near Osaka, and as he visited them from time to time, promised to get in touch with Kaneko to see how she was and if he could do anything to help her.

Nozawa was a handsome, athletic-looking fellow with a broad outlook and had been with the Oska Shosen Kaisha, in which company he had at one time served as a purser and visited Europe, South Africa, the United States and South America. We were to become good friends as far as this was possible in war time, and as with Shinozaki, who is now a neighbour, were able to fully realize our friendship at the end of the war.

Then I met John Gibson, a scholarly chap, fluent in German, French and Italian who was then studying Arabic. A graduate of Melbourne University, he had won a scholarship for study in Germany and Italy and on his return to Australia joined the Army, spent some time interrogating German and Italian prisoners of war from the Middle East and was then sent to New Guinea where he had fallen into the Japanese bag.

Within six weeks my health had vastly improved, thanks to the kindness and attention I received at the Navy hospital and I was very sorry when it was no longer necessary for me to go there, as the walk along the Bluff with one of the sailors was a great treat.

Soon I became calm and resigned to things and spent the days reading, and writing a novel about a leper colony in the South Pacific founded by an English nobleman who had contracted the disease. I had always been interested in lepers and leprosy since I had visited a leprosarium on an island near Singapore.

John had quite a number of books he'd acquired from second-hand shops in Motomachi, Yokohama, and told me that he was taken out from time to time to buy them by Nozawa or Shinozaki. Most of his books were on Arabic, Urdu, Hungarian, and other languages.

II

One day I asked Nozawa if it would be possible for him to arrange to take me to Maruzen's, meaning the book store, in Bentendori, Yokohama.

"I think I might be able to take you to Tokyo if you have some sort of civilian clothes," he replied.

At Omori, Eric Marsden had given me a rather peculiar suit

of clothes which he had acquired whilst in a prison camp in Formosa. It was blue, and made of some kind of staple fibre, and looked as if it might disintegrate if worn in the rain.

And so one afternoon Nozawa took me up to Tokyo. We stood all the way in the packed electric car, my eyes drinking in all around me—the people, the rather shabby looking foreigners, German sailors in uniform, the railway stations—all those old familiar names—Kawasaki, Omori, Hamamatsu-cho, Shimbashi.

Few people were on the streets and most of them elderly folk—in drab clothing—the men wearing military type caps and with their legs encased in puttees over their trousers; and most of the women in *mompei*.

The Ginza was almost deserted, like the city of London on a Sunday.

At Maruzen's we found the foreign-books department closed to the public, but Nozawa was able to persuade the manager to allow us in.

It was almost too good to be true! I could have stayed there for days, for the shelves were still packed with English books and I bought the *Oxford Books of English Prose and Poetry*, a small dictionary, and a bottle of bay rum. The sales people were most kind and polite, but of course, very curious.

A cup of green tea was all we could obtain for refreshment.

The pavements were cracked and scarred. Here and there were slit trenches dug in preparation for air raids and concrete tubs filled with water, and whole rows of wooden houses had been demolished to provide fire breaks.

I was immensely grateful to Nozawa for having given me the chance to see Tokyo, but on my return to Yokohama felt I did not wish to go there again, it was all too depressing.

And so I walked up and down the small garden, read my books, argued with John, wrote my novel, and lived with a perpetual hunger.

Early in November I managed to procure a small quantity of barley and decided to make some wine for Christmas and the New Year. I put it in a large bottle together with potato peelings, some raisins I had saved from a Red Cross parcel, a Yeast-Vite tablet which I'd kept since Hong Kong, and hoped for the best.

Ken Sato returned and said that Kaneko had visited him at his home, that she was quite well, and that if she could get to Yokohama he would find a way for her to come and see me.

The petty-officer was a good man, strict with the sailors yet fair and humane in all things. One day his old parents visited him from Tochigi prefecture, bringing with them such gifts as dried persimmons, sweet potatoes, and other things which were so hard to come by, and shared these equally among the sailors, John and myself.

One day he told me that he had agreed for my wife to visit me in secret and said that it would be within a few days. I waited anxiously.

Then came the first air raid on Tokyo.

The following day he brought me a white bag which contained some of my own woollen socks, a bottle of *Wakamoto*—yeast tablets—warm underwear, a shirt, a tin of home-made cheese, butter, home-made jam, cigarettes and soap! I could imagine how difficult it had been for Kaneko to obtain these foodstuffs and learned later that she had made the cheese and jam herself. But she did not appear and I did not care to say too much about it to Nozawa or Shinozaki, as I did not wish to embarrass them in any way. After the war I had Kaneko's story.

As an enemy alien, she was prohibited from leaving the Kobe area. However, one evening she mentioned to a friend whose husband was an army doctor, home on leave, that she could have the chance to see me providing she could get to Tokyo, and the doctor said: "There's a medical conference to take place in Tokyo shortly. Supposing you go there as a woman delegate?"

He wrote on his own name card to the effect that she was a delegate to the conference.

She arrived in Tokyo in the middle of the first real American bombing raid on the capital and went to a small hotel in Kanda. She'd dressed in trousers, had a scarf over her head, so as to be as inconspicuous as possible. The next morning she 'phoned to her contact in the Navy Ministry, who met her at Tokyo station where he took the white bag containing her gifts to me and told her to get back quickly to Kobe before she was found out.

III

We had a bath once a week when we could arrange it; but the water system and lack of fuel made this quite uncertain. Nearby was a public bath-house which the Japanese sailors used and I suggested to the petty-officer that we be allowed to go to the bath-house with the sailors early in the afternoon before the regular customers. He laughed, but added that it was a good idea and he saw nothing against it as long as we could keep it quiet and the "*kempei*" were not informed. That evening he went to see the bath-house master and John and I became secret patrons of the Yamate public bath-house.

A vast change had come over the Press since the fall of the Tojo Cabinet after the Americans had taken the island of Tinian. It was now rather more reserved. At Omori we kept a record of the *daihonyei*—Imperial Headquarters—sinkings of United States warships and, within the space of some six months or so, came to the conclusion that the United States Navy had ceased to exist.

The bombings became more frequent—starting with raids by three or four B–29s, they were now coming over in twenties and thirties and John and I watched them as they swept in from the direction of Mount Fuji, which was a perfect landfall. We often saw the fighters swarm in upon the great silver bombers but most of those shot down seemed to have been caught in the concentrated anti-aircraft fire.

One afternoon we were given an American Red Cross parcel each which had been sent from Omori and, as the sailors had generously shared with us their New Year's ration of cigarettes, sake, beer, and sweetmeats, which the petty-officer had brought from Yokosuka, we were happy to be able to give them such unobtainable delicacies as chocolate, and "Lucky Strike", "Chesterfield", or "Camel" cigarettes.

When Nozawa came I offered him a packet of cigarettes and some soap for his wife.

"I am sorry. I thank you for your offer, but I cannot accept anything from you while we are at war."

I thought of all the robbery of our Red Cross parcels that had taken place at Omori.

IV

The Americans were now well established in the Philippines; in February they landed at Iwo Jima to join in one of the most bloody battles of the Pacific War; in April they landed on Okinawa.

The bombings of Tokyo and other cities became intense. Night after night we watched the great bombers sweeping over us, their numbers increasing as the United States forces drew nearer and nearer to the Japanese mainland.

One night the B–29s came in singly, flying very low. Their target seemed to be somewhere in the Kawasaki area. They released their bombs, then turned sharp to port, and at this point several were shot down by anti-aircraft fire which concentrated on that one position. We saw at least a dozen planes hit. Some plunged straight to earth, others flew on afire for a while and we saw the crews descending by parachute amid the cheers of the people. Our hearts bled for those American fliers but it seemed to us that the low altitude at which they were flying was quite foolhardy. All over the area was a great glow of red and orange which floodlit the clouds and presented a fiery and angry scene such as might have been a painting by Turner of the "Day of Judgement".

Yokohama had still not been attacked, and we felt that perhaps the Americans wished to spare the port city for their own convenience.

On May 8th John and I celebrated VE Day with an extra cup of Red Cross coffee which we had hoarded for such occasion.

On the morning of May 29th, I was shaving. The air raid warnings had already sounded and I looked out of the window. A formation of some 25 bombers was approaching, then another formation came in sight and yet another. Suddenly great eruptions of black smoke soared skywards.

Within five minutes one could not see the sky for smoke and above it all was the roar of those great bombers and the bark of the anti-aircraft guns. Then came a noise like hailstones falling on a corrugated and iron roof, the wind started to roar, and soon the houses were burning all around us.

The petty-officer ordered us outside and I grabbed my duffle coat, stuffed a few small possessions in my pockets and followed him and the sailors down the road. You could hardly see your hand in front of your face. It was like a dense, black London fog and the wind was howling and flames licked out from the burning houses and trees like the tongues of giant serpents.

People bumped into us from out of the blackness which enshrouded everything, and that ghastly hail of incendiary bombs showered all around us, as wave after wave of B-29s passed overhead. We found the International Cemetery crowded with people who moved about with blankets over their heads to protect them from flames, and sparks and flying debris.

Old men, women and young children, moved about between the grave-stones amid the enveloping smoke like so many ghosts. We sat down in a group and then the petty-officer told us to mind their rifles while he and the sailors returned to the house to try to fight the fire. He handed me a packet of *Homare*. I lit one from a burning bush. An old woman with a blanket draped round her watched me as I inhaled, and came close and said, "Please give me one puff." I gave her a cigarette and lit it for her and watched her as she inhaled it hungrily.

The bombs still showered around us and clattered on the graves and monuments. Even the dead could not sleep in peace! A group of old people were huddled around a stone crucifix—it was as if they had instinctively hastened to Christ. "Come unto me all ye that labour, and I will give you rest!"

A middle-aged Japanese appeared with a European woman, probably French, for even though she wore trousers and had a blanket swathed around her—yet she retained that indescribable French chic. She clung to two Eurasian children. The man asked me for a light, obviously an excuse to speak, for there was no lack of fire all around us, and said: "You'll soon be free. Japan is finished; she cannot go on."

A sailor returned and told us to bring the rifles and return to the house. Despite the scorching air, the smoke and the noise, I could not help smiling as I realized the humorous sight we must have presented. Two prisoners of war carrying half a dozen Japanese rifles and escorted by a very short sailor!

The house was enveloped in smoke and inside were fires in a dozen places where bombs had penetrated the roof, but at about three o'clock the smoke started to clear and we had extinguished all the fires.

Practically every wooden building in Yokohama had disappeared.

Chapter Thirty

I

THE petty-officer, a new man named Kitahara, told me that henceforth we must go to the basement during a raid, as the Americans had announced they would shortly use a terrible bomb, more destructive than anything hitherto known to mankind. A sailor had picked up a pamphlet dropped the previous night. They talked about *genshi bakudan*.

I consulted my dictionary. *Genshi—Genko*, a manuscript. I could not imagine the Americans would start showering pamphlets over Japan in the hope of scaring the people. Some glimmer, some intuition led me to look up the Japanese for atom. I'd read of the atom being split, but the significance of this meant little to my unscientific mind.

Then the petty-officer told me that a terrible bombing had taken place at Hiroshima and the city was completely devastated.

Carrier-borne aircraft now came over Yokohama at will, flying at tree-top level so that we could see the pilots quite plainly.

One night there was a prolonged rumble as of thunder. The Allied fleets were bombarding the coast off Mito and the entire area shook and trembled as during a severe earthquake.

Then, one afternoon a number of senior Japanese naval officers arrived. The majority of them spoke English and were most cordial. One had been taught by the late Professor Frank Lee, at Etajima Naval Academy. Another gave me the sad news of the death of an old friend, Captain Mizuno, a great gentleman and Christian, who had at one time been aide-de-camp to the ill-fated Prime Minister, Admiral Minoru Saito, who had been assassinated by nationalist fanatics in 1936.

They sat about laughing, asking us about our families, talked of the weather, with the petty-officer and sailors standing there like statues in great awe of all this top brass.

"I hope you are receiving plenty of good food and an allowance of whisky and beer?" inquired one officer.

I laughed, and he called the petty-officer and wanted to know the reason why we were not being supplied with such luxuries. The poor man looked bewildered to say the least.

"I am sure he is doing his best for us, and I can assure you that he has always been extremely kind," I said.

"That is good. But as officers you should have the things you are accustomed to," he replied.

"Well, well," said John, "I'd better get back to my studies for it won't be long now."

The following day one of the sailors went to Yokosuka and returned with some beer, a bottle of sake, cigarettes and biscuits.

II

All morning I walked round and round the garden. The atmosphere was tense, a swarm of American carrier-borne fighters passed overhead and a few seconds later I heard the roar of their rockets as they attacked Atsugi airfield and Hachioji. Then, just before noon there was a deathly silence.

It was indeed so quiet that you could hear sounds of movements down in the city, and the petty-officer and sailors sat together round a table listening to a radio which I could not hear because the doors to the garden were shut.

From a house nearby a radio was turned to full volume; and suddenly, I heard a calm, dignified voice and stood quite still, for although I could not understand, I knew that with millions of Japanese I was listening for the first time to the voice of the Emperor of Japan.

My whole being surged with emotion, my blood for the moment seemed to boil within me, my face became wet with tears.

It was all over! I sank down on the grass, and then rushed into the house and bounded up the stairs.

"John! John! It's over! The Emperor has just announced Japan's acceptance of the terms of unconditional surrender!"

He looked at me, and did not even smile, as he said, "Well, that's good. But I would have liked to finish this Arabic!"

The petty-officer came up, saluted smartly and said: "Japan has surrendered by order of His Majesty the Emperor."

On August 19th we said good-bye to the sailors and I urged them to get away to their homes as soon as possible and to take with them anything which might be useful.

We drove to Omori in a truck. The devastation was simply indescribable. On both sides of the Tokyo-Yokohama road few buildings remained and people were existing in makeshift shelters put together from the debris.

And once again, though in vastly different circumstances, I walked over the Bamboo Bridge.

III

The camp was packed and now the prisoners were about 95 per cent. Americans. There were two entire huts of aircrews shot down whilst on bombing raids in the B–29s.

It was grand to see my old friends again. David James and "Poop" Badger, Harry Parker and Commander Maher, USN, and others.

Gone were Brown and Little Beast. They had been transferred

soon after my departure and apparently there had been a tremendous improvement in the general treatment.

Boyington, a US Marine flier, was acting as camp provost marshal. "Pappy" was a much decorated hero, a gay and charming fellow who was to record his own story in *Baa! Baa! Black Sheep*.

Some of the airmen had been beaten by civilians, many had been badly burned, and some were in a pitiful condition through being confined in various detention camps without food for long periods. At Omori, the colonel had given instructions that B–29 aircrew were not to receive medical treatment. Dr. Fuji, true to the medical code, disobeyed these instructions and treated men in secret. Ample proof of his humane behaviour was brought forward at his trial as an alleged war criminal and I believe that Hiroshi Fuji was responsible for saving the lives and preserving the health of hundreds of Allied prisoners.

I longed to get in touch with Kaneko but was refused permission to go to Kobe. I am sure I would not have been molested. I had complete faith in the Japanese people obeying faithfully the commands given them by their Emperor.

Carrier-borne planes now came over the camp and dropped supplies of food and cigarettes.

Then came the B–29s dropping five tons of food and clothing and cigarettes at a time.

I was sitting talking to Harry Parker when we heard a shout and ran outside just in time to miss a case of corned beef which wrecked the room.

"Christ! Fancy being killed now by a case of bully!" exclaimed Harry.

In another camp a prisoner *was* killed during the dropping of supplies.

Within two days we had thousands of pairs of boots, and food and clothing enough to last for months. But there was still no contact with our forces.

We were told that no prisoner would be released until the formal entry of General MacArthur.

"Trust 'Showman Doug' to make a ceremony of it," said one disgusted American.

At Omori there was only one incident, as far as I can remember, concerning prisoners taking reprisals against Japanese. The despicable colonel complained to our senior officer that someone had urinated in one of his boots and evacuated in the other. We could not of course countenance such behaviour, but he had always been most unpleasant to us and at most this was a pretty harmless way for the men to get even with him. We promised to find and punish the culprit, but the attempt to do so was rather half-hearted.

One afternoon we had a visit from the Swiss representatives of the International Red Cross accompanied by Tadatsugu Shimazu, of the Japanese Red Cross Society, and Yoshitomo Tokugawa. They promised to get in touch with Kaneko by telegram.

The Japanese now issued us with five thousand vitamin tablets apiece. These had come from the American Red Cross and had been in the camp for months!

I gave mine to Yoshitomo Tokugawa.

IV

When on August 29th warships were sighted out in the Bay, the men swarmed over the fences like a horde of excited children.

An hour later landing craft were seen approaching and the whole camp simply went mad and the men broke down the fences and some even swam out to meet the small vessels which were packed with armed sailors and marines. An American commander from the cruiser USS *San Juan* stepped ashore followed by marine officers and a naval doctor. The Japanese camp commandant came rushing up, looking angry as he said: "You can't land here, I have no instructions."

The Japanese stared at their colonel in amazement. The American commander replied: "I do not care about your instructions. These men have been here long enough and I intend to clear this camp tonight."

A Japanese sergeant said: "The commandant is quite mad—he's the kind of fellow who started this war. Even now he seems to think he can tell the Americans what to do."

"Point out those who've ill-treated you," said an American officer.

Commander Maher hastened to inform him that apart from the commandant the present camp staff had been very considerate. But I doubt if Brown or Little Beast would have got away unharmed had they still been there!

There was an abundance of surplus food, clothing and cigarettes, which had been dropped by the Americans, and we loaded these upon those Japanese who had been good to us. But most were frightened to accept for fear they might get into trouble if the Americans found them with such supplies, even though we wrote letters explaining these were gifts.

I said my goodbye to Yoshitomo, promised to see his friends in London, and to come back as soon as possible, shook hands with Gentleman Jim, Doctor Fuji, and Fukuda, the good and manly cookhouse sergeant who'd lost his home in the bombings, and Sergeants Konno and Katoh, and others. And I thought to myself —if it had not been for men like these—how many of us would have survived to see this day?

V

Late that evening I was one of the last to board a landing craft which headed out into the bay to berth alongside USS *Benevolence*, a beautiful white hospital ship. Its name was more than upheld, for never was such kindness, gentleness and understanding displayed as by the officers, nurses, doctors and men of that magnificent American vessel.

We were in a complete daze as we climbed the gangway and were led below through gleaming alleyways, our nostrils twitching with the clean smell of soap, floor polish and antiseptics, and the perfume in the hair of the nurses; our eyes bulging at the sight of silk-sheathed legs, wavy hair and make-up. And as for the *"WAVES"*—well—they were out of another world. One of our men could not restrain himself and exclaimed: "Well, I'll be b...d!"

"Now then, watch your language chum," said a comrade.

But the girls laughed and beamed like a bevy of Hollywood film stars.

"Sit down and get your clothes off," said a sick-bay steward. I looked at the sheets. It seemed vandalism to sit on them. He laughed, and gave me a push. I laid my face against the pillow— the smell of the linen was delicious.

"Get off all your clothes and we'll burn them."

"Yes, do but not my cap."

"All right, keep it. And here's another bag for your kit," he said, handing me a white kit bag into which I emptied my posses- sions from the zip fastener bag which did not zip and was fastened with a piece of rope. We then went into the baths where sick-bay men scrubbed our backs, and just wallowed in soap and hot water.

After this we were given a complete kit of American sailors' clothing, new shoes, a Red Cross bag donated by some kind ladies in Pennsylvania, which contained toilet goods, cigarettes, note- paper, and all manner of good and useful things, and then went off to eat.

In the mess hall our men were already tucking into sausages and bacon, steaks, eggs cooked in any way desired, cornflakes, porridge, and ice cream and fruit.

"Take it easy fellows," shouted a doctor. "You'll kill yourselves if you're not careful."

"What a glorious death! I can think of only one better," cracked "Tim" Callahan, our wild Irish petty-officer.

Tim had finished his third helping of bacon and eggs and was dealing with an enormous steak.

The following morning British, American and Australian news- paper correspondents came aboard and our small party of naval prisoners was visited by Admiral Sir Bruce Fraser, Commander- in-Chief of the British Pacific Fleet whose flagship, HMS *Duke of York*, was lying off Yokohama, and I was ordered to board a destroyer which came alongside.

Apart from my old cap and badge I was an American sailor in working kit. So with my kit bag and a bundle under my arm I boarded HMS *Whelper*, and was simply inundated with kindness.

A tall lieutenant gave me two hundred cigarettes and some pipe tobacco. I was to learn that he was none other than Lieutenant

Philip Mountbatten, now Duke of Edinburgh, and consort of HM Queen Elizabeth.

Off Yokohama there were warships and transports as far as the eye could see. Huge battleships like the USS *Missouri,* HMS *Duke of York,* aircraft carriers, cruisers, destroyers, frigates, submarines, landing craft and transports.

On the quarter-deck of *King George V* I met Vice-Admiral Sir Bernard Rawlings, RN, whom years before I had met at the Tokyo Club when he had been naval attaché.

In *Duke of York* a paymaster-commander named Jacobs fitted me out with a naval kit at his own expense. I drank much that evening but, strange to say, even after so long abstinence it did not seem to affect me. It was all most bewildering; gold braid everywhere, the vessel reeked of full captains and admirals and the like, and I found it almost impossible to find my way around. I wrote a report, and slept what seemed like dozens of decks below the waterline.

The Navy was making every effort to get in touch with Kaneko but had I known it she was at that moment in Yokohama searching for me and waiting about in the New Grand Hotel when General MacArthur arrived. Even security guards could not keep her out.

I was told that I should be sent home via Manila and that she would be flown down to join me there or else to England direct.

On September 1st, I joined my comrades aboard the aircraft-carrier, HMS *Speaker.* In the afternoon we were entertained to lunch by the commanding officer of USS *San Juan* who had taken us out of Omori. Those were hectic and bewildering days. The whole pattern of naval and military life had changed since we had been taken prisoners and even the new war-time language was at times quite incomprehensible.

The next morning, little more than a cable's length distant, history was in the making; the curtain about to be lowered on the war in the Pacific, in China and South-east Asia, as up the gangway to the quarterdeck of the grim, businesslike USS *Missouri* streamed the representatives of the Allies; top-hatted, morning-suited Japanese dignitaries, and high-ranking naval and military officers.

At eleven o'clock came a strange hush over the fleets, which recalled the moment only two weeks or so before when I'd heard the Emperor of Japan speak to his people for the first time. All eyes, telescopes and binoculars were trained on the quarterdeck of the American battleship, whose crew perched on turrets, guns, to glimpse the dramatic signing of the documents of Japan's surrender by Mr. Mamoru Shigemitsu, General Douglas MacArthur, whose powerful figure dominated the assembly, the representatives of the Commonwealth, China, the Netherlands, and the Soviet Union.

At mid-day, all hands spliced the mainbrace. The carrier's wardroom was packed with her own officers, former POWs, and our

American Allies who still suffered under a naval Volstead Act and in their own ships could obtain nothing stronger than Coca Cola.

The next morning all paraded on the flight deck as the carrier steamed slowly between the lines of flag-bedecked warships and transports and their cheering crews, while bands played, bells rang, whistles blew. There was not a dry eye around me.

"God!" exclaimed an Australian. "We are a lucky lot of bastards. Makes you weep to think of the poor sods we've left behind." I thought of the Canadians whose bones rested at Niigata, my friends buried in the hills of Hong Kong and at Stanley, and the countless strewn on battlefields scattered over Burma and Malaya, in New Guinea and Guadalcanal, Tarawa, Saipan, Okinawa, the Philippines. Yes, indeed, we had much for which to thank our God.

VI

We cleared the Miura Peninsula; ahead was the smoking volcano of Oshima, to starboard the snowless silhouette of Fuji San.

"Well, it's all over now, sir," said Mitchell, at my elbow.

"Yes, you'll soon be back in Pompey now, coxswain, to the missus and the boy you've never seen."

"Sorry they didn't get your wife aboard with us, sir."

"Well they tell me they're sending her to join us at Manila."

"Will you ever come back—back to Japan?" he inquired.

I gazed over the starboard quarter into the haze, and replied, "Yes, I know I shall come back, coxswain, and when I do you'll probably find me there, near the shore where I can hear the ocean and just behind a rocky point where a great general is said to have flung his sword into the sea while praying that the waters would recede so that he could attack the enemy without storming their defences in the hills."

"Oh, and what happened?"

"The tide went out and he worked round the point and won a famous victory."

"Hm, I dunno, they're a queer bunch all right. Don't think I could ever make 'em out, though. Look at that Brown, and that swine of a colonel, and the 'Pig' at Hong Kong. Tell you to look after your health with no bloody water or soap, keep our vitamin pills till we don't need 'em, pinch our Red Cross parcels, expect us to celebrate their Emperor's birthday with 'em, and all that cock about being sincere! Then look at Gentleman Jim, and Konno, and that cook and others, as nice blokes as you'd find anywhere. Still, maybe they'll learn a bit of common sense, 'cos it seems to me that with all their cleverness it's what they need most. Must be plenty more like Gentleman Jim and, by Christ! they're going to need 'em."

VII

We had a smooth passage down to Manila, marred only by the news that an aircraft with POWs had crashed in the Formosa Channel and there had been no survivors.

In Manila Bay were more ships than we'd seen at Yokohama. In preparation for the invasion of Japan, on shore stores were piled up like blocks of buildings. A few minutes after we berthed an Australian Army band arrived at the double and a brigadier came aboard profuse with apologies that they'd not been there as we came alongside. An American carrier arrived from Formosa with POWs, and to our intense amusement all were as bald as Yul Brynner. We'd stoutly resisted Japanese efforts to make us shave our heads, and laughed loud and long at these chaps who'd been made hideous by the Yanks.

The rehabilitation camp was a veritable town of duckboards and tents. Here to greet us and assist was Squadron-Leader Eric Williams RAF, whose amazing "Wooden Horse" escape from Germany is perhaps the greatest ever made.

Kaneko had not arrived and authority said she'd probably go to England via Hong Kong or USA or Canada, and assured me that she was being cared for and would be given a top priority for a passage. Harry, Quillie and I sat with John Gibson watching outdoor cinema in the rain and the antics, in glorious Technicolor, of a chap we'd never even heard of named Danny Kaye, when the senior naval officer in camp sent for me. He said that he and the captain and other officers of the ill-fated HMAS *Hobart* and *Perth* were going to Australia or New Zealand and that I could select nine other naval types for a record-breaking flight by an RAF Skymaster leaving the next morning for Blighty.

We took off from Nicholl's Field, and sixteen hours later made a belly landing at Alipore, Calcutta. Here we were wined and dined magnificently by our own people and Indians alike, then whisked off in a Dakota to Karachi where, after languishing for a couple of days in a deadly camp in the desert, boarded a fantastic looking aircraft called a Stirling bomber. We arrived at Lydda with an engine on fire, had a tyre burst leaving Castel Benito, and swooped down through low cloud with our fingers crossed and a prayer on our lips, to find our "green and pleasant land" at Lyneham, in Wiltshire.

Chapter Thirty-one

I

ONE afternoon, some thirteen months after VJ Day, Kaneko and I sat in the Allied Military train speeding us towards her birthplace from Iwakuni by the Inland Sea, where she had arrived the previous afternoon from England by BOAC flying-boat, to end our second separation.

We had exhausted all we had to say, and sat watching the picturesque countryside and the telegraph poles flashing by, among Americans, Australians, New Zealanders, bearded Sikhs from the Punjab, British and Indian WRNS, WVS girls, a couple of khaki-clad newspapermen, and officers and men of half a dozen units from the United Kingdom.

It seemed only yesterday since herself had stepped ashore at Southampton from SS *Highland Chieftain*, after four months on the voyage from Wakayama, in West Japan; since with my parents, my brother and sister-in-law we stood in a little Norman church in Essex to offer thanks that we had been spared.

Detained by the *"kempei"* at Hong Kong, she was unable to contact the Swiss or Swedish consuls and at the end of 1942 was placed aboard a transport for Japan, her few pieces of jewellery, her typewriter, being sold by her captors to pay for a passage she did not want.

On arrival at Kobe, after a harrowing trip at the bottom of a hold, during which she was protected by a former Hirosaki student, she was amazed to be asked why she had no entry visa, and who had sent her, a British subject and an enemy, to Japan!

She was then placed in an hotel under guard of a policeman until her brother arrived, but was allowed to go to Nagahama after he had provided guarantees.

But life in her birthplace became intolerable, and although they did not complain, she felt herself to be a terrible burden on her parents. The police and *"kempei"* made repeated searches of the house, the neighbours were instructed to report all her movements, children followed her crying obscenities whenever she went out; and so she wrote to the Swiss Consul at Kobe who found her a small house and took her under his care. She was, however, prohibited from leaving the area, and unable to attend her father's funeral.

Her sole companion was a small dog she had found who shared her paltry rations. Kaneko encountered much kindness sometimes from unexpected quarters, as in the case of the army doctor who assisted her on her ill-fated attempt to see me at Yokohama. Many years later I was to learn that our meeting had been arranged by several friends in the Navy who'd even booked a room in the Imperial Hotel, planned to bring me up from Yokohama for a day, and would have carried the project through if a certain person had not got cold feet. But she'd encountered much harshness, downright hatred, and had even been threatened by people who were to fall over backwards in pandering to American military government. We were to meet a woman who positively gushed over Kaneko, who could not disguise her scorn and loathing, and who replied when I questioned her attitude towards the woman:

"Just before the surrender she came and showed me a dagger, and said, 'When the Americans land we shall deal with you first.'"

She was now chatting with a young New Zealander, looking as chic, if more mature, than the day so many years before when we'd upset the harmony of her family.

Shortly after her arrival in England she'd had to go into hospital for a serious operation, long overdue. Then the Admiralty ordered me to return to Japan for another short spell before demobilization. And so, knowing that we had to go back, to pick up the broken threads, to do what we could for those we loved, and to start life anew, I accepted. It was an entry. For although when I joined up it was agreed that I be returned to my domicile on cessation of hostilities, it was well-known that the clique around General MacArthur was making it most difficult for any but Americans to return.

As the train flashed by the tiny coves and the small harbour towns, between cliffs of rugged pines, through fields where folk were busy gathering in the harvest, our companions seemed quite enamoured of all the beauty before them.

Hiroshima! A city of rubble, of shacks and ashes had invited much discussion; regrets that the atomic bombing had been necessary were freely expressed. But it was generally conceded that it had saved hundreds of thousands of Japanese, and Allied servicemen, who must have perished in an invasion.

As we slid to a stop at Okayama a train was moving away from the opposite platform crammed with ill-clad, miserable people, who even perched on the carriage roofs, on the steps, and as the last coach sped by there were two men sitting on the buffers.

"God! Makes you feel a bit of a heel to ride in comfort like this," expressed an American.

"Yeah, but wonder how we'd have been riding if the Nips had won?" retorted a companion.

A wretched Japanese ex-soldier, clad in what had once been a white hospital jacket, on his head a military cap from which the yellow star had been removed, stumbled along the platform on steel legs supporting himself with two sticks.

An American handed him two packets of cigarettes and some chocolate, a New Zealander gave him a packet of biscuits, and then an American MP started dressing them down for their charity.

Kaneko was watching, and I saw a tear. "No one cares now,"

she said. "When I went to look for you last August the people stopped the soldiers boarding the trains; jeered at them, called them cowards, said they'd brought on the war. It was shameful. They'd given the soldiers send-off parties, cheered them, praised their victories, and few of those men wanted to go to war."

"Can't understand it," remarked an American major. "I find them as nice folk as you'd meet anywhere. Don't seem possible they treated our boys so bad and raped and murdered in the Philippines and wherever else they went."

Understand! I preferred to hope it was simply a case of the small percentage who'd always been criminally minded and took advantage of the lack of discipline, of the license given them by war? Or was it merely because any evil perpetrated against the enemies of the Emperor became worthy of merit? Tokyo's Sugamo Prison was filled with those charged with war crimes, and the majority were nonplussed, bewildered at being there for what they apparently considered had only been committed in line of duty.

In that prison, I had interviewed Hiroshi Fuji, the excellent cadet doctor at Omori who was there through the deposition of someone who accused him of refusing medical treatment to B-29 aircrew. The fact was he'd treated patients at night in direct contravention of his colonel's orders and had I knew always done his best to uphold the medical code. I was thankful that I was able to assist in delivering him, and Heidelberg Henry, charged with command responsibility, from sentences of death demanded by the prosecutors. Colonel Suzuki did not complain, sought not to shift blame and took like a gentleman the responsibility for all that happened in the thirty or so camps under his command, and was to die in prison. Little Beast was to receive some such ridiculous term as forty or fifty years and was paroled after three; but Brown was never apprehended.

Tokugawa was tireless in the service of the Red Cross, Gentleman Jim appeared to be running a goat farm, and one day a stocky figure in khaki, with a pip on his shoulder, strode into my billet and to my surprise turned out to be none other than Cardiff Joe!

Matsuda San had held a British passport all the time, but this the Japanese would never recognize, and so he just went along with them and in doing so brought much comfort to POWs and to my knowledge saved many lives. After his return to Hong Kong with our draft he ran foul of the "*kempei*" and was removed from all dealings with POWs; but when the British forces entered the Crown Colony in 1945 Joe was taken care of and later given a commission. It was fitting that some years later the POW Association in Britain invited Joe to be their guest at their annual reunion, and unfortunate that he could not accept through the illness of his wife.

Day after day I ran into old students, some legless, some without an arm, and learned of those who'd perished.

Phelps Phelps, a kindly American captain I assisted in his investigations of Omori Camp, was an outstanding character who asked me to take him to the families of those in the prison to see if they were in want and seemed to spend his military pay on such charity.

"I don't know if those fellows are guilty," he'd say, "that's for the courts to decide. But the women and children must not suffer."

I prayed they'd get through with the war crimes trials with justice and without delay. A Japanese had told me: "A long drawn out demonstration will back-fire, people will start to wonder if they are really guilty if it takes too long to prove them so."

An old man said: "Why pick on them? We are all guilty for having permitted our affairs to be handled by such men"; and a housewife speaking over the radio in connection with the general foreign admiration for Japanese women had remarked: "I do not find this complimentary; to me it infers that we are a lot of docile dolls, and this is true otherwise we could never have permitted our men to commit such evils."

But were we entirely blameless? I thought of the brash RAF Regiment officer who boasted at a naval party of how he'd received the swords of three Japanese officers, shot them and then handed over their men to the Chinese who bayoneted all to death! There were the news pictures of hundreds of men being incinerated in caves with flame-throwers. The Occupation was probably the most benevolent in history, but shocking crimes were reported, chiefly rape and robbery with violence by the morons one finds in any army, but whereas similar crimes seemed to have been condoned by the Japanese Army, when the Occupation authorities caught the culprits in most cases justice was swift and relentless.

Early morning saw us passing through devastated Kobe and Osaka; then came the hills surrounding Kyoto, spared destruction through the efforts of a fine American, the late Dr. Langdon Warner, and above a platform seething with hungry-looking, shoddy people, I glimpsed a triumphal arch erected by an American regiment which proclaimed that it had been first here and first there. There was one like it as you entered Tokyo and these seemed to me somewhat childish if intended as morale builders, or to impress the populace.

"Well, my dear," I said with a smile, as we approached Maibara, "we'd better get ready . . . and I hope your buttons are secure today."

II

A charcoal-burning taxi bore us across the familiar countryside to Nagahama. Little had changed, more barley and potatoes were being cultivated, there was little for sale in the wayside shops and in the villages. The same shrine of the Fox God, the same grey-roofed temples, the bamboo groves, the pines and cryptomeria below majestic Mount Ibuki, and near the lake the imposing image of Kwannon whose expression reminded me of great-aunt Esther.

We might have been royalty for the reception accorded us. There was no doubt about the sincerity of the family and relatives, but Kaneko remarked, "They are so kind aren't they, but not so long ago many here heaped scorn upon me and my family and certain shopkeepers even refused to serve us."

"Oh, well, that is war . . . now they probably feel ashamed."

It was a joyous family gathering, but I wished so much that bull-necked old father-in-law could have been with us, even the crotchety old aunt from Formosa, and Kimi with the Fox in her stomach, and One-armed Cho. The war had been too much for Hidesaburo's ancient mother, but he was as jolly as ever and voted the Australian Corio whisky I'd brought along as the finest to pass his lips; he told me he had been experimenting with such dangerous spirits as industrial alcohol which blinds or kills less hardy characters. In the middle of our party a policeman arrived to tell me that I should telephone Military Government at Otsu who'd told him that I'd no right in the area. "Well, tell them to come here and see me about it," I replied.

At the bath-house an ancient woman in the ticket-box was vastly startled to see me in blue naval battledress. An old man hastened to introduce us, and chuckled, "They used to call him Honourable Mr. Nose-Paper!"

I sat in the bath recalling old Ogawa, and Yano, and Ishii, the jolly policeman, and other friends. Mount Fuji was a little more steamed and faded, and the mirror with the geisha at top and bottom unrecognizable as such. My presence appeared to cause a sudden rush on the establishment, heads peeked over from the women's department and I listened to a perfect chorus of reminiscences concerning my idiosyncrasies in other days. On my way back to the small hotel I noticed that all the houses in Cat Street bore the sign OFF LIMITS.

In one of the better quarters of Tokyo I had noticed many private houses with the sign, VD KEEP OUT, on their gateposts and was astounded when I found a similar sign outside the home of an old friend. He laughed when I expressed surprise, and said, "Well, sometimes drunken soldiers come around looking for girls and so people think this is one way to keep them out."

The very handsome and dignified wife of a former ambassador and court official had been surprised one evening by half a dozen GIs seeking entrance to her home and, in her impeccable English, inquired what they wanted.

"Just dames, ma'am, girls, broads!" one cried. "All were young enough to be my grandsons," she told me, "and I stifled a smile and pointed to the house opposite and said, 'Well, if I were you I'd go over and ask your general, for his house is always filled with very pretty women!'"

My friend who ran the restaurant and who'd always been suspected of Communist leanings was overjoyed to see me and opened a precious bottle of Old Parr he said he'd preserved for some special occasion. He told me that Hideya, the geisha, had died of tuberculosis soon after her marriage.

"Our defeat is a great blessing," he remarked. "In no other way could our people have been taught a lesson. But wait till they know, are a little more convinced that the Americans don't want to keep them down, and then from out their present despond they'll rise to repair and build out of the greatest typhoon we've ever experienced to create a free and better Japan."

A jeep, marked with a white star and Military Government Shiga, stood outside the hotel. Upstairs I found Kaneko and her relations with two American officers who appeared quite at home and enjoying my Corio and water.

"Hell, I'm glad to meet you," said the major. "We guessed that another bunch of thieves was in town. Last week some GIs with a jeep played hell in Cat Street and got away with a load of silk from a warehouse. By rights you, too, are not supposed to be here, but I guess you've a better right than any." They were nice fellows, told me that GIs already had a blackmarket distribution organization in the prefecture, and said that with some characters people were wise to keep their womenfolk out of sight.

We paid our respects at the family graves, trudged across the fields past the water-wheel of "blood churning" fame and the lightning-riven tree beside the stone Jizo, saviour of little children, to visit Hidesaburo and his family; renewed so many other old friendships, and then left that town where I'd received so many of my first impressions of this land I had come to love, and from which not even war and prison camps could tear me away, eager for demobilization and to pick up the old threads.

Chapter Thirty-two

I

THE scars of war were almost healed; with the end of the war crimes trials and the signing of the San Francisco Peace Treaty it seemed the reaction of the millions crammed into the archipelago was like that of the dried earth after long-awaited rain, to bring a veritable whirlwind of activity in every field of human endeavour.

From out of the rubble sprang factories and office buildings, concrete apartment houses appeared and spread from suburbs into the countryside, then the television towers, and below ground new subways were being burrowed under Tokyo and other great cities.

It seemed a lifetime since I'd first gazed upon the Pacific Ocean from the beach at Kamakura, sat in the glow of sunset at Inamuragasaki and made my vow that someday here we should make our home, and but yesterday since I'd gazed shorewards from the flight deck of HMS *Speaker* to repeat my desire to Petty Officer Mitchell as the shores of Sagami Bay faded into the horizon. Now that dream was fulfilled, in a somewhat ramshackle but charming Japanese style home, but a stone's throw from the point where centuries before Nitta Yoshisada cast his sword into the ocean, and prayed the tide might soon start to ebb.

Here the murmur of the great ocean lulls us to sleep, and in its roaring, angry mood, warns us to fasten well the wooden shutters against the dread typhoons. In spring and late autumn the shrike nests in the flowering camellias, on moonlit nights the owls hoot from the cryptomeria on the hillside, and from my window, especially in winter or before a storm, peerless Mount Fuji can be seen in all her glory like some presiding deity above the lesser peaks and hills and the ribbon-like bridge connecting the mainland with Enoshima—Picture Island, and seawards the smoke rises from the never-slumbering volcano on Oshima.

There are now but few thatched roofs in the hamlet; television antennae stab the skyline with the pines and telegraph poles, and along the beach road speeds the new generation on its motorcycles, *Pigeon* and *Rabbit* scooters, clad in leather jackets and crash helmets, with Miss Japan clinging on behind. Toyopets and Datsuns speed by with the Hillmans and Renaults and Chevs and Fords, and purring softly over the concrete come the enormous Cadillacs with company presidents lolling back, lords of all they survey like *daimyo* of old.

Over the hill the excursion buses disgorge their fares, along with the tourists, chiefly from the USA, to admire and photograph the great image of the Lord of Boundless Light. On the beaches henna-haired, scarlet-nailed, and bikini-clad Japanese Brigitte Bardots pose before the gadget-encrusted cameras of their boy-friends, trade unionists cavort in the dances of the USSR and wave their red flags, while helicopters shower down rubber balls or pamphlets for the benefit of the manufacturers of foam mattresses, caramels, motorcycles, transistor radios, cameras, vitamin and liver pills.

Each day in all seasons the tall chimney of the salt-water bath-house smokes merrily away and into this establishment troop mostly elderly folk from the rural areas to enjoy the brine from Sagami Bay, eat, drink and make merry, and perhaps watch base-ball, pro-wrestling, or kabuki on the television. Like everything else the public bath-house is no longer the simple establishment I knew in Omi. It is most hygienic in every way, there are even notices about washing your clothes in the establishment, some even charge women extra for washing their hair, and in many there is no longer the *sansuké* to massage and wash your back, since some women objected that he was but another vestige of feudalism.

Now, folk without television time their visits to the bath-house to coincide with the broadcasting of "Twenty Questions," "I Love Lucy," or other favourite programmes.

Inamura and Kamakura are no longer exclusive villa resorts for the aristocrat and wealthy, and each morning the electric car from our little station bears the factory worker, clerk and shop-girl, with the former ambassador or cabinet minister, one-time admirals and generals, painters, composers, poets, priests and newspapermen, with the svelte fashion model, the air hostess, the business executive, the policeman, fishmonger, greengrocer, pedlar, the school-children and university students, scientists, engineers, radio announcers and television stars to their various activities in Kamakura, Yokohama, or Tokyo, the most densely populated city on earth.

Old folk often sigh and mourn the passing of more conservative days, bewail the changes in the habits of youth, the new pleasures and the new freedoms of which their generations never dreamed. Our fishmonger speaks with certain pride of the great mansion which once stood nestled in the trees of the little promontory, of the comings and goings of the mighty, even Imperial princes, and of the gentle Italian silk merchant who built the house, in which the famous painter and his gifted wife and daughter now live, who used to set out across the hills to Yokohama each day in a coach and pair and clad in morning suit and silk hat with a flower in his buttonhole. And my charming old friend, diplomat, professor of commonsense, as he likes to style himself, and excel-lent raconteur, tells me of the Great Earthquake, and the tidal wave which almost inundated Inamura in 1923, of the days of his youth and life in a dozen capitals in Europe, and North and South America. He thrives on the new order of things, and seems to bend all his energies most successfully towards leaving the world a better place than when he entered it.

It is a far cry from our little house in Omi with the banana tree outside the porch, and One-armed Cho to visit me each morning, and Hidesaburo and his "Buckingham Palace" whisky; from Hirosaki, and Yamagata, and Hong Kong where rests our dear Joan, the Airedale we could never forget.

Norman, the dour Scottie, his son O'Niichan, and Kuro and Nick, the mongrels, now appear to run our household and yelp their displeasure at the jet fighters, the helicopters, or airliners which disturb the sanctity of what they seem to regard as their own private sky.

Every hour or so, the night silence is broken by the clappers of the night watchman to warn us against fire and to lock our doors tight, and sometimes from up the hill come the strains of the bamboo Japanese flute in plaintive notes which seem to focus the mind on days of which we've only read or dreamed; of quiet Zen monasteries, of footsore travellers beneath a harvest moon, and of fishing boats sailing in from deep waters.

Here is our haven, the little port we made after squall, rain and sunshine, glowering storm, the tempest, and the calm. And here amid the ever-changing moods and amenities of the space age there is still a fundamental kindness and gentleness and ways as time-honoured as the gnarled pines on the promontory, where once we sat with the salt wind in our hair at the beginning of our journey along the Road to Inamura.

Other TUT BOOKS available:

UNBEATEN TRACKS IN JAPAN: An Account of Travels in the Interior Including Visits to the Aborigines of Yezo and the Shrine of Nikko *by Isabella L. Bird*

ZILCH! The Marine Corps' Most Guarded Secret *by Roy Delgado*

Please order from your bookstore or write directly to:

CHARLES E. TUTTLE CO., INC.
Suido 1-chome, 2–6, Bunkyo-ku, Tokyo 112

or:

CHARLES E. TUTTLE CO., INC.
Rutland, Vermont 05701 U.S.A.